american education

education

second edition

American Education
a problem-centered approach

Lita Linzer Schwartz

*the pennsylvania state university,
ogontz campus*

Holbrook Press, Inc.
boston

to

my parents, *who taught and inspired me*

my husband, *who encouraged and sustained me*

our sons, *who may profit if this helps to bring them fine teachers*

Library of Congress Catalogue Card Number: 73-93285

contents

Preface to the Second Edition **x**
Preface to the First Edition **xii**

1 **Historical Roots of Education** 3

   The Ancient Cultures
   The Early and Medieval Church
         st. jerome/*Letter to Laeta*
   Islam
   Individual Contributors
   What Flourishes from These Roots?
   Summary

2 **American Education and Educational Goals** 27

   The Colonial Period
   The Federalist Period
   At the Turn of the Century
         john dewey/*Democracy and Education*
         mortimer smith/*Fundamental Differences Do Exist*

v

3   **Philosophical Orientation**   65

Idealism
    robert m. hutchins/*A Liberal Education*
Realism
    aristotle/*Ethics and Politics*
Pragmatism
    george f. kneller/*Pragmatism, Reality and
        Education*
    john dewey/*Resulting Modifications of the
        School*
    clarence j. karier/*Pragmatic Conceptions of
        Man and Society*
Essentialism
Existentialism
Summary

4   **Governmental Responsibility for
    Education**   101

The National Level
    thomas d. bailey/*The Folklore of Local Control*
The State Level
The Local Level
    robert l. drury and kenneth c. ray/*School Board
        Rules and Regulations*
    john c. pittinger/*School Board Most Harrowing
        Job in Education*
Consolidation and Corporation
    compact for education/*Preamble and Selected
        Articles from the Constitution*
Problems and Issues which Continue

5   **Economics and Education**   131

Poverty and Mobility
    james b. conant/*Slums and Suburbs*

The Problem of the Dropout
The Disadvantaged
    education news/*The Crossover Phenomenon*
    william g. mather/*The Unskilled and*
                      Automation
The Costs of Education
The Magnitude of the Problem

6 Federal Aid to Education 169

The Development and Expansion of Federal Aid
Arguments Advocating Federal Aid
Arguments Against Federal Aid
The Kennedy-Johnson Administrations
The Nixon Years
An Estimate of the Future

7 Religion and Education 193

Historical Background
The Federal Aid Controversy—Pro
    carl n. degler/*Why Not Federal Aid to Parochial*
                  Schools?
The Federal Aid Controversy—Con
    r. freeman butts/*Public Funds Should Not*
                  Support Parochial Schools
The Court Decides
How Much Religion in the Schools?
Conclusions

8 Segregation and Education 223

Historical Background
Reactions to School Desegregation
Summary

9   Excellence and Education   247

The Quality of Education
    john w. gardner/*Toning Up the Whole Society*
Teacher Recruitment and Retention
The Curriculum
    james b. conant/*The Comprehensive High
        School*
Research and Development
What Do Teachers Teach?
Where Do We Begin?
    earl j. mcgrath/*The Meaning of Academic
        Excellence*
Summary

10   Professional Preparation of Teachers   283

Historical Background
    edward everett/*The Purpose of the New
        Normal Schools*
A Defense of Mann and the Normal Schools
    horace mann/*Tenth Annual Report of the
        Massachusetts State Board of
        Education, 1846*
Professional Selection and Preparation
    james b. conant/*Teacher Certification*
Sample Curricula
    lynn l. weldon/*Is Teacher Education an
        Illusion?*
Teachers in the Field
    frank g. jennings/*Most Dangerous Profession*

11   Academic Freedom and Responsibilities   319

What Is Academic Freedom?
    sterling m. mcmurrin/*Academic Freedom in
        the Schools*

richard m. nixon/*The Four Academic Freedoms*
henry steele commager/*The Nature of*
Academic Freedom
Faculty and Student Responsibility
national education association/*A Code of Ethics*
donald s. seckinger/*Freedom and Responsibility*
in Education
Loyalty Oaths

12 A National Educational Policy   353

The Problems
Patterns at Home and Abroad
Implementing a National Education Policy
frederick m. raubinger/*A National Testing*
Program—No
joshua a. fishman and
paul i. clifford/*Mass-Testing in American*
Education
robert l. ebel/*A National Testing Program—*
Yes
Summary

13 Anticipations and Conclusions   383

14 A Concluding Statement 393

Periodicals of Interest   **395**

Index   **401**

preface to the second edition

Even children today comment on how quickly time seems to move, and everyone, not only the elderly and traditional, is aware of the rapid changes occurring in society. It is not change itself that frightens us, but its rapidity; not the coming of the future, but an anxiety that the future will be here before we have become accustomed to the changes in the present. There is a growing realization that 1980 is no longer distant, but less than a decade away; and that five- and ten-year programs are outdated after only one or two years. These situations have been particularly apparent in education and related fields, hence the need for revising a book published only five years ago.

Among the major concerns of the '70s in education is the fiscal belt-tightening that is in such marked contrast to the affluence and expansion of the 1950s and 1960s. Population control, environmental conservation, antipollution movements, education of the culturally different, rights of exceptional children, means of supporting public and nonpublic schools, and the impact of collective bargaining by teachers at all levels are principal issues in education today. These issues will be discussed in the appropriate chapters.

This second edition of *American Education: A Problem-centered Approach* retains the basic format of the original text.

The first three chapters present the historical and philosophical foundations of contemporary American education. The problem-centered chapters each have a presentation of the historical background of their respective problems. Since the "One World" of the 1940s has shrunk even more in the 1970s because of jet transportation and telecommunications satellites, the opportunity for educators around the world to influence each other's work has increased markedly. This opportunity is reflected throughout the book, although with greater depth in the chapter on comparative education. A new chapter presents some of the ideas currently being projected for implementation in the near future, particularly with reference to adult and informal education. The second edition also includes recently available publications.

Acknowledgements

The helpful comments of colleagues across the country who have used the original text are much appreciated, and can be acknowledged only in this way since the list of colleagues is too long to be included.

At Holbrook Press, John J. DeRemigis, Manager, and Paula E. Carroll, Production Editor, have contributed suggestions and confidence that have been most valuable.

Many thanks, too, are due to Sunnie R. Spiegel, Harvey Spiegel, and Jerome Staller for their contributions of information and expertise.

As always, the emotional support and encouragement of my husband, Melvin J. Schwartz, and our sons, Arthur, Joshua, and Frederic, are deeply appreciated. Without these, no books would ever be written in our house, nor perhaps would there be an inner need to write them.

Lita Linzer Schwartz

preface to the first edition

Schools are not isolated from the rest of society, or from the national heritage, or from the ideals of the various sub-cultures which comprise the United States as we know it. The problems of schools are similarly not set apart from the rest of the community. As parents, teachers, students, and/or taxpayers, almost every member of the community has some legitimate concern with the problems of education.

The present book has a problem-centered approach to enable and encourage the reader to focus on a single particular critical area in education. To "set the stage," a chapter of general historical background of education, including non-Western influences, and one on philosophical views serve as bases for each of the subsequent chapters. Excerpts from various authors' works are interwoven with the text, each where it is most directly relevant, rather than at the conclusion of the chapter or in a separate book of readings. There has been a conscious attempt to present divergent points of view both in the text and in the reading selections, for there is generally some merit to be found in arguments on both sides of an issue. Reference is made to additional opinions in the text, often via brief quotations which illuminate further the problem being considered.

The problems discussed in this volume are of two kinds, basically: one type consists of philosophical and legal questions, such as the concept of Federal aid to education, public aid to parochial schools, teacher education, academic freedom, and the efforts to gain quality in education; the other type emphasizes practical problems, such as the cost to the nation of having under-educated citizens, the ways in which education can be and is being improved for the "educationally disadvantaged," the costs of educating those who are now in school, the desegregation of schools in the most feasible fashion. As teachers and as citizens, these are the crucial issues with which each generation has to deal.

Extensive bibliographical references and suggested films are included to aid the reader in probing more deeply into each area of controversy under discussion. There is also included an annotated list of periodicals which publish articles relevant to the problems in education at all levels. Relevant material from the fields of sociology, psychology, economics, law, and theology may be combined with appropriate chapters with ease for greater depth of understanding.

Educational crises are reported in the news media daily. An understanding of the foundations of current educational problems is, therefore, basic to an informed and rational discussion of the issues involved. Although public attention is focused mainly on one or two issues at a time, all of the problems discussed here are controversial current events. It is very interesting, really, to study the pattern and texture of education today because it is revealed as a fabric made up of many fibers arranged in exciting and different ways. Education at all levels is intimately involved with how we relate to each other as individuals and as groups, how we vote, and how we think. It is exciting, too, to know that some of these problems are two thousand and more years old and were resolved through the centuries in a variety of ways. The use of a problem-solving approach thus serves one of the prime purposes in education as a whole: to stimulate each individual to think logically, rationally, and, hopefully, creatively in reaching decisions.

Acknowledgements

In any writing effort, there are people who help the author in many ways. They deserve not only private expressions of gratitude, but also public acknowledgement of their contributions. And so, my thanks to:

My students at the Ogontz Campus of The Pennsylvania State University who have shared with me their reactions to this mode of presentation, and their ideas of the "ideal textbook;"

Donald G. Tarbet of the University of North Carolina, Valentine R. Glockner of Northern Illinois State College, and John E. Sturn of the State University College at Buffalo for their constructive criticism of the manuscript.

Janet Snowdon and Barry Fetterolf of Holbrook Press for their guidance and patience;

The publishers who have generously granted permission to reprint the several selections and illustrations incorporated into the text, as well as individual authors and illustrators who shared their work with me;

Melvin J. Schwartz for being a husband with abundant patience and fortitude during the book's production; and

Arthur, Joshua, and Frederic Schwartz for their cooperation during countless working hours.

LITA LINZER SCHWARTZ

1

historical roots of education

Educational problems are not new to the world. The ways in which they have been approached and resolved have changed, from one civilization to another, and from one period of history to another. Yet, as is often observed, "Nothing is new under the sun." Many of our current educational practices originated among the ancient Greeks and Hebrews, and much of our knowledge stems from discoveries by Mohammedan scholars. It is the purpose of this chapter to survey the diverse roots of American education and to show the relationships of the emphases of earlier cultures to those of today.

The Ancient Cultures

In ancient Greece, there are several views of what public education should be, who should be educated, and the methods to be used. The underlying philosophies of both Plato and Aristotle are merely introduced here as part of the historical survey, but will be expanded upon in another chapter.

Plato (427–347 B.C.), an idealist, believed that education was designed to serve the state by providing it with "good citizens" who could work intelligently toward the ideal and better society. He felt that an elementary practical education for both boys and girls destined to be either soldiers or rulers should teach only the truth via good examples. Sensory impressions were not part of Plato's technique. He preferred the "dialectic" method in which students would break down definitions, and by questioning, arrive at new and more truthful definitions. In all subjects, he would start with the simple and build up to the complex, anticipating contemporary teachers by some 2300 years.

Aristotle (386–322 B.C.), a realist, on the other hand, favored public education as a means of creating constructive citizens, and also as a means of creating an intellectual elite based on ability. Contrary to Plato's view that citizens should serve the state, Aristotle believed that it was the obligation of the state to provide the good life for its citizens. His basic curriculum included reading, writing, and drawing as tools for further knowledge, as well as for their intrinsic usefulness. Like Comenius and Dewey centuries later, Aristotle believed that "what you do, you learn." He also stressed knowledge for its own sake, achieved through observation and sensory impressions. Aristotle's curriculum was divided into four stages of emphasis: 1) from birth to five years, spontaneous bodily activity; 2) from five to seven years, observation of future learning; 3) from age seven to puberty, training the irrational soul (related to Freud's "Id") with catharsis through gymnastics; and 4) from puberty to age 21, an emphasis on reason and training of the rational soul through a study of science, philosophy, and literature. Aristotle's theories were later to serve as the basis for medieval philosophy and church education.

In Sparta, the militaristic Greek city-state, education was free for all children. This was so that they might serve the state intelligently. Physical and military training, ancestors of the modern-day R.O.T.C., were necessarily an integral part of Spartan education. Some aspects of Spartan education must also have served as a model for modern Israeli training and philosophy of education and citizen-soldiers.

Although the Greeks put forth many educational ideals, and believed that their greatest work of art was the creation of a man, they did not practice their ideals very successfully. According to one viewpoint, "They were the first to regard education as a means of moulding human character in accordance with an ideal."[1] This "moulding" in Plato's views and in Spartan practice has dangers, of course, but should not reduce our recognition of the concept's underlying value. In our own schools, much of what is taught is designed to "mold" the pupil to fit into society in general, and to fit the school's pattern specifically. Education in ancient Greece was not as widespread as works of Plato and Aristotle would suggest, but Greeks were among the best-educated people of the ancient Western world.

During the Hellenistic Age, 300–150 B.C., Greek learning was widespread, largely through the conquests of Alexander the Great. The use of libraries was already important, one of the most famous being that of the Ptolemies in Alexandria, Egypt. Because of the stress on an harmonious development of the intellectual, the esthetic, the physical, and the military in education, there was an increasing lack of respect for manual labor. Emphasis was placed on the intellectual and the artistic, as well as on physical well-being. The glory of Greece in this period, however, was reflected in the changing values as well as in the contemporary literature and growing scientific knowledge of all peoples with whom the Hellenes came in contact.

Among the ancient Hebrews, and even among modern ones, literacy and learning were emphasized for all, and held in high regard. Learning and doing were considered a life-long process, with some compulsory education as a beginning. The emphasis on literacy was bound to the need to be able to read the Torah (Five Books of Moses) and other religious texts for oneself. A scholar, Rabbi Eleazar Ben Azariah, wrote: ". . . Where there is no Torah, there's no right conduct; where there is no right conduct, there's no Torah. Where there is no wisdom, there's no fear (of God); where there is no fear (of God), there's no wisdom. . . ."[2] Concern with reading the Law for oneself was stressed later by the Bible-oriented Puritans when they established schools in the seventeenth-century Massachusetts Bay Colony.

It is interesting to note here that nineteenth and twentieth century Jewish immigrants brought the love of learning with them to this country, and used learning as a means of rising from the big-city ghettos in which they had settled. Also stressed in education was the doctrine of responsibility, or service to humanity.

In 17 A.D., there were 394 schools in Jerusalem offering courses in Torah, Talmud (Rabbinical interpretations of the Torah), history, and vocational training. Adult study groups existed in addition to the schools. Two modern aspects of educational psychology were important to the Hebrews: recognition of individual differences and the importance of motivation in learning. Individuals were characterized as comprehending readily but forgetting readily; slow to learn but slow to forget; a "good portion" as one who comprehends readily and forgets slowly; and a "bad portion" as one who comprehends slowly and forgets quickly. Repetition, group discussion, and clarification were used to increase motivation. The principles of education in ancient Palestine are being carried on in American secular education today, as well as by the descendants of the Hebrews in Israel and elsewhere.

In ancient Rome, contrary to the examples above, education was available chiefly to the aristocracy, often by tutors who were themselves Greek-trained.

E. B. Castle contrasts Roman and Greek education in the following excerpt:

> When . . . we compare the education of the Roman youth in the first century of our era with that of the Greek boy of good family in the fifth and fourth centuries B.C., we find several conditions of good education sadly lacking. The moral, social, and intellectual climate was not healthy; there was no grand conception of the education of the whole man that, at least in theory, was so evident in Athens; there was a narrow view of the content of literary education and small respect for philosophical thinking; and the peculiar weaknesses of Greek education persisted —the servile schoolmaster and the crude disciplinary methods.[3]

Earlier, education of freemen was by means of the apprenticeship system. However, when fathers were unable to train their sons for a life which became increasingly complicated, they turned to more formal schemes of education. The *ludus* or elementary school taught reading, writing, and arithmetic—our own basic "three R's." The grammar school was an idea borrowed from Hellenistic Greece, and boys attended there from age 12 to about age 16. Emphasis in the grammar or secondary school was on Greek and Roman literature, grammar, history, and mythology. Education was then continued in rhetorical schools where the techniques of oratory, so important in the Roman Republic, were taught. All of these schools were privately supported and were voluntary, not compulsory. Roman girls received only an informal education, usually in the home. Those from wealthy families sometimes had a private tutor, and in the later periods of Roman history studied grammar and philosophy. By 300 A.D., the Roman curriculum consisted largely of the seven liberal arts: grammar, rhetoric, and dialectic, which were the *trivium*; and arithmetic, geometry, music, and astronomy, which were the *quadrivium*.[4] The seven liberal arts formed the basis for later medieval education as well. Public education was subsidized on a limited basis from the time of the first Caesar, and succeeding emperors paid teacher's salaries, exempted them from banishment from Rome, and relieved them of some taxes.

Ancient China's basic educational pattern continued through centuries until the advent of Westernized mission schools and finally the current rule of the Chinese Communists. The Taoistic emphasis on the "mean" and the Confucian concern with the goodness of the individual as part of society were the guiding principles of education and Chinese life in general. Private instruction was given in China as early as the Chou dynasty (1122 B.C.), and formal education was urged from the T'ang period (620 A.D.) on. The purpose was to serve the social order by educating prospective officials. (Examinations for what were essentially civil service positions were open to all, but relatively few could afford to go to school to learn the information necessary for passing them.) The "six arts" of Chinese education at that time included music, archery, charioteering, "rites," writing, and mathematics.[5] Although, as indicated, it was theoretically possible for the "peasant" to rise upward in Chinese society by becoming a government servant, the training for the government examinations was not education as we view it today. The would-be student found that he had to memorize classical writings for years at a time, imitate his teachers, and spend time in contemplation. There was no room for creative thinking in the curriculum. The bulk of education, then, was available to the nobility and the very bright. It became the duty of the nobility to set an example for the "common people" and to educate them. Yet, with these limitations, the Chinese were highly inventive mechanically, and advanced in their philosophy and literature, much to the surprise of early travelers from the West.

The Early and Medieval Church

Early Christianity was dominated by faith, not reason. It ignored philosophy and science, and denounced Graeco-Roman literature as pagan, and therefore not to be studied. Emphasis was placed on the writings of Christian saints and theologians as the content of the curriculum. St. Jerome (340–420 A.D.) was one of those who sought to limit the content of learning, but he was also an astute educator, as may be seen in his "Letter to Laeta." This letter was written in 403 A.D. in answer to Laeta's request for instruction on how to bring up her infant daughter, Paula.

st. jerome

Letter to Laeta

4. Thus must a soul be educated which is to be a temple of God. It must learn to hear nothing and to say nothing but what belongs to the fear of God. It must have no understanding of unclean words, and no knowledge of the world's songs. Its

In Ulich, Robert (ed.). *Three Thousand Years of Educational Wisdom* (Cambridge, Mass.: Harvard University Press, 1963), pp. 164–169.

tongue must be steeped while still tender in the sweetness of the psalms. Boys with their wanton thoughts must be kept from Paula; even her maids and female attendants must be separated from worldly associates. For if they have learned some mischief they may teach more. Get for her a set of letters made of boxwood or of ivory and called each by its proper name. Let her play with these, so that even her play may teach her something. And not only make her grasp the right order of the letters and see that she forms their names into a rhyme, but constantly disarrange their order and put the last letters in the middle and the middle ones at the beginning that she may know them all by sight as well as by sound. Moreover, so soon as she begins to use the style upon the wax, and her hand is still faltering, either guide her soft fingers by laying your hand upon hers, or else have simple copies cut upon a tablet; so that her efforts confined within these limits may keep to the lines traced out for her and not stray outside of these. Offer prizes for good spelling and draw her onwards with little gifts such as children of her age delight in. And let her have companions in her lessons to excite emulation in her, that she may be stimulated when she sees them praised. You must not scold her if she is slow to learn but must employ praise to excite her mind, so that she be glad when she excels others and sorry when she is excelled by them. Above all you must take care not to make her lessons distasteful to her lest a dislike for them conceived in childhood may continue into her maturer years. The very words which she tries bit by bit to put together and to pronounce ought not to be chance ones, but names specially fixed upon and heaped together for the purpose, those for example of the prophets or the apostles or the list of patriarchs from Adam downwards as it is given by Matthew and Luke. In this way while her tongue will be well-trained, her memory will be likewise developed. Again, you must choose for her a master of approved years, life, and learning. . . . Things must not be despised as of small account in absence of which great results cannot be achieved. The very rudiments and first beginning of knowledge sound differently in the mouth of an educated man and of an uneducated. Accordingly, you must see that the child is not led away by the silly coaxing of women to form a habit of shortening long words or of decking herself with gold and purple. Of these habits one will spoil her conversation and the other her character. She must not therefore learn as a child what afterwards she will have to unlearn. . . . Early impressions are hard to eradicate from the mind. When once wool has been dyed purple who can restore it to its previous whiteness? . . . We are always ready to imitate evil; and faults are quickly copied where virtues appear unattainable. Paula's nurse must not be intemperate, or loose, or given to gossip. Her bearer must be respectable, and her foster-father of grave demeanour. . . .

9. And let it be her task daily to bring to you the flowers which she has culled from scripture. Let her learn by heart so many verses in the Greek, but let her be instructed in the Latin also. For, if the tender lips are not from the first shaped to this, the tongue is spoiled by a foreign accent and its native speech debased by alien elements. You must yourself be her mistress, a model on which she may form her childish conduct. Never either in you nor in her father let her see what she cannot imitate without sin. Remember both of you that you are the parents of a consecrated virgin, and that your example will teach her more than your precepts. Flowers are quick to fade and a baleful wind soon withers the violet, the lily, and the crocus. Let her never appear in public unless accompanied by you. Let her never visit a church or a martyr's shrine unless with her mother. Let no young man greet her with smiles; no dandy with curled hair pay compliments to her. . . . Let her take as her model some aged virgin of approved faith, character, and chastity, apt to instruct her by word and by example. She ought to rise at night to recite prayers and psalms; to sing hymns in the morning; at the third, sixth, and ninth hours to take her place in the line to do battle for Christ; and, lastly, to kindle her lamp and to offer her evening sacrifice. In these occupations let her pass the day, and when night comes let it find her still engaged in them. Let reading follow prayer with her, and prayer again succeed to reading. Time will seem short when employed on tasks so many and varied. . . .

11. When you go a short way into the country, do not leave your daughter behind you. Leave her no power or capacity of living without you, and let her feel frightened when she is left to herself. Let her not converse with people of the world or associate with virgins indifferent to their vows. . . .

12. Let her treasures be not silks or gems but manuscripts of the holy scriptures; and in these let her think less of gilding, and Babylonian parchment, and arabesque patterns, than of correctness and accurate pronunciation. Let her begin by learning the psalter, and then let her gather rules of life out of the proverbs of Solomon. From the Preacher let her gain the habit of despising the world and its vanities. Let her follow the example set in Job of virtue and of patience. Then let her pass on to the gospels never to be laid aside when once they have been taken in hand. Let her also drink in with a willing heart the Acts of the Apostles and the Epistles. As soon as she has enriched the storehouse of her mind with these treasures, let her commit to memory the prophets, the heptateuch (i.e. Genesis, Exodus, Leviticus, Numbers, Deuteronomy, Joshua, Judges), the books of Kings and of Chronicles, the rolls also of Ezra and Esther. When she has done all these she may safely read the Song of Songs but not before: for, were she to read it at the beginning, she would fail to perceive that, though it is written in fleshly words, it is a marriage song of a spiritual bridal. And not understanding this she would suffer hurt from it. Let her avoid all apocryphal writings, and if she is led to read such not by the truth of the doctrines which they contain but out of respect for the miracles contained in them; let her understand that they are not really written by those to whom they are ascribed, that many faulty elements have been introduced into them, and that it requires infinite discretion to look for gold in the midst of dirt. . . . Let her take pleasure in the works and wits of all in whose books a due regard for the faith is not neglected. But if she reads the works of others let it be rather to judge them than to follow them.

13. You will answer, "How shall I, a woman of the world, living at Rome, surrounded by a crowd, be able to observe all these injunctions?" In that case do not undertake a burden to

which you are not equal. When you have weaned Paula as Isaac was weaned and when you have clothed her as Samuel was clothed, send her to her grandmother and aunt; give up this most precious of gems, to be placed in Mary's chamber and to rest in the cradle where the infant Jesus cried. Let her be brought up in a monastery, let her be one amid companies of virgins, let her learn to avoid swearing, let her regard lying as sacrilege, let her be ignorant of the world. . . .

As was common in that period, Paula had been dedicated to the Church prior to her birth, so that the instructions given by St. Jerome were even more stringent in terms of avoiding "worldliness" than usual. Also of interest in this letter, particularly, is paragraph four. In more modern language, these might be the words of a contemporary teacher or psychologist. In fact, St. Jerome's injunction to guide the learner's hand in writing antedates Maria Montessori's method by some 1500 years. Similarly, teaching the alphabet by sight and sound is basic to the phonics and Initial Teaching Alphabet methods of teaching reading today. Many other ideas of St. Jerome are also still in practice, but are better known to us as part of learning theory or part of John Dewey's methods of education.

Under the Roman Catholic Church, particularly during the Dark Ages and Counter-Reformation periods, the state was subordinate to the Church, and education, too, was completely dominated by the Church. This retarded the acceptance of the idea of education as a function of the state for centuries. Church philosophy leaned heavily on misinterpretations of Aristotelian philosophy, with the practical result that education was designed for an elite—mostly clergy—in a highly agrarian and feudal society.

Since this was an age of faith, questioning of dogma or any teachings was heresy, and this resulted in the stagnation of knowledge. The trials of Copernicus and Galileo are cases in point. Copernicus, a Polish astronomer, published a book in which he proved that the earth was only one part of the solar system, a system which was centered on the sun. This was contrary to the accepted view of the earth as the center of the universe, so Copernicus had kept his discovery a secret for many years for fear of persecution during the period of religious unrest of the early sixteenth century. Galileo, an Italian scientist, demonstrated the validity of Copernicus' teachings in 1610. Since this was still heresy, he was called to Rome by the Pope, sent to prison, and forced to recant publicly his heretical findings. Many of his contemporaries in the Scientific Renaissance condemned both Galileo and the Copernican theory of telescopic investigation which he supported.

The telescopic method of investigation was denounced by those theologians who, following Aquinas, held that the only true method was that of reasoning theologically from the Scriptures, and by those who believed that Aristotle had said the last word about the world of nature. Telescopic observation, it was held, could reveal nothing in the heavens which Aristotle did not know.[6]

In addition to the schools which trained the clergy, there were song and parish schools for poor and lay students, still religiously-oriented; guild schools for apprentices in various cities for the different crafts; charity schools; and palace schools such as that operated in Charlemagne's court. There, fortunate boys chosen to be pages at the court were taught obedience, manners, and those techniques they would later need as squires and knights. A literary description of such a court school may be found, incidentally, in the *Story of Roland*.

It was not until the expansion of commerce, the various voyages of discovery and exploration, the rise of the bourgeosie, and the growth of political units in the fourteenth to sixteenth centuries that there was a move toward state rather than family or church responsibility for education. The rise of Humanism in Italy created greater awareness of the need for education, but still limited it to an aristocracy. In Germany, however, Luther's protests against the corruption of the Church led him to urge the expansion of knowledge to all the people. Luther wanted the Bible published in the vernacular, feasible because of the recent invention of the printing press, and pointed out that to spread God's word, it would be necessary to have a literate population. In his "Letter to the Mayors and Aldermen of all the cities of Germany in behalf of Christian schools," Luther wrote:

> Therefore it will be the duty of the mayors and council to exercise the greatest care of the young. For since the happiness, honor, and life of the city are committed to their hands, they would be held recreant before God and the world, if they did not, day and night, with all their power, seek its welfare and improvement. Now the welfare of a city does not consist alone in great treasures, firm walls, beautiful houses, and munitions of war; indeed, where all those are found, and reckless fools come into power, the city sustains the greater injury. But the highest welfare, safety, and power of a city consists in able, learned, wise, upright, cultivated citizens, who can secure, preserve, and utilize every treasure and advantage. . . .
>
> Since, then, a city must have well-trained people, and since the greatest need, lack, and lament is that such are not to be found, we must not wait till they grow up of themselves; neither can they be hewed out of stones nor cut out of wood; nor will God work miracles, so long as men can attain their object through means within their reach. Therefore, we must see to it, and spare no trouble or expense to educate and form them ourselves. For whose fault is it that in all the cities there are at present so few skillful people except the rulers, who have allowed the young to grow up like trees in the forest, and have not cared how they were reared and taught? . . .
>
> Even if there were no soul, (as I have already said), and men did not need schools and the languages for the sake of Christianity and the Scriptures, still, for the establishment of the best schools everywhere, both for boys and girls, this consideration is of itself sufficient, namely, that society, for the maintenance of civil order and the proper regulation of the household, needs accomplished and well-trained men and women.[7]

Although basically his purpose in seeking education for all was in the service of religion, Luther did recognize the necessity for having a literate and educated citizenry for the improvement of local government. His pressure on mayors, aldermen, and princes of the German states led to the first real State responsibility for education. The German pride in their educational system thus has long roots. In later centuries, Horace Mann was deeply impressed by the quality and practices of Prussian education, and the German universities were held in high esteem throughout the Western world until their debasement by the Nazi regime in the 1930's.

In medieval France, education was also dominated by the Church, and this continued until the time of Napoleon, who instituted a national system of education. Although there were teachers and classes, usually heterogeneous, for children, the emphasis was on the university with its faculties of theology, letters, and arts. "Until the nineteenth century, there was no term for elementary education in everyday French. The term *petite école*, corresponding to 'little school' or 'petty school' in English, did not appear until the seventeenth century."[8] The later national system began with the primary school and, by rigid selection methods, proceeded through the university level. Some flexibility has been introduced into the French school system in recent years, as will be seen in Chapter 12.

Islam

Our heritage from Islam is a rich one. This was a highly cultured empire, with many scholars and universities. The fields of learning which were taught included literature, science (mathematics, medicine, engineering, astronomy), architecture, and philosophy. Alkendhi (ninth century), a neo-Platonist and Aristotelian, helped to popularize Indian arithmetic. He also believed that truth should be accepted from wherever it comes. Avicenna, a Moslem physician, was a leading figure in the rediscovery of Aristotle, and was the author of an encyclopedia which included sections on the liberal arts.

It was Ibn Khaldoun, however, who made a notable contribution to the transmission, if not the substance, of Mohammedan knowledge. He emphasized the "faculty of understanding," in which he stressed that in order to become master of a field, one must know and understand its foundations. Such understanding could be obtained not only through listening and retention, but also through perception. Ibn Khaldoun was also one of the earliest to recognize the effects of cultural background on intelligence.

> . . . To be sure, if one compares a city dweller with an inhabitant of a desert one will discover in the first a mind endowed with penetration and sagacity. Therefore, the peasant feels inferior in nature and intelligence to the city dweller. However, he deceives himself. The superiority of the latter comes from the perfect acquisition of the faculties which facilitate the exercise of the various arts and from the observation of the customs imposed upon him by the usage of habits of a sedentary life; all these are things of which the man of the desert has no idea. When people understand the practice of arts . . . all the individuals who miss them imagine that the other owes them to the superior nature of his intelligence and that the mentality of the inhabitants of the desert is inferior in organization and nature to the city dweller. But this is not the case.[9]

It took until the second quarter of the twentieth century for this sage observation to be rediscovered in terms of American education.

Individual Contributors

One of the leading contributors to modern American education was John Amos Comenius (1592–1670), a Moravian bishop who sought social justice for all and believed that science was the key to the improvement of society. He was a pansophist. That is, he believed that reforms in the world could be accomplished if all men were taught all things from all points of view. He was a prolific author, writing about desirable educational principles in *The Great Didactic* and methods of applying them in numerous textbooks. "Comenius . . . laid the foundation of a systematic understanding of the teaching and learning process by applying Bacon's inductive method to education; . . ."[10] He also advocated the use of one teacher and one textbook per subject; movement of learning from the simple to the complex and the specific to the general; and urged that children be taught through activity and independent study. These concepts were later emphasized by John Dewey in the United States, and have been perpetuated by Comenius' native Czechoslovakia even to the present day. All subjects were to be correlated, much like the "core curriculum" fashionable in this country during the 1930's, 1940's, and 1950's. Comenius wanted to create a public school system with equal educational opportunities for all, regardless of sex, and in which advancement after the common six-year curriculum would be on the bases of merit and ability. This is the system used in much of Western Europe even today, although schooling is offered beyond six years with differentiated curricula and goals.

Jean Jacques Rousseau, an eighteenth-century romanticist, agreed with Comenius on the importance of considering nature in connection with education, but went further in that he wanted to substitute nature for education, whereas Comenius would have used nature as a guide in education. Rousseau believed that the main influences on education should be man, nature, and things. Thus sensory impressions were valuable, à la Aristotle, and essential to cognitive learning. Rousseau also emphasized the importance of motivation and placed considerable emphasis, in his *Émile*,[11] on spontaneous expression rather than habit in children's activities. This naturalistic approach antecedes Dewey's "child-centered curriculum," England's (and now the United States') "open classroom," and several of the contemporary alternatives to traditional education, including "free schools."

Emile and other works by Rousseau were protests against the distortion of human nature by society. He did not see the goal of education as being in the service of the state or religion, but rather as being directed toward the fullest natural development of the individual as a person. Moral instruction was to be given in early childhood through experience, e.g., the consequences of Emile's behavior, and good examples. During adolescence, the teacher was to develop Emile's intellect, following his natural interests, and making the utilitarian value of his studies apparent to the youth.

Emile and its emphasis on nature strongly influenced Pestalozzi (1746–1827), a Swiss experimental educator. As he worked in his own schools, he attempted to make intellectual studies meaningful through the use of concrete examples. Use of Pestalozzi's object-lessons, incidentally, was one of the first successful efforts to introduce psychology into the curriculum. He believed that education should take place in a warm teacher-pupil atmosphere, in which the innate or natural powers of the individual could unfold, much as a plant unfolds during its growth. Ulich comments that "Pestalozzi is still right when he demands the education of the head, the heart, and the hand, and with intelligent youth the last element in the triad of education will not take away undue time and strength from the first two. On the contrary, some practically constructive activity will support the general learning."[12] Pestalozzi viewed the goal of education, in a common or public school system, as the natural growth of the individual, leading to the ability to help himself and indirectly to reform society. His thoughts and educational practices were widely adapted in Prussia, and later in the United States. Although Pestalozzi's methods were introduced in this country as early as 1806 by Joseph Neef (1770–1854), it was Horace Mann who included many of them in the reforms he recommended and instituted in the following decades.

Even more influential in the introduction of psychology to the curriculum was Johann Friedrich Herbart (1776–1841), a German philosopher and educator. He was, contrary to Rousseau and Pestalozzi, interested in education as the means of developing a religious and moral man, and in the relationship of man to his social environment. However, he was in agreement with his contemporaries, Pestalozzi and Froebel, in considering that ". . . any education that disconnects itself from a comprehensive philosophical understanding of man and his role in the universe seemed amateurish and by necessity aimless. Metaphysics, logic, psychology, ethics, and education have to form a whole."[13]

Herbart tried to intellectualize a science of education which included five basic steps in instruction: 1) *Preparation*, which included a review of earlier relevant material; 2) *Presentation* or introduction of new material; 3) *Assimilation*, the connection of the old and the new material; 4) *Generalization*, in which general principles were abstracted from the assimilated material; and 5) *Application* of the acquired knowledge.[14] These pedagogical steps are still used at all levels of education. He also placed strong emphasis on interest as a means and end of instruction, which was a valuable contribution to pedagogical practice.

More under the influence of Pestalozzi was the German educator Friedrich Froebel (1782–1852). American education is particularly indebted to him for the introduction of the kindergarten. Incorporated into Froebel's educational theories was a recognition of children's native capacities and the educational value of activity, i.e., play and creativity in the curriculum. These are still aspects of modern American pre-school and kindergarten curricula. Like his contemporaries, Froebel was deeply religious, and felt that the child could be made aware of the working of God within himself through spontaneous activities. In his *The Education of Man*, Froebel envisaged education as, "that specifically human activity by which man participates purposefully in the evolution of the world from lower to higher stages of consciousness. Every step in this divine-natural unfolding is as characteristic of the whole as every other. Thus, childhood and play are not merely preparations for adulthood, to be passed over as quickly as possible, but are significant stages, to be respected and cultivated."[15]

The significance of these contributors to education in America cannot be under-estimated. Their ideas were brought to these shores by Horace Mann, and by their students. They helped to shape European education in general (the remaining effects of which may be seen in Chapter 12 in the discussion of comparative education), which was in turn to have great influence on American education as it developed.

What Flourishes from these Roots?

The variety of ideals and practices in education from ancient times through the nineteenth century abroad not only influenced American education as it developed, but also led to a major controversy in the philosophy of American education: do we educate the individual that he may function more intelligently and effectively as a citizen, or that as a socially-conscious individual he may effect changes in society? The concern of several schools of thought on the question of what are our educational goals will be explored more fully in Chapter 2, followed by a survey of philosophical positions in Chapter 3.

Another area of concern in education is economic in orientation. The cost of poverty to the nation, as well as the cost of education to the individual and the nation, will be discussed in Chapter 5. The interrelationship of economics and education is further intimately involved with the contemporary problem of how to secure adequate financial support for school programs, which are now administered on a local level, as agent for the state, without incurring Federal domination of such programs. The problems of governmental responsibility in education are explored in Chapter 4. The need for financial aid from some source is admitted in most quarters, but fear continues to exist that Federal support will result in loss of control by state and local boards of education. Chapter 6 will include the presentation of arguments by those in favor of and those opposed to Federal aid to education.

Another major problem in education today is whether public aid should be given to non-public, primarily parochial, schools. The development of this problem from the passage of the First Amendment to the Constitution up to the current day, and the opinions of various authorities on this question, will be the subject of Chapter 7.

The civil rights conflicts of today, particularly in relation to school desegregation, provide daily headlines in the press. In Chapter 8, the history of segregated education, changing court decisions, and reaction to school integration measures will be examined.

The focus of Chapter 9 is on excellence and education. In this chapter, what is meant by excellence, how to attain quality, and where to begin such programs, while maintaining our positive efforts toward a maximum quantity of education for all, will be considered. Among the final chapters, Professional Preparation of Teachers, Chapter 10, and a National Educational Policy, Chapter 12, are closely related to Chapter 9, for the high quality of teaching personnel and a way to evaluate the effectiveness of education are vital aspects of the problem of excellence in education. Also related to the chapter on teacher preparation is Chapter 11 on academic freedom. The question of teacher strikes and their appropriateness to the profession is another problem confronting us in the daily press. There are, clearly, many problems and many controversies in modern education—the fruit of centuries-old roots.

Summary

As we have demonstrated in this historical overview of the antecedents of American education, the state assumes responsibility for education when society feels the need to preserve itself for and in future generations. In addition to historical factors, the nature of the education provided or encouraged in any given period or culture depended heavily on the socio-economic conditions of the society and the philosophies dominant in the society.

The influence of various individual contributors to modern American educational practices and to the rise of public education as a function of the state were also discussed in this chapter. Many philosophers and educators were omitted from examination because their work overlapped or resembled too closely that which was included. Some of those omitted here, or mentioned only briefly, will be dealt with in other chapters where the reader will be spared the redundancy which would have occurred with two presentations of a man's work.

This chapter can be viewed in the historical and cultural perspective, with which we will continue in Chapter 2, or by grouping the ideas presented into several principal orientations in education, the subject of Chapter 3.

Endnotes

1. Castle, E. B. *Ancient Education and Today* (Baltimore: Penguin Books, 1961), p. 102.
2. Goldin, Judah trans., *The Fathers According to Rabbi Nathan*, Yale Judaica Series, X (New Haven: Yale University Press, 1955), p. 100.
3. Castle, *op. cit.*, p. 124.
4. Mulhern, James. *A History of Education* (2nd Ed.; New York: The Ronald Press Co., 1959), pp. 251 ff.
5. Woody, Thomas. *Life and Education in Early Societies* (New York: The Macmillan Co., 1949).
6. Mulhern, *op. cit.*, p. 335.
7. In Ulich, *op. cit.*, pp. 224–232.
8. Aries, Phillippe. *Centuries of Childhood*, transl. Robert Baldick (New York: Alfred A. Knopf, 1962), p. 286.
9. In Ulich, *op. cit.*, p. 201.
10. Ulich, Robert. *The Education of Nations* (Cambridge, Mass.: Harvard University Press, 1961), p. 55.
11. Rousseau, Jean Jacques. *Émile*, trans. Barbara Foxley (London: J. M. Dent and Sons, Ltd., 1911).
12. Ulich, 1961, *op. cit.*, p. 308.
13. *Ibid.*, p. 204.
14. Mulhern, *op. cit.*, p. 470.
15. Ulich, 1961, *op. cit.*, p. 204.

For Further Reading

ARIES, PHILLIPPE. *Centuries of Childhood*, transl. Robert Baldick (New York: Alfred A. Knopf, 1962).

BRAMELD, THEODORE. *Cultural Foundations of Education: An Interdisciplinary Exploration* (New York: Harper and Row, 1957).

BRUBACHER, JOHN S. *A History of the Problems of Education,* second edition (New York: McGraw-Hill Book Company, 1965).

BUTTS, R. FREEMAN. *A Cultural History of Education,* second edition (New York: McGraw-Hill Book Company, 1955).

CASTLE, E. B. *Ancient Education and Today* (Baltimore: Penguin Books, 1961).

CUBBERLEY, ELLWOOD P. *Readings in Public Education in the United States* (Boston: Houghton-Mifflin Company, 1934).

CUBBERLEY, ELLWOOD P. *The History of Education* (Boston: Houghton-Mifflin Company, 1922).

FROST, S. E., JR. *Historical and Philosophical Foundations of Western Education* (Columbus, Ohio: Charles E. Merrill, 1966).

GOLDIN, JUDAH. transl. *The Fathers According to Rabbi Nathan,* Yale Judaica Series, Vol. X (New Haven: Yale University Press, 1955).

GROSS, CARL H., STANLEY P. WRONSKI, and JOHN W. HANSON, eds. *School and Society: Readings in the Social and Philosophical Foundations of Education* (Boston: D. C. Heath, 1962).

HODGKINSON, HAROLD L. *Education in Social and Cultural Perspectives* (Englewood Cliffs, N.J.: Prentice-Hall, 1962).

MEYER, ADOLPHE E. *An Educational History of the Western World* (New York: McGraw-Hill Book Company, 1965).

MULHERN, JAMES. *A History of Education* (New York: The Ronald Press Company, 1959).

NASH, PAUL, ANDREAS M. KAZAMIAS, and HENRY J. PERKINSON, ed. *The Educated Man: Studies in the History of Educational Thought* (New York: John Wiley and Sons, Inc., 1965).

ROUSSEAU, JEAN JACQUES, *Émile,* transl. Barbara Foxley (London: J. M. Dent and Sons, Ltd., 1911).

SMITH, WILFRED C. *Islam in Modern History* (Princeton, N. J.: Princeton University Press, 1957).

THUT, I. N. *The Story of Education* (New York: McGraw-Hill Book Company, 1957).

ULICH, ROBERT. *History of Educational Thought* (New York: American Book Company, 1950).

ULICH, ROBERT. *The Education of Nations* (Cambridge, Mass.: Harvard University Press, 1961).

ULICH, ROBERT, ed. *Three Thousand Years of Educational Wisdom: Selections from Great Documents*, second ed. (Cambridge, Mass.: Harvard University Press, 1954).

VON GRUNEBAUM, G. E. *Medieval Islam: A Study in Cultural Orientation*, second ed. (Chicago: University of Chicago Press, 1953).

WOODY, THOMAS. *Life and Education in Early Societies* (New York: The Macmillan Company, 1949).

2

*american education
and
educational goals*

The purposes or goals of education have varied in our country in different periods of its history from an emphasis on religious training to concern for excellence, with other goals at intermediate stages. These changing aims reflect socio-economic conditions, historical developments, and the philosophical approaches of each period.

The Colonial Period

The early settlers in New England brought to these shores deep religious convictions and a belief that the ability to read the Bible was of critical importance (following Luther's pleas of a century before). The state, specifically Massachusetts, therefore assumed responsibility for and instigated the beginnings of education early in American colonial history. The leaders of Massachusetts passed legislation in 1642 providing for children's basic education for religious purposes, the first compulsory education law, and in 1647 added the principle of public tax support. The goal of education stated in the "Ould Deluder" Act of 1647 was the literacy of townsmen in order that they might more effectively fight the Devil. This famous act, passed in November 1647, reads as follows:

It being one cheife proiect of ye ould deluder, Satan, to keepe men from the knowledge of ye Scriptures, as in former times by keeping ym in an unknowne tongue, so in these lattr times by perswading from ye use of tongues, yt so at least ye true sence & meaning of ye originall might be clouded by false glosses of saint seeming deceivers, yt learning may not be buried in ye grave of or fathers in ye church and commonwealth, the Lord assisting or endeavrs, — It is therefore ordred, yt evry towneship in this urisdiction, aftr ye Lord hath increased ym number to 50 householdrs, shall then forthwith appoint one within their towne to teach all such children as shall resort to him to write and reade, whose wages shall be paid eithr by ye parents or mastrs of such children, or be ye inhabitants in genrall, by way of supply, as ye maior part of those yt ordr ye prudentials of ye towne shall appoint; provided, those yt send their children be not oppressed by paying much more yn they can have ym taught for in othr townes; and it is furthr ordred, yt where any towne shall increase to ye number of 100 families or householdrs, they shall set up a grammar schoole, ye mr thereof being able to instruct youth so farr as they shall be fited for ye university, provided, yt if any towne neglect ye performance hereof above one yeare, yt evry such towne shall pay 5 £ to ye next schoole till they shall performe this order.[1]

Obviously, the practical value of reading, writing, and calculation, while not completely ignored, were subordinate to the religious reasons behind this Act. It was the first mandate for publicly-supported education in the New World. Connecticut, in 1650, enacted its own educational legislation, but incorporated the entire Massachusetts law in its own.

Dame schools, taught by a housewife who combined supervision and instruction with her domestic duties, were established, where the children learned the rudiments of reading, writing, arithmetic, and religion. It was a situation equivalent, perhaps, to our contemporary kindergarten and first grade, with the addition of cooking and sewing for the girls and the rudiments of religiously-oriented reading for the boys. The "dame," and teachers at more advanced levels, continued the use of materials first studied in the home—the Bible, the Horn Book, the New England Primer, the catechism, and the classics. The catechism was the basis for a "core curriculum" at the primary level, on which was founded exercises in reading, writing, and ciphering (or arithmetic). The schoolmaster demanded obedience and conformity from the boys in his charge, and was little concerned with problems of "adjustment" to either the curriculum or his rigid demands.

In sizable communities of New England, Latin grammar schools were established to prepare boys aged 8–16 years for college and for leadership. The boys studied Latin, Greek, religion, and slightly more advanced mathematics, in order to qualify for admission to Harvard or Yale. These colleges, as well as the College of William and Mary in Virginia, specialized in education for the ministry via a classical education. The University of Pennsylvania, a later outgrowth of the eighteenth century Philadelphia Academy founded by Benjamin Franklin, also offered some scientific training as a result of the practical and scientific interests of its founder. Law and college teaching were later included as "respectable" courses of study in these and other universities.

Because of religious diversity and the desire of each denomination to train its children in its own faith, there was no parallel development of free schools in the Middle Atlantic colonies. There were denominational schools, some of which exist even today, and a few charity schools for paupers. The Quakers and Moravians of Pennsylvania admitted girls to some of their schools. The Dutch in New York had public church-affiliated schools in the seventeenth century, and under British rule later on, even had some public aid for secondary schools. It was in the Middle Atlantic colonies, however, that the academy, forerunner of the modern high school, was founded to provide a college preparatory program for boys. Franklin's Philadelphia Academy was the leading secondary school of the mid-eighteenth century.

Benjamin Franklin was a leader in eighteenth century American education. He favored charity education for the poor, academies for the wealthy, and utilitarian education for the middle class. His own Academy offered a broader and more practical curriculum than did most others in the Middle colonies or the Latin grammar schools of New England. The American

Philosophical Society, successor to the Junto, also founded by Franklin, recognized the need for a school system serving the state and nation, and implied the concept of free compulsory education at the elementary level, with scholarships for the talented in secondary school. Franklin's work in education formed a cornerstone of the developing American educational system.

In the Southern colonies, a third pattern of education, also closely tied to religion, was emerging.

In Virginia, plans were submitted by the Virginia Company of London in the period 1607–1624 for a college at Henrico and a preparatory school for it. Although plans were made and construction was underway, the financial failure of the Virginia Company and an Indian massacre, both in 1624, caused the abandonment of the project. However, the colonists persisted in their quest for educational facilities, and during the period 1624–1699, when Virginia was a royal colony, were able to establish schools at the elementary level as well as the College of William and Mary. "A strong interest in education, a sense of personal responsibility, self-reliance, and the cooperation of individuals, communities, and local officials seem to be the keys to the educational developments of the seventeenth century."[2] Unique to the educational developments during this period in Virginia were the endowed free schools.

The purpose of the endowment was to reduce or abolish altogether the charges for tuition either of all the pupils or of the pupils of a certain group or section. The first endowment for an educational institution in English North America was provided in Virginia by the will of Benjamin Syms, February 12, 1635. Syms gave two acres of land, the proceeds from the sale of milk, and the increase of eight cows, for a school to be located in Elizabeth City County and to afford free education to children within that county. Since this bequest for educational purposes was the first gift of the kind in the colony, it was confirmed by the General Assembly of March, 1643.[3]

The great distances between plantations was a major factor in the development of boarding schools rather than local day schools, and the alternative of resident tutors at many of the self-sufficient plantations. Thus, for the wealthy, Southern education was a choice between Anglican church-dominated private boarding schools or private education at home. For the poor, the choice was largely between pauper schools and apprenticeship programs. In the latter, the masters were supposed to instruct the boys in the "4 R's" (including religion), as well as their trade, but this was a responsibility often taken lightly.

It was recognized in the colonies that education could also serve the purpose of training the community's workers and leaders, which aided economic and political growth, but this was decidedly secondary to the religious goals of colonial education. Despite the fact that religion and other freedoms were the goals of the early settlers, in all the Colonies, sectarian, class, and racial prejudice marked the educational scene. As nationhood approached, elementary education and apprenticeships in practical, commercial, and manual fields were for the masses wherever such programs existed. Secondary and higher education were reserved for the privileged.

The Federal Period

Although eighteenth century philosophers introduced the concepts of the inherent dignity of man and the worth of the individual, concepts which led to political and social revolutions for the following two hundred years, education at the beginning of the Federal period was still dominated by concern for spiritual salvation. When we became the United States of America, several states, as provided in the Tenth Amendment to the Constitution, passed their own constitutional provisions for public education. These stressed greatly the virtues of education for religious or moral purposes. In Pennsylvania, for example, a 1776 provision stated that:

A school or schools, shall be established in every county by the legislature, for the convenient instruction of youth, with such salaries to the masters, paid by the public, as may enable them to instruct youth at low prices; and all useful learning shall be duly encouraged and promoted in one or more universities. . . . Laws for the encouragement of virtue, and prevention of vice and immorality, shall be made and constantly kept in force. . . .[4]

Federal interest in and contributions to education came as early as the 1780's, and expanded from that time on. The Northwest Ordinance of 1787 provided for public education in newly-acquired territories, since "religion, morality, and knowledge" were considered essential to good government. The last phrase, "essential to good government," is indicative, however, of the growing awareness that the welfare of the new nation required an informed citizenry. This would seem to be the first change in the pattern of educational goals. The emphasis was beginning to shift from the idea of state responsibility to serve religion to a concept of educating the individual for knowledgeable citizenship and for his own benefit.

In the same period, Thomas Jefferson presented an education bill to the Virginia legislature, the intent of which was the strengthening of democracy. He was among the first to view education as being in the service of the government rather than the service of religion. Jefferson's plan, never enacted into law, included numerous three-year schools open to all free (i.e., non-slave) children in Virginia; several grammar or secondary schools open to intellectually able boys selected from the primary school population, and public scholarships for a limited number of grammar school graduates to attend the College of William and Mary. Jefferson's comprehensive bill included provisions for public supervision of the program, and for the evaluation and selection of pupils for the higher levels. The most democratic aspect of the plan was the removal of the stigma of charity then attached to *free* elementary schools. In its exclusion of slaves and girls, the plan was non-democratic from today's point of view.

The rapid growth of the country contributed to the spread of the New England pattern of education. Recognition of the practical as well as the spiritual applications of learning came as the need increased for people competent in surveying, cartography, keeping court records, and practicing the arts of democracy. Education for citizenship had begun to displace education for salvation by the beginning of the nineteenth century. Newer concepts of educational goals and patterns continued to emerge as Pestalozzi's philosophy of the "Common School Movement" was accepted in this country, and as laws were passed, particularly in nineteenth-century New England, implementing these goals.

Horace Mann, often called the "Father of the Public School," held to the basic premise stated in the Declaration of Independence that all men were created equal. He came along at the right time in our early national history, the 1830's and 1840's, to push education as a social and political force, to decrease the distance between educational theory and practice, and to create via education, a population, which could contribute knowledgeably to the Industrial Revolution, as well as to the developing democratic institutions of the time.

The historical setting of Mann's work was a complex web of changing patterns, conflicting philosophies, and the impingement of world events on the young nation's development. The second quarter of the nineteenth century saw the expansion of both our frontiers (to the Pacific and the Rio Grande by 1850), and our population (due to increasing immigration from Europe). Although our economy was predominantly agricultural, the growth of the textile industry in Massachusetts foreshadowed the rapid developments of the Industrial Revolution in the New England and Middle Atlantic states particularly. The doctrine of individualism was in the air, preached widely by Alcott, Emerson, and Thoreau. The rights and dignity of man were of increasing concern, both here in the abolition-slavery controversy, and in Europe where nationalist revolutions occurred in the late 1840's. The spirit of ferment characterized this era and meshed perfectly with the dedication and vision of Horace Mann.

A lawyer and public official, Mann was early convinced of the virtues of and need for an educated populace. In a Fourth of July oration in 1823, at the age of 27, Mann warned that the hard-won blessings of freedom could only be preserved through intelligence, which ". . . like the blood sprinkled upon the door-posts of the Hebrew houses, will prevent the destroying angel of despotism from entering."[5] Elected to the Massachusetts State Senate in 1835, Senator Mann only two years later sponsored legislation which would apply the surplus revenue of the state to education. When the state board of education was created that same year, he became its first secretary. As a state legislator, Mann was also active in the creation of normal schools for better teacher preparation, and the encouragement of public-supported local schools. In his crusade on behalf of education, Mann was strongly influenced by the views of Pestalozzi, by the political support of Governor Edward Everett of Massachusetts, by the financial support of Edmund Dwight (a mill-owner who, concerned about the illiteracy of his millhands and their children, felt that there should be good schools available to them, as well as school attendance laws), and by the theories of George Combe, a prominent Scottish phrenologist.

As secretary to the Massachusetts State Board of Education, Mann wrote twelve annual reports. These reflect both the problems of the times and his own interests. The Fifth Annual Report (1842), stressed the economic value of education, and was an appeal to the industrialists of the day to support universal education. He was one of the first to emphasize investment in education as an investment in productivity. Mann's seventh report was concerned with comparative education. This followed a trip to England, France, Prussia, and Scotland. He concluded that the government could and should play an important and beneficial role in education, as it did in Prussia, rather than the minor role it played in Britain. He also praised the Scottish and graded Prussian school systems for their teachers' awakening of motivation and interests in their pupils, rather than instruction based solely on authoritarian indoctrination. The findings of this journey were an important weapon in Mann's war for school reform, but they aroused strong controversy because of his criticisms, none too subtle, of the Boston schoolmasters and their superiors.

Mann's Eighth Annual Report was concerned with the value of education to the state.

If we do not prepare children to become good citizens;—if we do not develop their capacities, if we do not enrich their minds with knowledge, imbue their hearts with love of truth and duty, and a reverence for all things sacred and holy, then our republic must go down to destruction as others have gone before it . . .[6]

Mann himself had attended school only about ten weeks each year until he was 16 years old. Yet, in his Tenth Annual Report, he advocated compulsory, universal, state-supported education for children aged four to 16 years, ten *months* per year. He felt that universal free education was the nation's best safeguard against mobocracy, confiscatory legislation, and the Jacksonian spoils system—all crucial problems of his time.

In his Twelfth Annual Report, he again stressed the need for free education, but as partial recompense for the low wages of industrial workers. He condemned the then increasing economic inequalities which were responsible for privations and suffering, and relied on the free public schools to eliminate the social ills of industrial capitalism. Education was seen as the great equalizer of men. In fact, according to Mann and other leading educators of the day, "The aim of education was to fit children for society as well as for a rich personal life; the two aims were in fact inseparable."[7]

Horace Mann's contribution to Massachusetts education has had a profound and lasting effect on American education in general. As a legislator and educator, he was responsible for the establishment of state-supported and controlled schools; the foundation of schools for the blind and the deaf; the establishment of state normal schools; the introduction of written essay examinations to furnish exact and equal means of testing students' achievements; opposition to sectarian religious instruction in public schools, although the Bible could be read without comment (still a problem today despite Supreme Court rulings); and for urging reforms in curriculum, teaching methods, school organization, and teacher education. Later, as president of Antioch College, he also encouraged coeducation, laid the foundation for student self-government, and used the honor system. Much of what he did and said remains applicable to contemporary American education. His work, as seen in the twelve annual reports, is indicative of what one individual can do in shaping goals, methods, and practices.

The Industrial Revolution, as Mann and others pointed out, made universal literacy an important national goal more for economic than religious reasons, a trend which has increasingly characterized educational thinking since that time. The New England Primer of Colonial times was replaced by Mc-Guffey's *Eclectic Reader* and Webster's *The American Speller.* These were still highly moralistic in tone, but not as harshly Puritanical as the Primer. They also included some patriotic material, contributing to the growing nationalism of this era.

The basic questions of nineteenth century New England education were who should be taxed, whether the schools were intended to help preserve democracy, state versus Federal control, the development of a uniform curriculum, the establishment of uniform annual attendance requirements, and the issuance of teaching licenses.

Compulsory education really began with the Massachusetts Act of 1852, which provided that:

> Every person who shall have any child under his control between the ages of eight and fourteen years, shall send such child to some public school within the town or city, in which he resides, during at least twelve weeks, . . . in each and every year during which such child shall be under his control, six weeks of which shall be consecutive.[8]

Another issue, that of state control versus private control of liberal arts colleges had been resolved in the Dartmouth College case of 1819. Private liberal arts colleges, it had been determined, could not be taken over by the state.

The issue of public tax support for secondary education was settled in the Kalamazoo (Mich.) case of 1872, in which such support was ruled constitutional by the state. The ruling was based on the fact that the citizens of Michigan had adopted articles submitted to them by a constitutional convention which provided, in part, ". . . for the establishment of free schools in every school district for at least three months in each year, and for the university."[9] Since preparation was needed for the university, and since both private schools or the means to send children abroad for preparatory work were rare in Michigan, the judges involved in this case wrote: "The inference seems irresistible that the people expected the tendency towards the establishment of high schools in the primary school districts would continue until every locality capable of supporting one was supplied."[10] The appeal against public support of high schools was thus denied.

By the late nineteenth century, then, education in New England and other northern states was set on the path leading to our modern educational system. Some retardation had been experienced in the North and West during the Civil War, but recovery and expansion as the growth of the country continued, were rapid.

In the South, however, the Civil War destroyed the existing educational patterns. The social, economic, and political breakdown of that region led ultimately to the creation of a new state-controlled educational system. During the Reconstruction Period, there was also the foundation of a school program for the newly-freed Negroes, designed to help them become a knowledgeable force in the population. As will be discussed in Chapter 8, however, the good intentions of the Freedman's Bureau and various Negro educators became embroiled in conflict and controversy which often negated those intentions. Up to the end of the nineteenth century, no southern state had enacted a compulsory school attendance law, although most of the other states had done so. In 1901, President Dabney of the University of Tennessee, spoke out on this problem, and in the course of so doing, revealed other Southern problems vis-a-vis education as well.

. . . One thing is certain, ninety days' school with an average attendance of only 30 to 40 percent of the school population will never educate the people.

The laws designed to disfranchise illiterate whites and blacks are likely to have a beneficent influence upon the educational situation in the South. Such laws, if impartially

drawn and fairly carried out, will do almost as much good
in promoting the elementary education, of males at least,
as compulsory laws. The uneducated people of the southern
states, both whites and blacks, esteem their ballot to a
degree that is almost ridiculous. In states like North Carolina where the educational qualification has been applied,
the colored people are already showing an earnest desire
to get the little education required to qualify as voters.
But these laws, even at best, touch only one-half the population. The only perfect solution of the problem is a compulsory attendance law, carefully designed to reach every
healthy child. We must put all the children in school, but
before we do this we must have the schools and the
teachers.[11]

At the Turn of the Century

Late in the nineteenth century, education acquired yet another
purpose. This was a social function. Immigration from Europe
was increasing at a rapid rate. The growth of industrialization
and consequent migration from farms to cities was also increasing. It fell to education to fit these migratory masses into
the mainstream of the American culture. As President John F.
Kennedy pointed out:

> But the very problems of adjustment and assimilation pre-
> sented a challenge to the American idea—a challenge
> which subjected that idea to stern testing and eventually
> brought out the best qualities in American society. . . .
> the public school became a powerful means of preparing
> the newcomers for American life. The ideal of the "melting
> pot" symbolized the process of blending many strains into
> a single nationality . . .[12]

Many of the immigrants, poor in everything except aspirations and the culture which they brought with them, clutched at
education as the means by which their children, if not they
themselves, would become Americans both in name and sub-

stance. Those who could not attend the public schools gladly spent their few free hours at settlement house classes or libraries where they were prepared for citizenship, taught English, taught new trades, and became part of their new community. Acculturation, then, has been a major function of American education in the period beginning about 1885 and lasting, in varying degrees, until the present time. (The present efforts of the schools to assimilate minority and culturally different groups will be examined at length in Chapter 5.)

It was in this era and setting, therefore, that the first major change in American education took place—a revolution in the quantity of education provided and in the quantity of population reached by education. From the Massachusetts Act of 1852, *supra*, to 1918, legislation was passed in every state providing for some degree of compulsory school attendance. We were late in this development compared to other countries, as we were in areas such as workmen's compensation laws, provisions for Social Security, and other social legislation. Prussia, France under the Napoleonic Code, and other European states had made education compulsory before our Civil War. Contemporaneous with this development, moreover, there was an increase in legislation regulating child labor which made it possible for children to attend school rather than work. Limits were set in the child labor laws on minimum age for working, maximum hours of labor per day, and the conditions under which and industries in which children might be employed.

Not only did elementary and secondary education expand, but, in California, the movement for public junior colleges succeeded by 1910 in founding such institutions. It was believed that they were needed because of the expense of four-year colleges, the distance the student would have to travel to attend four-year colleges on a day basis, and the training needs for minor technical and professional occupations. (In the 1960's, publicly-supported two-year or community colleges were becoming common in the several states because of popular demands for post-high school education, and the physical limitations of four-year institutions to accept and accommodate all applicants.)

With the resultant great increase in school population, and because of the increasing application of psychological theories to education, school practices as well as goals were changing. John Dewey, in particular, was a major force in revamping both educational goals and the curricula. He believed that education was a necessity of life—that living beings have to be able to use the world about them as well as to develop their capacity for continuing growth. To Dewey, education *was* life, not a preparation for it. In his laboratory school at the University of Chicago, and later as professor at Columbia University, Dewey introduced the child-centered, experiential curriculum (within the limitations of "child-centered" as Dewey saw it).

From Rousseau, Dewey had learned that education was not something to be forced upon youth. It involved rather a process of growth antedating the pupil's admission to the school and extending beyond his departure from it. In teaching it was essential always to take account of the conditions of learning, to impart the ability to read, to write, and to use figures intelligently in terms that were themselves meaningful and real. That meant at the lower grades an emphasis on activities over abstractions, not as ends in themselves but as means of evoking stimulating questions.[13] Dewey was much concerned that educational goals and practices were stagnating while the world in which they existed was changing markedly. He was a pragmatist, a point which will be discussed further in the next chapter, believing that educators should consider the cultural, scientific, and technological forces which produce change in the society, estimate their probable direction and level of success, and then consciously strive to ally them and the schools. In his later years, criticizing the educational patterns of the 1920's and 1930's, Dewey wrote: "The educational system must move one way or another, either backward to the intellectual and moral standards of a prescientific age or forward to ever greater utilization of scientific method in the development of the possibilities of growing, expanding experience."[14]

Dewey was a critic of the traditional subject-centered curriculum because, to him, it was an unreal compartmentalization of the child's "outer world." As he pointed out in *The Child and the Curriculum* (1902), the child does not see the world in terms of arithmetic, spelling, geography, etc. To the contrary, the child perceives the world through his contacts with it and reacts to it as a totality. Therefore, according to Dewey, the child's experiences must be an integral part of the curriculum, being used, for example, to introduce new subject-matter. The aims of education to him were, therefore, to arise from the free growth (albeit guided by the teacher's experience and knowledge) of individual experience. Included in Dewey's aims were: 1) stimulating the individual to continue his growth and education; 2) the development of orderly, progressive, purposeful activity; 3) habituation of the individual to social control without subordinating his natural powers to authority, so that he might more effectively contribute to society as a citizen; and 4) the cultivation of cultural ideas and appreciation. Thus, Dewey saw education both in the service of the individual and, indirectly, the state. Like Mann before him, he believed that the nation would benefit from an educated citizenry. The school served as an instrument of society for socializing individuals in a simplified social environment.

john dewey
Democracy and Education

1. The Nature and Meaning of Environment.—We have seen that a community or social group sustains itself through continuous self-renewal, and that this renewal takes place by means of the educational growth of the immature members of

Dewey, John. *Democracy and Education* (New York: The Macmillan Co., 1922), Chapter II, pp. 12 ff.

the group. By various agencies, unintentional and designed, a society transforms uninitiated and seemingly alien beings into robust trustees of its own resources and ideals. Education is thus a fostering, a nurturing, a cultivating, process. All of these words mean that it implies attention to the conditions of growth. We also speak of rearing, raising, bringing up—words which express the difference of level which education aims to cover. Etymologically, the word education means just a process of leading or bringing up. When we have the outcome of the process in mind, we speak of education as shaping, forming, molding activity—that is, a shaping into the standard form of social activity. In this chapter we are concerned with the general features of the *way* in which a social group brings up its immature members into its own social form.

Since what is required is a transformation of the quality of experience till it partakes in the interests, purposes, and ideas current in the social group. Things can be physically transported in space; they may be bodily conveyed. Beliefs and aspirations cannot be physically extracted and inserted. How then are they communicated? Given the impossibility of direct contagion or literal inculcation, our problem is to discover the method by which the young assimilate the point of view of the old, or the older bring the young into likemindedness with themselves.

The answer, in general formulation, is: By means of the action of the environment in calling out certain responses. The required beliefs cannot be hammered in; the needed attitudes cannot be plastered on. But the particular medium in which an individual exists leads him to see and feel one thing rather than another: it leads him to have certain plans in order that he may act successfully with others; it strengthens some beliefs and weakens others as a condition of winning the approval of others. Thus it gradually produces in him a certain system of behavior, a certain disposition of action. The words "environment," "medium" denote something more than surroundings which encompass an individual. They denote the specific *continuity* of the surroundings with his own active tendencies. . . . The things with which a man *varies* are his genuine environment. . . .

3. The Social Medium as Educative.—Our net result thus far is that social environment forms the mental and emotional disposition of behavior in individuals by engaging them in activities that arouse and strengthen certain impulses, that have certain purposes and entail certain consequences. A child growing up in a family of musicians will inevitably have whatever capacities he has in music stimulated, and, relatively stimulated more than other impulses which might have been awakened in another environment. Save as he takes an interest in music and gains a certain competency in it, he is "out of it"; he is unable to share in the life of the group to which he belongs. Some kinds of participation in the life of those with whom the individual is connected are inevitable; with respect to them, the social environment exercises an educative or formative influence unconsciously and apart from any set purpose. . . .

Just as the senses require sensible objects to stimulate them, so our powers of observation, recollection, and imagination do not work spontaneously, but are set in motion by the demands set up by current social occupations. The main texture of disposition is formed, independently of schooling, by such influences. What conscious, deliberate teaching can do is at most to free the capacities thus formed for fuller exercise, to purge them of some of their grossness, and to furnish objects which make their activity more productive of meaning.

While this "unconscious influence of the environment" is so subtle and pervasive that it affects every fiber of character and mind, it may be worth while to specify a few directions in which its effect is most marked. First, the habits of language. Fundamental modes of speech, the bulk of the vocabulary, are formed in the ordinary intercourse of life, carried on not as a set means of instruction but as a social necessity. . . . Secondly, manners. Example is notoriously more potent than precept. . . . Thirdly, good taste and aesthetic appreciation. If the eye is constantly greeted by harmonious objects, having elegance of form and color, a standard of taste naturally grows up. . . . To say that the deeper standards of judgments of value are framed by the situations into which a person habitually enters is not so much to mention a fourth point, as it is to point out a fusion of those already mentioned. We rarely recognize the extent in which our conscious estimates of what is worth while and what is not, are due to standards of which we are not conscious at all. But in general it may be said that the things which we take for granted without inquiry or reflection are just the things which determine our conscious thinking and decide our conclusions. And these habitudes which lie below the level of reflection are just those which have been formed in the constant give and take of relationship with others.

4. The School as a Special Environment.—The chief importance of this foregoing statement of the educative process . . . is to lead us to note that the only way in which adults consciously control the kind of education which the immature get is by controlling the environment in which they act, and hence think and feel. We never educate directly, but indirectly by means of the environment. Whether we permit environments to do the work, or whether we design environments for the purpose makes a great difference. And any environment is a chance environment so far as its educative influence is concerned unless it has been deliberately regulated with reference to its educative effect. . . . schools remain, of course, the typical instance of environments framed with express reference to influencing the mental and moral disposition of their members.

Roughly speaking, they come into existence when social traditions are so complex that a considerable part of the social store is committed to writing and transmitted through written symbols. Written symbols are even more artificial or conventional than spoken; they cannot be picked up in accidental intercourse with others. In addition, the written form tends to select and record matters which are comparatively foreign to everyday life. The achievements accumulated from generation to generation are deposited in it even though some of them have fallen temporarily out of use. Consequently as soon as a community depends to any considerable extent upon what lies beyond its own territory and its own immediate generation, it must rely upon the set agency of schools to insure adequate transmission of all its resources. . . .

. . . The first office of the social organ we call the school is to provide a *simplified* environment. It selects the features which are fairly fundamental and capable of being responded to by the young. Then it establishes a progressive order, using the factors first acquired as means of gaining insight into what is more complicated.

In the second place, it is the business of the school environment to eliminate, so far as possible, the unworthy features of the existing environment from influence upon mental habitudes. It establishes a purified medium of action.

. . . In the third place, it is the office of the school environment to balance the various elements in the social environment and to see to it that each individual gets an opportunity to escape from the limitations of the social group in which he was born, and to come into living contact with a broader environment. . . .

In the olden times, the diversity of groups was largely a geographical matter. There were many societies, but each, within its own territory, was comparatively homogeneous. But with the development of commerce, transportation, intercommunication, and emigration, countries like the United States are composed of a combination of different groups with different traditional customs. It is this situation which has, perhaps more than any other one cause, forced the demand for an educational institution which shall provide something like a homogeneous and balanced environment for the young. Only in this way can the centrifugal forces set up by juxtaposition of different groups within one and the same political unit be counteracted. The intermingling in the school of youth of different races, differing religions, and unlike customs creates for all a new and broader environment. Common subject matter accustoms all to a unity of outlook upon a broader horizon than is visible to the members of any group while it is isolated. The assimilative force of the American public school is eloquent testimony to the efficacy of the common and balanced appeal.

The school has the function also of coordinating within the disposition of each individual the diverse influences of the various social environments into which he enters. One code prevails in the family; another, on the street; a third, in the workshop or store; a fourth, in the religious association. As a person passes from one of the environments to another, he is subjected to antagonistic pulls, and is in danger of being split into a being having different standards of judgment and emotion for different occasions. This danger imposes upon the school a steadying and integrating office.

Although the progressive education movement is popularly associated with Dewey's pragmatic theories and practices, it stemmed in reality from the progressive program of social and political reform which was current prior to the turn of the century. The school was to be a fundamental instrument in this program, just as it had been for Horace Mann. "From the beginning, progressivism cast the teacher in an almost impossible role: he was to be an artist of consummate skill, properly knowledgeable in his field, meticulously trained in the science of pedagogy, and thoroughly imbued with a burning zeal for social improvement."[15] He was not to let the pupils run rampant in the classroom, but was to encourage more freedom of exploration than the restricting and authoritarian nineteenth century educational pattern permitted. Much of the criticism of progressive education, and of Dewey, in later years developed because of excessive permissiveness and concern with "adjustment" of the child which were caricatures rather than characteristics of the movement.

The reform aspects of progressive education were introduced at a time when other influences on educational goals (as reflected in the curriculum) were also being felt. Up to the twentieth century, education had had as its goal the development of a literate population in terms of the masses, and the preparation of ministers, lawyers, and scholars among the elite. However, in the first decade of the new century, when compulsory education laws had been passed in most states, when the ethnic background of the school population had begun to change (as Dewey mentioned), when the economy had become increasingly industrialized to a point where the "3 R's" were no longer adequate preparation for good jobs, and when the psychological testing movement had been newly introduced, there was recognition of the fact that simple literacy and transmission of the culture were no longer adequate educational goals. There had been a movement for vocational and industrial education since the post-Civil War years, with particular impetus from the Russian industrial education exhibit at the Philadelphia Centennial Exposition in 1876.

Although vocational education in the public schools was a threat to the apprenticeship programs of unions, many employers welcomed the prospect of well-trained men as new and competent employees rather than "helpers." Farmers were anxious to have their children trained in agricultural methods.

The 1900's, then, brought not only a powerful rural demand for vocationalism as the key to educational reform, but a sharpening definition of the content of agricultural studies and their place in a reconstituted school curriculum. Notwithstanding traditional rural-urban antipathy, it was inevitable that this rural phase of the larger industrial education movement would eventually join forces with its urban counterpoint. The two streams tended to run parallel during the first years of the twentieth century; but the National Society for the Promotion of Industrial Education did its work well, and after 1906 they began to converge. Groups that were at best strange bedfellows found themselves lobbying together in Congress toward the common goal of a federal vocational education bill.[16]

After much lobbying and study, a vocational education bill was finally passed—the Smith-Hughes Act of 1917. It provided for educational programs in agriculture, home economics, trade, and industrial subjects as part of all-day secondary school programs, in part-time schools for working adolescents, and in evening adult schools. This marked the real beginning of differentiated secondary curricula in terms of the needs both of the individual and of society. The academic or common secondary curriculum continued to focus on the transmission of culture from one generation to the next, and was the college preparatory course as it had traditionally been.

American entrance into World War I brought this period to a close. Our involvement in world affairs at this time represented, in a sense, the coming-of-age of American democracy, with a consequent decline in the European domination of our educational and other processes. After the war, a distinctly American educational philosophy arose, with emphasis on life adjustment. The National Education Association's Commission on the Reorganization of Secondary Education, in 1918, stated what came to be known as the "Seven Cardinal Principles." These goals for education included: health, worthy home membership, competence in the fundamental learning processes, vocational efficiency, worthy use of leisure time, and ethical character. Compare this list to the statement of the Educational Policies Commission more than a generation later (see page 47), after another world conflict and subsequent world political developments.

The Past Fifty Years

In the 1920's and 1930's, reconstructionist educational philosophers such as Brameld, Counts, and Rugg, urged a change in curriculum goals from the perpetuation of society to innovation in society. Dewey's pragmatism and the progressive education movement were attacked as being unconcerned with building a better society. The schools were seen instead as the agency to change society, since educational and social reconstruction movements had to work together. Education, according to Rugg, was to develop a socially cooperative, not competitive, philosophy and to produce a man fit to live in the modern world.[17] The study of discrete subjects in the curriculum was to be abandoned for an integrated "core curriculum," utilizing longer blocks of time, activity projects in groups, and units of study emphasizing a community viewpoint. The school was to become the focal community institution, and all of its activities were to be part of the curriculum. Some indoctrination of ideas would be necessary under this plan, but so would the understanding and discussion of controversial issues for consent to the ideas. Rugg wrote, "We cannot create a whole theoretical design for a new society and impose a specific course of action upon a people if we wish to continue the tradition of consent in a democratic society."[18] Brameld had a utopian view of education as a means for maximum self-realization of the great masses of people in a democratic welfare state. Somewhat restated, this utopian goal still exists today. The approach of the reconstructionists might be summed up by the title of one of Counts' books: *"Dare the School Build a New Social Order?".*[19]

This philosophy was unquestionably influenced by Marxism and the fact that that philosophy was successfully changing the character of the Russian society of the times. Its influence in this country was somewhat stronger than it might have been because of the severe economic depression of the 1930's.

Reconstructionism was not the only philosophy of this period, however. Bertrand Russell and Alfred North Whitehead, realists, believed that the goal of education was knowledge for its own sake and for the advancement of science. Bagley, an essentialist, also saw an intrinsic value in certain prescribed courses, with an emphasis on method and content rather than on creative thinking.

There was, in general, however, an emphasis on adaptation to the present with a corresponding revolt against external authority in this period (except for the stress on group interaction). This situation, to which the public was generally apathetic, was encouraged by the disintegration of empires in the political sphere, an acceptance of mediocrity and relative rather than absolute values, a rise in the crime rate, and widespread cynicism. Educational goals, as well as individual self-discipline, became "watered down."

The idealists and other traditionalists fought this pattern and persisted in emphasizing absolute truths, the ordered presentation of prescribed subject matter, and self-realization as the ultimate aim of education. Their influence was limited in the second quarter of the century. Criticisms of society-oriented education and the emphasis on "life adjustment" as its goal included those of the late Senator Joseph McCarthy of Wisconsin, who viewed such a philosophy as Communist-dominated.

The philosophy of group-centered learning and a curriculum geared to adjustment to the group continued to be dominant until the Russians launched Sputnik I in October, 1957. Then, the public and its representatives were startled into action. Bills for Federal aid to education were resurrected, culminating in the National Defense Education Act of 1958 (see Chapter 6). Since that reaction to Russian scientific prowess, the stress in educational goals has been on the education of the individual in terms of quality (e.g., the "talent search") so that he can be a more effective contributor to the state and society. Every person is to be aided to maximum self-development. In the wake, also, of the 1954 Supreme Court desegregation decision (see Chapter 8), which obligated the several states to provide equal educational opportunity for all, the stage was set for what has been called the third revolution in American education. To Francis Keppel, former Assistant Secretary of Health, Education, and Welfare, this is the necessary revolution in education—a revolution of quality.[20]

Current views on educational goals reflect certain basic national aims: universal, free, publicly supported and controlled, compulsory, non-sectarian education. Despite public concern about school integration and desegregation, curricula, and standards, conflicts in the implementation of these goals remain. We waver between competition (emphasis on the individual) and cooperation (necessary for the smooth operation of society), between traditional academic curricula and "preparation for living," and between emphasis on the past in transmitting our heritage and stress on the emergence of new patterns and social change. Even the compulsory aspect of education is being challenged.

Admiral Hyman Rickover, an ardent critic of education in the 1950's and 1960's, believes that our schools ". . . must return to the traditional task of formal education in Western civilization—transmission of the nation's cultural heritage, and

Figure 1.1

"If education is compulsory,
how come I'm still ignorant?"

preparation for life through rigorous training of young minds to think clearly, logically, and independently."[21] His concern with educational aims was, of course, intensified by Russian achievements in science and technology. The goals of Soviet education, however, were *not* so rigorous, although they may have appeared so to Rickover. Soviet goals include: producing citizens ". . . for participation in their society's life with a feeling of belonging . . . to prepare men and women for creative enjoyment of life; and to prepare them for intelligent contributions to the production and advancement of the material basis of society."[22] A comparison of Russian, English, and United States curricula shows that there was less variation in the primary schools than Rickover stated.

Table 1.1   **Comparison of relative places reserved for subjects taught in Russian, English, and American
schools, 1958[23] (In percentages.)**

Subject	Russia	England	U.S.A.
1. Language	53.00	23.00	46.50
2. Mathematics	18.50	11.50	11.50
3. Natural and physical sciences	10.00	4.50	16.00
4. Moral educ. and social sciences	3.50	5.00	10.00
5. Practical activities	4.00	16.00	4.00

Other activities complete the 100 percentage points. The relatively large percentage of practice activities in the English
primary curriculum reflects the early terminal education policy
of that country which was still in practice at the time of the
report.

At hearings before the House Committee on Appropriations in August, 1959, Rickover had more clearly delineated
his concept of an educated man; that is, the ultimate product
of our educational system, as ". . . a man with broad knowledge in all the fundamentals that make the world around him
intelligible; a man whose mind has been sharpened so that he
can use it effectively. He accepts ideas, thinks about them,
imparts something of himself into them, and comes forth with
something new. Because of his broad general knowledge, the
educated man sees things in perspective, in relation to other
things and in an interconnected way."[24] It is interesting to note
that Rickover defined, at least in part, what psychologists today
call the "creative" man.

A somewhat different point of view is that of Bruner, a
highly respected psychologist. In the course of reviewing education as a social invention, he came to several conclusions
which suggested general educational policies:

The first has to do with what is taught. It would seem, from
our consideration of man's evolution, that principal emphasis in education should be placed upon skills—skills in
handling, in seeing and imaging, and in symbolic operations, particularly as these relate to the technologies that
have made them so powerful in their human expression. . . .

This brings us immediately to a second conclusion. . . . A curriculum should involve the mastery of skills that in turn lead to the mastery of still more powerful ones, the establishment of self-reward sequences. . . .

A corollary of this conclusion (one I have urged before) is that there is an appropriate version of any skill or knowledge that may be imparted at whatever age one wishes to begin teaching—however preparatory the version may be. The choice of the earlier version is based upon what it is one is hoping to cumulate. The deepening and enrichment of this earlier understanding is again a source of reward for intellectual labors.

The third conclusion relates to change. If there is any way of adjusting to change, it must include, . . . the development of a metalanguage and "metaskills" for dealing with continuity in change. . . .

A further speculation about preparation for change is that we are bound to move toward instruction in the sciences of behavior and away from the study of history. Recorded history is only about five thousand years old . . . Most of what we teach is within the last few centuries, for the records before that are minimal while the records after are relatively rich. . . .

Finally, it is plain that if we are to evolve freely as a species by the use of the instrument of education, then we shall have to bring far greater resources to bear in designing our educational system. For one thing, if we are to respond to accelerated change, then we shall have to reduce turn-around time in the system. To do this requires greater participation on the part of those at the frontiers of learning.[25]

Perhaps the key to Bruner's thinking about the need to adapt to our constantly changing society is in his statement that we need to study the possible rather than the achieved.[26]

A third example of a contemporary approach to educational goals, this one by professional educators, states that the central purpose of the school is to develop the rational powers of the human mind which are crucial to establishing and preserving the freedom of the individual and society. The Educational Policies Commission, in 1961, iterated the traditional obligation of the school to develop in students the ability to think and to reason. This is basic to the achievement of other goals of education: health, worthy home membership, vocational competence, effective citizenship, worthy use of leisure, and ethical character. This list of worthy objectives is almost identical to the one issued by a similar commission in 1918.[27]

There are many additional statements about what our educational goals should be, but basically they are all related to one of the three viewpoints already expressed: traditional subject-matter orientation, education for a changing world, and "life adjustment." In fact, one may classify statements of goals as being oriented to intellectual training or to all-inclusive purposes.

mortimer smith

Fundamental Differences Do Exist

The advocate of basic education maintains that education as carried on in schools must deal primarily with intellectual training, with making young people literate in the essential fields of human knowledge, with transmitting the heritage and culture of the race. He acknowledges that formal education also plays a role in the social adjustment of the individual child, that it contributes to his physical welfare, the development of his personality, and his vocational competence . . . At the same time, however, he would insist that schools must have some priorities . . . The school, he insists, cannot be responsible for our total education, for the sum of experiences, information, and skills we acquire as we go through life.

Smith, Mortimer. "Fundamental Differences Do Exist," in *American Education Today* eds. Paul Woodring and John Scanlon, (New York: McGraw-Hill Book Company, 1963), pp. 28–29.

In contrast to this viewpoint, an all-inclusive view of the purpose of education and schools has gained momentum during the last thirty or forty years. This viewpoint has been summed up by a professor of education who says: "The chief goal of education is the development of physical health, mental and emotional stability, fine personality, and effective citizenship." . . .

On this matter of priorities in education, the picture seems clear: One group believes that the school must maintain its historic role as the chief institution of intellectual training; another group—and perhaps the dominant one in public education—maintains that intellectual training is only a part of the school's total program, and not necessarily the most important part.

Politicians, too, have contributed their views concerning educational goals. In 1963, the late President Kennedy, in his message on education to the 88th Congress, said, "For the Nation increasing the quality and availability of education is vital to both our national security and our domestic well being. . . . improved education is essential to give new meaning to our national purpose and power."[28] He added that, for the individual, education leads to the power of knowledge which enriches life and makes for good citizenship in the world. In requesting Federal aid for educational purposes, Kennedy named as national educational goals the following: 1) improving the quality of education at all levels; 2) expanding educational facilities to meet the needs of an expanding population; and 3) ". . . increasing the opportunities and incentives for all Americans to develop their talents to the utmost."[29]

Two years later, President Johnson echoed these sentiments and added emphases of his own. He proposed that a national goal of full educational opportunity be declared for the sake of the individual as well as the nation. Both Kennedy and Johnson were requesting Federal aid funds to implement their aims. We can see the results of their proposals in the many new programs now extant—Operations "Head Start" and "Get Set," special reading programs, expansion of school library programs, supplementary education for the talented, programs for the mentally retarded, aid to State education agencies, and many other programs.

During the Nixon administration, many of these programs were continued and others added, although funds for education remained among the lower priorities in appropriations during the early 1970's. A National Institute of Education was established in 1972 to coordinate and disseminate the findings of multitudinous research projects related to the field of education. Social pressures caused Congress to pass new legislation or amend earlier laws in efforts to increase educational opportunities for both the culturally different and the handicapped. In passing the Education Amendments of 1972, Congress introduced the establishment of the National Institute of Education with a firm commitment, supported by both parties, that stated:

> "The Congress hereby declares it to be the policy of the United States to provide to every person an equal opportunity to receive an education of high quality regardless of his race, color, religion, sex, national origin, or social class. . . ."[30]

To summarize the contemporary views of educational goals, we must attempt to visualize and anticipate the kind of world we expect to have in the next fifty years. This means that we must educate youth not only with facts and basic skills, ethics and morality, but also with the techniques of problem-solving and adaptation so that they are prepared for whatever social, economic, political, and technological changes may occur. As Bruner pointed out, change is occurring at an accelerated pace. At this point in time we cannot even foresee some of what will be commonplace ten years hence, let alone the needs of individuals and society half a century from now. Such a viewpoint implies, also, that we must consider now how best to use the resources and opportunities currently available in order to meet the challenges which lie—unknown—before us.

Toffler, in *Future Shock*, and Drucker, in *The Age of Discontinuity*, among others, offer some clues to these unknown challenges as well as some suggestions as to how we may be able to meet them. From Toffler's viewpoint, we will need to change the direction of education from a focus on the past and tradition to a focus on the future. As we grapple with our current problems, many of which will be explored in the coming chapters, we must learn to try to anticipate the unknown and to use the lessons of the past as a means to preparing alternatives for the future.

Endnotes

1. Records of the Governor and Company of the Massachusetts Bay in New England, vol. II, p. 203 (Boston: 1835). In Cubberley, Ellwood P., *Readings in Public Education in the United States* (Boston: Houghton-Mifflin Company, 1934), pp. 18–19.

2. Ames, Susie M. *Reading, Writing and Arithmetic in Virginia, 1607–1699* (Williamsburg, Va.: Virginia 350th Anniversary Celebration Corporation, 1957), p. 6.

3. *Ibid.*, p. 8.

4. In Knight, Edgar W. *Readings in Educational Administration* (New York: Henry Holt and Co., 1953), pp. 2–3.

5. Tharp, Louise Hall. *Until Victory* (Boston: Little, Brown & Co. 1953), p. 55.

6. Mann, Horace. *Eighth Annual Report,* in *The Republic and the School,* ed. Lawrence Cremin, (New York: Columbia Teachers College, 1957).

7. Curti, Merle. *The Social Ideas of American Educators* (New York: Charles Scribners' Sons, 1935), p. 132.

8. Knight, *op. cit.*, p. 229.

9. *Ibid.*, p. 251.

10. *Ibid.*, p. 251.

11. *Ibid.*, pp. 269–270.

12. Kennedy, John F. *A Nation of Immigrants* (New York: Harper and Row, 1964), p. 67.

13. Handlin, Oscar. "John Dewey's Challenge to Education," in *Dewey on Education: Appraisals*, ed. R. D. Archambault, (New York: Random House, 1966), p. 30.

14. Dewey, John. "Means and End of Education." From *Experience and Education* (New York: Macmillan, 1938), p. 113. Quoted in *Intelligence in the Modern World: John Dewey's Philosophy*, ed. J. Ratner (New York: Random House Modern Library, 1939), p. 681.

15. Cremin, Lawrence A. *The Transformation of the School* (New York: Vintage Books (Random House), 1964), p. 168.

16. *Ibid.*, pp. 49–50.

17. Rugg, Harold. *American Life and the School Curriculum* (Boston: Ginn and Company, 1936).

18. *Ibid.*, p. 299.

19. Counts, George S. *Dare the School Build a New Social Order?* (New York: The John Day Co., Inc. 1932).

20. Keppel, Francis. *The Necessary Revolution in American Education* (New York: Harper and Row, 1966), p. 17.

21. Rickover, H. G. *Education and Freedom* (New York: E. P. Dutton and Company, Inc., 1960), p. 18.

22. Cohen, Robert S. "On the Marxist Philosophy of Education," *Modern Philosophies and Education*, NSSE: Fifty-fourth Yearbook, Part I (Chicago, University of Chicago Press, 1955), p. 203.

23. *Preparation and Issuing of the Primary School Curriculum*, Twenty-first International Conference on Public Education, Geneva, 1958 (Paris: UNESCO, 1958), p. LVIII.

24. Rickover, *op. cit.*, "Reports on Russia by Vice Admiral Rickover Before the Committee on Appropriations, House of Representatives, August 18, 1959, p. 60.

25. Bruner, Jerome S. *Toward a Theory of Instruction* (Cambridge, Mass.: Belknap Press of Harvard University Press, 1966), pp. 34–37.

26. *Ibid.*, p. 36.

27. Educational Policies Commission, National Education Association, *The Central Purpose of American Education*, (Washington NEA, 1961), pp. 3–12. © 1960, 1961, 1963 by Saturday Review, Inc.

28. Kennedy, John F. *Education Message to the 88th Congress*, Jan. 29, 1963.

29. *Ibid.*

30. Education Amendments of 1972, Amendment to the General Education Provisions Act (title IV of Public Law 90–247), Part A, Sec. 405 (a) (1).

For Further Reading

ALLEN, FREDERICK LEWIS. *The Big Change: America Transforms Itself, 1900–1950* (New York: Harper and Row, 1952).

ARCHAMBAULT, R. D., ed., *Dewey on Education: Appraisals* (New York: Random House, 1966).

BAILYN, BERNARD. *Education in the Forming of American Society* (New York: Random House, 1960).

BAYLES, ERNEST E., and BRUCE L. HOOD. *Growth of American Educational Thought* (New York: Harper and Row, 1966).

BESTOR, ARTHUR E. *Educational Wastelands: The Retreat from Learning in Our Public Schools* (Urbana, Ill.: University of Illinois Press, 1953).

BLANSHARD, BRAND, ed., *Education in the Age of Science* (New York: Basic Books, Inc., 1959).

BRAUNER, CHARLES J. *American Educational Theory* (Englewood Cliffs, N.J.: Prentice-Hall., 1964).

BRUNER, JEROME S. *Toward a Theory of Instruction* (Cambridge, Mass.: Belknap Press of Harvard University Press, 1966).

BUTTS, R. FREEMAN, and LAWRENCE A. CREMIN. *A History of Education in American Culture* (New York: Holt, Rinehart, and Winston, 1953).

CARTER, HAROLD J., ed., *Intellectual Foundations of American Education* (New York: Pitman Publishing Company, 1965).

CHILDS, JOHN L. *American Pragmatism and Education* (New York: Henry Holt and Company, Inc., 1956).

COMMAGER, HENRY STEELE. "McGuffey and His Readers." In *Social Foundations of Education*, ed. Jonathan C. McLendon (New York: The Macmillan Company, 1966).

CONANT, JAMES BRYANT. *Thomas Jefferson and the Development of American Public Education* (Berkeley, Calif.: University of California, 1960).

COUNTS, GEORGE S. *Dare the School Build a New Social Order?* (New York: The John Day Company, Inc., 1932).

CREMIN, LAWRENCE A. *American Education: The Colonial Experience (1607–1783)*. (New York: Harper & Row, 1970).

CREMIN, LAWRENCE A. *The Genius of American Education* (New York: Vintage Books, 1965).

CREMIN, LAWRENCE A. *The Republic and the School: Horace Mann* (New York: Teachers College, Columbia University, 1957).

CREMIN, LAWRENCE A. *The Transformation of the School* (New York: Vintage Books, 1964).

CUBBERLEY, ELLWOOD P. *Public Education in the United States* (Boston: Houghton Mifflin Company, 1947).

CUBBERLEY, ELLWOOD P. *Readings in Public Education in the United States* (Boston: Houghton Mifflin Company, 1934).

CURTI, MERLE, *American Paradox: The Conflict Between Thought and Action* (New Brunswick, N.J.: Rutgers University Press, 1956).

CURTI, MERLE. *The Social Ideas of American Educators* (New York: Charles Scribners' Sons, 1935).

CURTI, MERLE. "The Social Ideas of American Educators: the Last Twenty-Five Years." In *Social Foundations of Education*, ed. Jonathan C. McLendon (New York: The Macmillan Company, 1966).

DEWEY, JOHN. *Democracy and Education* (New York: The Macmillan Company, 1922).

DE YOUNG, CHRIS A., and RICHARD WYNN. *American Education* (New York: McGraw-Hill Book Company, 1955).

DRUCKER, PETER F. *The Age of Discontinuity.* (New York: Harper and Row, 1969).

General Education in a Free Society (Cambridge, Mass.: Harvard University Press, 1945).

GROSS, CARL H., and CHARLES C. CHANDLER, ed. *The History of American Education through Readings* (Boston: D. C. Heath and Company, 1964).

KEATS, JOHN. *Schools Without Scholars* (Boston: Houghton-Mifflin Company, 1958).

KENNEDY, JOHN F. *A Nation of Immigrants* (New York: Harper and Row, 1964).

KIMBALL, SOLON T., and JAMES E. MCCLELLAN, JR. *Education and the New America* (New York: Vintage Books, 1962).

KING, EDMUND J. *Society, Schools, and Progress in the U.S.A.* (Oxford, England: Pergamon Press, 1965).

KNIGHT, EDGAR W. *Readings in Educational Administration* (New York: Henry Holt and Company, 1953).

LEVINE, DANIEL U. "The Community School in Historical Perspective." *Elementary School Journal*, 67, (Jan. 1967), 192–195.

MEAD, MARGARET. *The School in American Culture* (Cambridge, Mass.: Harvard University Press, 1951).

National Society for the Study of Education. *Social Forces Influencing American Education*, Sixtieth Yearbook, Part II (Chicago: University of Chicago Press, 1961).

Preparation and Issuing of the Primary School Curriculum. Twenty-first International Conference on Public Education, Geneva, 1958. (Paris: UNESCO, 1958).

RATNER, J., ed. *Intelligence in the Modern World: John Dewey's Philosophy* (New York: Random House (Modern Library edition), 1939).

RICKOVER, H. G. *Education and Freedom* (New York: E. P. Dutton Company, 1960).

RIESMAN, DAVID. *Constraint and Variety in American Education* (Lincoln, Nebr.: University of Nebraska Press, 1956).

RIPPA, S. ALEXANDER. *Education in a Free Society* (New York: David McKay Company, 1967).

ROSENMEIER, JESPER. "The Teacher and the Witness: John Cotton and Roger Williams." *William and Mary Quarterly*, 25 (July 1968), 408–431.

RUGG, HAROLD. *American Life and the School Curriculum* (Boston: Ginn and Company, 1936).

RUSSELL, JAMES E. *Change and Challenge in American Education* (Boston: Houghton-Mifflin Company, 1965).

SCOTT, C. WINFIELD, HILL, CLYDE M., and HOBERT W. BURNS. *The Great Debate: Our Schools in Crisis* (Englewood Cliffs, N.J.: Prentice-Hall, Inc., 1959).

SELAKOVICH, DANIEL. *The Schools and American Society* (Waltham, Mass.: Blaisdell Publishing Company, 1967).

SIDWELL, ROBERT T., and JOHN HARDIN BEST. *The American Legacy of Learning* (Philadelphia: J. B. Lippincott Company, 1967).

SMITH, MORTIMER, "Fundamental Differences Do Exist." In *American Education Today*, ed. Paul Woodring and John Scanlon (New York: McGraw-Hill Book Company, 1963).

TOFFLER, ALVIN. *Future Shock*. (New York: Random House, 1970).

TOQUEVILLE, ALEXIS DE. *Democracy in America* (New York: New American Library, 1956).

WRIGHT, LOUIS B. *The Cultural Life of the American Colonies: 1607–1763* (New York: Harper and Brothers, 1957).

3

philosophical orientation

Each of the eras of the past just discussed had its own dominant philosophy which was applied to life in general and education in particular. In some cases, the philosophy was mainly
theoretical. That is, it was an attempt by the thinkers of the
day to explain the nature of man and society. In other instances,
philosophers attempted to define "the good life" or "the good
man" and to tell specifically how either of these goals might
be attained. In so doing, the philosophers often analyzed the
existing society and/or pattern of education, pointed out
strengths and deficiencies, and offered what they believed to
be constructive criticism. Much of the writing vis-a-vis education today is in the last category, although the writers might
not view themselves or be viewed as philosophers.

In this chapter, we will survey several philosophical orientations: idealism, realism, pragmatism, existentialism, and
others. The emphasis will be on the applications of the various
philosophical positions to the field of education.

Idealism

The Idealists, who believe in universal and eternal truth, and
who are favorable to what has been done in the past, base
their views on Plato's writings. "Idealism declares that values
are absolute and unchanging. Goodness and beauty are not man-
made but rather part of the very structure of the universe.

65

School policy must, therefore, be founded on enduring principles."[1] Idealists also see the material world as a projection of the mind, not a reality to be explored by sensory impressions.

In *The Republic*, Plato traced the development of the real state and projected the ideal state as he saw it. To him, the purpose of education was to provide good citizens for the state by providing a practical (elementary) education for all. Females were to be included equally with males in this broadly-based educational system. The ideal state was to have three classes of citizens: the philosopher-kings, or governors of the Republic, were to lead the people toward absolute truth; the tradesmen and workers were to cater to the needs of the citizenry; and the guardians, or soldiers. The last class was to receive training in gymnastics for the body, music for the mind and soul, and additional abstract studies.

Although Plato believed that abstract knowledge is the best kind, he was sufficiently aware of the principles of growth and development to prescribe beginning with simple concepts and building to the complex. However, only good examples could be used to teach true knowledge, as may be seen in the following selection. Socrates was the "voice" (and former teacher) of Plato and speaks the principal part:

> "And shall we just carelessly allow children to hear any casual tales which may be devised by casual persons, and to receive into their minds ideas for the most part the very opposite of those which we should wish them to have when they are grown up?
> "We cannot.
> "Then the first thing will be to establish a censorship of the writers of fiction, and let the censors receive any tale of fiction which is good, and reject the bad; and we will desire mothers and nurses to tell their children the authorised ones only."[2]

Plato was also aware that skepticism might arise in the process of education, but was convinced that it would later be mediated by the overwhelming goodness of truth.

Plato also wrote that sensory impressions were false. The way of true knowledge was through the dialectic method. This technique consisted basically of breaking down definitions, and then by questioning, arriving at new ones. An illustration of this might be to take the word "knowledge," for example, as it is defined in the dictionary. A student, or a group of students, together with the instructor, would question the validity of every phrase in the definition, and would ultimately redefine the word. In a sense, we use the dialectic method every time we ask someone to explain what he means or to define his terms. React to the word "peace." Is peace simply the absence of war? Is it passive or active? Do the Russian Communists define it in the same way as the Chinese Communists? What is "peace?" This was, incidentally, the origin of the examination system.

Yet another aspect of Plato's idealism is the concept that individual talents should be sought out, trained, and put to social use. That is, the status of philosopher-king or guardian would be attained by individual ability rather than birth or wealth. Plato's scheme for this selection is rather interesting.

"Therefore, as I was just now saying, we must enquire who are the best guardians of their own conviction that what they think the interest of the State is to be the rule of their lives. We must watch them from their youth upwards, and make them perform actions in which they are most likely to forget or to be deceived, and he who remembers and is not deceived is to be selected, and he who fails in the trial is to be rejected. That will be the way?"

"Yes."

"And there should also be toils and pains and conflicts prescribed for them, in which they will be made to give further proof of the same qualities.

"Very right," he replied.

"And then," I said, "we must try them with enchantments— that is the third sort of test—and see what will be their behaviour; like those who take colts amid noise and tumult to see if they are of a timid nature, so must we take our youth amid terrors of some kind, and again pass them into pleasures, and prove them more thoroughly than gold is proved in the furnace, that we may discover whether they are armed against all enchantments, and of a noble bearing always, good guardians of themselves and of the music which they have learned, and retaining under all circumstances a rhythmical and harmonious nature, such as will be most serviceable to the individual and to the State. And he who at every age, as boy and youth and in mature life, has come out of the trial victorious and pure, shall be appointed a ruler and guardian of the State; he shall be honoured in life and death, and shall receive sepulture and other memorials of honour, the greatest that we have to give. But him who fails, we must reject. I am inclined to think that this is the sort of way in which our rulers and guardians should be chosen and appointed."[3]

In theory, and sometimes in practice, our nation espouses this ideal of selection by ability even today. The Horatio Alger novels of fifty years ago were based on this creed. Our preferences among politicians are based in part on how they have comported themselves in crises. As John Dewey pointed out, however, Plato's three classes had static limits and did not allow for the uniqueness of the individual, nor for the utilization of his specific and variable qualities.[4] Indeed, some of what Plato taught was anti-democratic and even narrow-minded.[5]

What of the teacher in this philosophy? What is his responsibility to the student and to the state?

The idealist teacher presides, like Socrates, over the birth of ideas, regarded not as things external to the student but as possibilities within him, which need to be realized. He does not expect the student to mature in accordance with rules of development that have been decided by other people but seeks to awaken within him his own latent capacities. The idealist teacher also believes with Kant that knowledge is best "wrung out" of the student rather than "poured into" him, although the content of education is not something that the student decides for himself. It is only the *approved* subject matter that the teacher may "wring out." Finally, the idealist teacher is supposed to be a person whom the student may emulate. In idealism, then, the teacher is accorded more importance than he is in any other educational philosophy.[6]

It is interesting to note that contemporary Communist teachers practice idealism in the classroom rather than what is considered pure Marxist theory. This is particularly evident in the concept of responsibility and obligation to the group. The individual student is constantly reminded that his behavior reflects on the group or community, and that when he misbehaves he is selfish, willful, and neglectful of his obligation to his fellows. On a more limited scale, teachers in the United States also use this argument, particularly on class "field trips."

The ancient Chinese followed many of the same principles expounded by Plato, especially his emphasis on the beauty and goodness of truth. Alkendhi, the islamic scholar, tried to modify Platonic philosophy and to reconcile it with the Aristotelian philosophy of realism. How difficult a task this was will be evident shortly. In the New World of the seventeenth century, the Puritans, who were classical humanists (an offshoot of idealism), were equally concerned with the education of their leaders-to-be.

> Since the classical mind could conceive of just political action only in terms of just and virtuous leaders, the central question which concerned most educational theorists was: What kind of education will produce the good ruler, the good statesman? This statesman would be the agent through which culture would be joined with action; it was, therefore of utmost concern that he be educated to receive the vision of the good life, behave justly in all action, and exemplify the ideal of virtue.[7]

This philosophy pervaded Colonial education and later higher education through the nineteenth century, producing the "liberally educated gentleman."

Closely allied to idealism in the modern era is the philosophy of perennialism. Perennialism also stresses eternal and absolute Truth which can be learned via a thorough study of the classical literature in many fields. To Perennialists, human nature and truth are both constants upon which education should be focused. Emphasis should be placed on developing the power of reason, not sensory impressions. This is a subject-centered philosophy which is best exemplified in the

"Great Books" curriculum favored by Mortimer Adler, Robert Hutchins, and Mark Van Doren, and practiced primarily at St. John's College, Annapolis, Maryland. It is, however, an education more appropriate for the "few" than the "many;" for Plato's philosopher-kings, as it were, although Hutchins appears to deny this in the following article.

robert maynard hutchins
A Liberal Education

The obvious failures of the doctrines of adaptation, immediate needs, social reform, and of the doctrine that we need no doctrine at all may suggest to us that we require a better definition of education. Let us concede that every society must have some system that attempts to adapt the young to their social and political environment. If the society is bad, in the sense, for example, in which the Nazi state was bad, the system will aim at the same bad ends. To the extent that it makes men bad in order that they may be tractable subjects of a bad state, the system may help to achieve the social ideals of the society. It may be what the society wants; it may even be what the society needs, if it is to perpetuate its form and accomplish its aims. In pragmatic terms, in terms of success in the society, it may be a "good" system.

But it seems to me clearer to say that, though it may be a system of training, or instruction, or adaptation, or meeting immediate needs, it is not a system of education. It seems clearer to say that the purpose of education is to improve men. Any system that tries to make them bad is not education, but

Hutchins, Robert Maynard. *The Conflict in Education* (New York: Harper and Row, Publishers, Inc., 1953), pp. 67–76.

something else. If, for example, democracy is the best form of society, a system that adapts the young to it will be an educational system. If despotism is a bad form of society, a system that adapts the young to it will not be an educational system, and the better it succeeds in adapting them the less educational it will be.

Every man has a function as a man. The function of a citizen or a subject may vary from society to society, and the system of training, or adaptation, or instruction, or meeting immediate needs may vary with it. But the function of a man as man is the same in every age and in every society, since it results from his nature as a man. The aim of an educational system is the same in every age and in every society where such a system can exist: it is to improve man as man.

If we are going to talk about improving men and societies, we have to believe that there is some difference between good and bad. This difference must not be, as the positivists think it is, merely conventional. We cannot tell this difference by any examination of the effectiveness of a given program as the pragmatists propose; the time required to estimate these effects is usually too long and the complexity of society is always too great for us to say that the consequences of a given program are altogether clear. We cannot discover the difference between good and bad by going to the laboratory, for men and societies are not laboratory animals. If we believe that there is no truth, there is no knowledge, and there are no values except those which are validated by laboratory experiment, we cannot talk about the improvement of men and societies, for we can have no standard of judging anything that takes place among men or in societies.

Society is to be improved, not by forcing a program of social reform down its throat, through the schools or otherwise, but by the improvement of the individuals who compose it. As Plato said, "Governments reflect human nature. States are not made out of stone or wood, but out of the characters of their citizens; these turn the scale and draw everything after them." The individual is the heart of society.

To talk about making men better we must have some idea of what men are, because if we have none, we can have no idea of what is good or bad for them. If men are brutes like other animals, then there is no reason why they should not be treated like brutes by anybody who can gain power over them. And there is no reason why they should not be trained as brutes are trained. A sound philosophy in general suggests that men are rational, moral, and spiritual beings and that the improvement of men means the fullest development of their rational, moral, and spiritual powers. All men have these powers, and all men should develop them to the fullest extent.

Man is by nature free, and he is by nature social. To use his freedom rightly he needs discipline. To live in society he needs the moral virtues. Good moral and intellectual habits are required for the fullest development of the nature of man.

To develop fully as a social, political animal man needs participation in his own government. A benevolent despotism will not do. You cannot expect the slave to show the virtues of the free man unless you first set him free. Only democracy, in which all men rule and are ruled in turn for the good life of the whole community, can be an absolutely good form of government.

The community rests on the social nature of men. It requires communication among its members. They do not have to agree with one another; but they must be able to understand one another. And their philosophy in general must supply them with a common purpose and a common concept of man and society adequate to hold the community together. Civilization is the deliberate pursuit of a common ideal. The good society is not just a society we happen to like or to be used to. It is a community of good men.

Education deals with the development of the intellectual powers of men. Their moral and spiritual powers are the sphere of the family and the church. All three agencies must work in harmony; for, though a man has three aspects, he is still one man. But the schools cannot take over the role of the family and the church without promoting the atrophy of those institutions and failing in the task that is proper to the schools.

We cannot talk about the intellectual powers of men, though we can talk about training them, or amusing them, or adapting them, and meeting their immediate needs, unless our philosophy in general tells us that there is knowledge and that there is a difference between true and false. We must believe, too, that there are other means of obtaining knowledge than scientific experimentation. If knowledge can be sought only in the laboratory, many fields in which we thought we had knowledge will offer us nothing but opinion or superstition, and we shall be forced to conclude that we cannot know anything about the most important aspects of man and society. If we are to set about developing the intellectual powers of men through having them acquire knowledge of the most important subjects, we have to begin with the proposition that experimentation and empirical data will be of only limited use to us, contrary to the convictions of many American social scientists, and that philosophy, history, literature, and art give us knowledge, and significant knowledge, on the most significant issues.

If the object of education is the improvement of men, then any system of education that is without values is a contradiction in terms. A system that seeks bad values is bad. A system that denies the existence of values denies the possibility of education. Relativism, scientism, and anti-intellectualism, the Four Horsemen of the philosophical apocalypse, have produced that chaos in education which will end in the disintegration of the West.

The prime object of education is to know what is good for men. It is to know the goods in their order. There is a hierarchy of values. The task of education is to help us understand it, establish it, and live by it. This Aristotle had in mind when he said: "It is not the possessions but the desires of men that must be equalized, and this is impossible unless they have a sufficient education according to the nature of things."

Such an education is far removed from the triviality of that produced by the doctrines of adaptation, of immediate needs, of social reform, or of the doctrine of no doctrine at all. Such an education will not adapt the young to a bad environment, but it will encourage them to make it good. It will not overlook immediate needs, but it will place these needs in their proper relationship to more distant, less tangible, and more important goods. It will be the only effective means of reforming society.

This is the education appropriate to free men. It is liberal education. If all men are to be free, all men must have this education. It makes no difference how they are to earn their living or what their special interests or aptitudes may be. They can learn to make a living, and they can develop their special interests and aptitudes, after they have laid the foundation of free and responsible manhood through liberal education. It will not do to say that they are incapable of such education. This claim is made by those who are too indolent or unconvinced to make the effort to give such education to the masses.

Nor will it do to say that there is not enough time to give everybody a liberal education before he becomes a specialist. In America, at least, the waste and frivolity of the educational system are so great that it would be possible, through getting rid of them, to give every citizen a liberal education and make him a qualified specialist, too, in less time than is now consumed in turning out uneducated specialists.

A liberal education aims to develop the power of understanding and judgment. It is impossible that too many people can be educated in this sense, because there cannot be too many people with understanding and judgment. We hear a great deal today about the dangers that will come upon us through the frustration of educated people who have got educated in the expectation that education will get them a better job, and who then fail to get it. But surely this depends on the representations that are made to the young about what education is. If we allow them to believe that education will get them better jobs and encourage them to get educated with this end in view, they are entitled to a sense of frustration if, when they have got the education, they do not get the jobs. But, if we say that they should be educated in order to be men, and that everybody, whether he is a ditch-digger or a bank president, should have this education because he is a man, then the ditch-digger may still feel frustrated but not because of his education.

Nor is it possible for a person to have too much liberal education, because it is impossible to have too much understanding and judgment. But it is possible to undertake too much in the name of liberal education in youth. The object of liberal education in youth is not to teach the young all they will ever need to know. It is to give them the habits, ideas, and techniques that they need to know to continue to educate themselves. Thus the object of formal institutional liberal education in youth is to prepare the young to educate themselves throughout their lives.

I would remind you of the impossibility of learning to understand and judge many of the important things in youth. The judgment and understanding of practical affairs can amount to little in the absence of experience with practical affairs. Subjects that cannot be understood without experience should not be taught to those who are without experience. Or, if these subjects are taught to those who are without experience, it should be clear that these subjects be taught only by way of introduction and that their value to the student depends on his continuing to study them as he acquires experience. The tragedy in America is that economics, ethics, politics, history, and literature are studied in youth, and seldom studied again. Therefore the graduates of American universities seldom understand them.

This pedagogical principle, that subjects requiring experience can be learned only by the experienced, leads to the conclusion that the most important branch of education is the education of adults. We sometimes seem to think of education as something like the mumps, measles, whooping cough, or chicken pox. If a person has had education in childhood, he need not, in fact he cannot, have it again. But the pedagogical principle that the most important things can be learned only in mature life is supported by a sound philosophy in general. Men are rational animals. They achieve their terrestrial felicity by the use of reason. And this means that they have to use it for their entire lives. To say that they should learn only in childhood would mean that they were human only in childhood.

And it would mean that they were unfit to be citizens of a republic. A republic, a true *res publica*, can maintain justice, peace, freedom, and order only by the exercise of intelligence.

When we speak of the consent of the governed, we mean, since men are not angels who seek the truth intuitively and do not have to learn it, that every act of assent on the part of the governed is a product of learning. A republic is really a common educational life in process. So Montesquieu said that, whereas the principle of a monarchy was honor, and the principle of a tyranny was fear, the principle of a republic was education.

Hence the ideal republic is the republic of learning. It is the utopia by which all actual political republics are measured. The goal toward which we started with the Athenians twenty-five centuries ago is an unlimited republic of learning and a world-wide political republic mutually supporting each other.

All men are capable of learning. Learning does not stop as long as a man lives, unless his learning power atrophies because he does not use it. Political freedom cannot endure unless it is accompanied by provision for the unlimited acquisition of knowledge. Truth is not long retained in human affairs without continual learning and relearning. Peace is unlikely unless there are continuous, unlimited opportunities for learning and unless men continuously avail themselves of them. The world of law and justice for which we yearn, the world-wide political republic, cannot be realized without the world-wide republic of learning. The civilization we seek will be achieved when all men are citizens of the world republic of law and justice and of the republic of learning all their lives long.

Realism

Aristotle, the Realist, sought to discover truth in a different way—objectively—and questioned whether "truths" so found conformed to reality. Although he also saw the possibility of a born slave with great ability becoming a master, in his view education was primarily for the intellectual elite and not for the masses. Contemporary applications of this philosophy can be seen in the school systems of Western Europe, where secondary and higher education are for the intellectual elite, not for the masses. He believed, too, that moral and intellectual training of the people was necessary for good government, but his emphasis was more on the needs of individuals and the existing state than on a remote ideal. Much of what Aristotle thought stemmed from his twenty-odd years of study with Plato. However, his emphasis was on research rather than reason, and he organized his Lyceum like a modern research institute.[8] Aristotle's views are particularly apparent in the following excerpt.

aristotle

Ethics and Politics

No one will doubt that the legislator should direct his attention above all to the education of youth; for the neglect of education does harm to the constitution. The citizen should be moulded to suit the form of government under which he lives.

. . . since the whole city has one need, it is manifest that education should be one and the same for all, and that it should be public, and not private—not as at present, when every one looks after his own children separately, and gives them separate instruction of the sort which he thinks best; the training in things which are of common interest should be the same for all. . . .

McKeon, Richard, ed., *The Basic Works of Aristotle* (New York: Random House, 1941), pp. 1305–1308. *Also:* Benjamin Jowett, trans., *The Oxford Translation of Aristotle*, Book VIII, "Politics," ed. W. D. Ross (Oxford: The Clarendon Press, 1921), Vol. X.

That education should be regulated by law and should be an affair of state is not to be denied, but what should be the character of this public education, and how young persons should be educated, are questions which remain to be considered. As things are, there is disagreement about the subjects. . . . The existing practice is perplexing; no one knows on what principle we should proceed—should the useful in life, or should virtue, or should the higher knowledge, be the aim of our training; all three opinions have been entertained. Again, about the means there is no agreement; for different persons, starting with different ideas about the nature of virtue, naturally disagree about the practice of it. There can be no doubt that children should be taught those useful things which are really necessary, but not all useful things; for occupations are divided into liberal and illiberal; and to young children should be imparted only such kinds of knowledge as will be useful to them without vulgarizing them. And for any occupation, art, or science, which makes the body or soul or mind of the freeman less fit for the practice or exercise of virtue, is vulgar; wherefore we call those arts vulgar which tend to deform the body, and likewise all paid employments, for they absorb and degrade the mind. . . .

The customary branches of education are in number four; they are—1) reading and writing, 2) gymnastic exercises, 3) music, to which is sometimes added 4) drawing. Of these, reading and writing and drawing are regarded as useful for the purposes of life in a variety of ways, and gymnastic exercises are thought to infuse courage. . . . There remains, then, the use of music for intellectual enjoyment in leisure; which is in fact evidently the reason of its introduction, this being one of the ways in which it is thought that a freeman should pass his leisure . . .

. . . To be always seeking after the useful does not become free and exalted souls. Now it is clear that in education practice must be used before theory, and the body be trained before the mind; and therefore boys should be handed over to the trainer, who creates in them the proper habit of body, and to the wrestling-master, who teaches them their exercises.

Because, according to Aristotle, man has a free will, moral virtue can be the result of conscious choice or habit training in "goodness" before the age of reason is reached. Part of the moral life was to avoid excesses (a pre-Freudian way of saying that the ego should mediate between the id and the super-ego); that is, to strive for the "Golden Mean" in all things.

Aristotle believed further that all objects and persons have a potential even before they come into being, which is limited by their capacity to become and regulated by their purpose. That is, since substances derive from material, they resemble their source, e.g., the child resembles his parents; a desk made from wood is a wooden desk, not a plastic one. The source, or material, from which they derive determines the potentiality of substances. Their actuality is determined by a formal reason or pattern assumed. The truth about substances can be discovered objectively, based on observations or sensory impressions. The knowledge thus gained is for its own sake. This entire concept is clearly different from that held by Plato and other Idealists.

Aristotle, included in his basic education, as was seen above, reading, writing, and drawing, which were tools for further organization and acquisition of knowledge as well as being practical for daily life. Even more, for the realist, the purpose of education is to enable the individual

> . . . to become a tolerant and well-adjusted person, in harmony mentally and physically with his physical and cultural environment. . . . When we speak of adjustment . . . we also mean adjustment to the individualism, creativity, curiosity, and personal enterprise that really are present in human nature. The realist conception of adjustment is not hostile to spontaneity and individualism.[9]

The duty of the state, therefore, was to provide the good life so that its citizens might be happy as well as constructive citizens. They were to be evaluated, in fact, in terms of how they used their leisure time.

Later misinterpretations of Aristotelian philosophy strongly influenced Church-sponsored education and theology through the Dark Ages and medieval history. On a more positive note, Aristotle influenced many individuals. Ibn Khaldoun emphasized sensory perception as a means of education. (Good modern illustrations of this practice are Anne Sullivan Macy's work with the young Helen Keller, and Montessori's methods with pre-school and retarded children.) Montaigne, stressing the objective search for truth, asked, "What do I know?" Or call the roll of post-Reformation scientists—Copernicus, Kepler, Galileo, Newton—and you can see the rise of inquiry regarding formerly-held "absolutes."

Francis Bacon, another Realist, was the first man to turn men's minds to the discovery of new and useful truths by the inductive method. In his *Novum Organum* (1620), he offered this technique ". . . by means of which men would be able to distinguish true from false, learn to see straight, create useful knowledge, and fill in the great gaps in the learning of the time by actually working out new knowledge from the unknown."[10] Also in this work, Bacon discussed "idols" which were barriers to truth. There were "idols of the tribe," which were inadequate human receptors or human errors in experimentation, which kept humanity from truth. The "idols of the den" were those experiences which caused the individual to perceive in error. The "idols of the market" were difficulties in the communication of concepts, and the "idols of the theatre" were various philosophies and abstruse metaphysics. These barriers today are discussed in psychological terms as bases for interpersonal difficulties or individual eccentricities of behavior.

Aristotle's concern with substance and its potential also influenced John Locke; his stress on sensory perception affected Rousseau's thinking (although some class the latter as an Idealist). Contemporary philosophers who lean on Aristotelian principles include Bertrand Russell, Alfred North Whitehead, and George Santayana. In Whitehead's discussion of educational goals, his orientation as a Realist is quite evident.

> The result of teaching small parts of a large number of subjects is the passive reception of disconnected ideas,

not illumined with any spark of vitality. Let the main ideas which are introduced into a child's education be few and important, and let them be thrown into every combination possible. The child should make them his own, and should understand their application here and now in the circumstances of his actual life. From the very beginning of his education, the child should experience the joy of discovery. The discovery which he has to make, is that general ideas give an understanding of that stream of events which pours through his life, which is his life. . . . Pedants sneer at an education which is useful. But if education is not useful, what is it? Is it a talent, to be hidden away in a napkin? Of course, education should be useful, whatever your aim in life. . . . It is useful, because understanding is useful.

I pass lightly over that understanding which should be given by the literary side of education. Nor do I wish to be supposed to pronounce on the relative merits of a classical or a modern curriculum. I would only remark that the understanding which we want is an understanding of an insistent present. The only use of a knowledge of the past is to equip us for the present. No more deadly harm can be done to young minds than by depreciation of the present. The present contains all that there is. It is holy ground; for it is the past, and it is the future.[11]

Whitehead continues, in the following quotation, sounding almost like a Pragmatist. This should not be too surprising, though, since pragmatism is among the descendants of realism.

. . . There is only one subject-matter for education, and that is Life in all its manifestations. Instead of this single unity, we offer children—Algebra, from which nothing follows Geometry, from which nothing follows; Science, from which nothing follows; History, from which nothing follows; a Couple of Languages, never mastered; and lastly, most dreary of all, Literature, represented by plays of Shakespeare, with philological notes and short analyses of plot and character to be in substance committed to memory. Can such a list be said to represent Life, as it is known in the midst of the living of it? The best that can be said of it is, that it is a rapid table of contents which a deity might run over in his mind while he was thinking of creating a world, and had not yet determined how to put it together.[12]

Certainly a sharp criticism of modern education, although this point of view in later years was strongly criticized itself.

Pragmatism

A third major school of philosophy is pragmatism. It is related to the British empiricist tradition which stresses the gaining of knowledge by sensory experience, and is itself related to realism. The empiricist tradition, and later pragmatism, advocated the "learning by doing" philosophy which has had such a strong influence on American education. It is, of all the schools of philosophy being surveyed, the one uniquely American. Pragmatism itself is a term coined by Pierce, but it is also called experimentalism or instrumentalism (Dewey) and functionalism (William James).

Four major principles of pragmatism are that truth is relative, not absolute; a human being is always capable of learning; education should be focused on the pupils rather than the subject-matter; and practical results should be emphasized. All of these were to function within a democratic atmosphere, for Pragmatists considered democracy a way of life. Although pragmatism is, as indicated earlier, basically an American philosophy, there were earlier proponents of these and similar principles in other cultures and other countries.

Comenius' pansophy (Chapter 1) is one forerunner of pragmatism. Rousseau, who seems ubiquitous, saw nature, man, and things as teachers, thus supporting the pragmatic and realistic concept that the material world exists and is not merely a projection of the mind as the Idealists averred. Pestalozzi was another who practiced the principle of learning through actual activity, as did Whitehead in the passage quoted above.

george f. kneller

Pragmatism, Reality, and Education

Pragmatists agree with realists that the material world exists in its own right and is not just a projection of the mind. They maintain, however, that the world is neither permanent nor independent of man. Change being the essence of reality, we cannot be sure that anything will endure forever. Moreover, reality itself is not simply external to man but is created by the interaction of the human organism with its surroundings; reality is the sum total of what we experience. Man and his environment, therefore, are "coordinate." Both are equally responsible for what is real.

The world is only meaningful to the extent that man is able to read his own meaning into it. If the universe itself possesses some deeper purpose, it is hidden from man and cannot be part of his philosophy. What man cannot experience cannot have reality for him. Pragmatism is humanist in temper, subscribing to the old Greek maxim that "Man is the measure of all things." The difference between Jamesean pragmatism and the pragmatism of Pierce and Dewey is that James emphasized the individual's right to create his own reality, whereas the latter declared that the facts of reality were established primarily by the scientist.

If, like the Pragmatist, we believe that change is the essence of reality, we always must be prepared to alter the way that we do things. The ends and means of education must be flexible and open to constant revision. They should also be

Kneller, *op. cit.*, pp. 46–47.

adopted scientifically in the light of all relevant facts and values rather than speculatively on the basis of reason alone. There is also an intimate connection between ends and means; ends and means are reciprocal. Means are indigenous to their ends, and ends may derive from their means. Thus, in education interest is not opposed to discipline, but rather discipline grows out of interest. Similarly, the psychological method of learning complements the logical organization of subject matter.

Since reality is created by the interaction of man with his environment, we must learn to study the world as it affects *us*. The child should regard reality, not as impervious to man, but as intimately responsive to him and capable of serving him in countless ways. Just as man is not a being apart from his environment, so the school is not separate from life itself. Education *is* life and not a preparation for it. School should use real-life situations rather than depend primarily on formal academic studies.

John Dewey, a prime exponent of pragmatism, believed that learning could be motivated by pupil interest and curiosity concerning practical problems. If the subject-matter could be made more relevant and meaningful, then the three R's themselves would be more readily mastered for use as tools in further learning. If you look back for a moment to the quotations from Aristotle and Whitehead about the nature of subject-matter, it will be readily apparent that these two educational philosophies are close to agreement. Both of them stress the utilitarian aspects of education. Dewey, in one of his early books, showed the need for transforming the education prevalent at the turn of the century.

john dewey

Resulting Modifications
of the School

If we go back a few centuries, we find a practical monopoly of learning. The term *possession* of learning was, indeed, a happy one. Learning was a class matter. This was a necessary result of social conditions. There was not in existence any means by which the multitude could possibly have access to intellectual resources. These were stored up and hidden away in manuscripts. Of these there were at best only a few, and it required long and toilsome preparation to be able to do anything with them. A high-priesthood of learning, which guarded the treasury of truth and which doled it out to the masses under severe restrictions, was the inevitable expression of these conditions. But, as a direct result of the industrial revolution this has all been changed. Printing was invented; it was made commercial. Books, magazines, papers were multiplied and cheapened. As a result of the locomotive and telegraph, frequent, rapid, and cheap communication by mails and electricity was called into being. Travel has been rendered easy; freedom of movement, with its accompanying exchange of ideas, indefinitely facilitated. The result has been an intellectual revolution. Learning has been put into circulation. While there still is, and probably always will be, a particular class having the special business of inquiry in hand, a distinctively learned class is henceforth out of the question. It is an anachronism. Knowledge is no longer an immobile solid; it has been liquefied. It is actively moving in all the currents of society itself.

Dewey, John, *The School and Society* (Chicago: University of Chicago Press, 1899); in Cubberley, E. B. *Readings in Public Education in the United States* (Boston: Houghton-Mifflin Co., 1934), pp. 402–404.

It is easy to see that this revolution, as regards the materials of knowledge, carries with it a marked change in the attitude of the individual. Stimuli of an intellectual sort pour in upon us in all kinds of ways. The merely intellectual life, the life of scholarship and learning, thus gets a very altered value. Academic and scholastic, instead of being titles of honor, are becoming terms of reproach.

But all this means a necessary change in the attitude of the school, one of which we are as yet far from realizing the full force. Our school methods, and to a very considerable extent our curriculum, are inherited from the period when learning and command of certain symbols, affording as they did the only access to learning, were all-important. The ideals of this period are still largely in control, even where the outward methods and studies have been changed. . . .

Our present education is highly specialized, one-sided and narrow. It is an education dominated almost entirely by the medieval conception of learning. It is something which appeals for the most part simply to the intellectual aspect of our natures, our desire to learn, to accumulate information, and to get control of the symbols of learning; not to our impulses and tendencies to make, to do, to create, to produce, whether in the form of utility or of art. The very fact that manual training, art, and science are objected to as technical, as tending towards mere specialization, is of itself as good testimony as could be offered to the specialized aim which controls current education. Unless education has been virtually identified with the exclusively intellectual pursuits, with learning as such, all these materials and methods would be welcome, would be greeted with the utmost hospitality . . .

But why should I make this labored presentation? The obvious fact is that our social life has undergone a thorough and radical change. If our education is to have any meaning for life, it must pass through an equally complete transformation. This transformation is not something to appear suddenly, to be executed in a day by conscious purpose. It is already in progress. These modifications of our school system which appear often—even to those most actively concerned with them, to say nothing of their spectators—as mere changes of detail, mere improvements within the school mechanism, are in reality signs and evidences of this change. The introduction of active occupations, of nature study, of elementary science, of art, of history; the relegation of the merely symbolic and formal to a secondary position; the change in the moral school atmosphere; in the relation of pupils and teachers—of discipline; the introduction of more active, expressive, and self-directing factors—all these are not mere accidents, they are necessities of the larger social evolution. It remains but to organize all these factors, to appreciate them in their fullness of meaning, and to put the ideas and ideals involved in complete, uncompromising possession of our school system. To do this means to make each one of our schools an embryonic community life, active with types of occupations that reflect the life of the larger society, and permeated throughout with the spirit of art, history, and science. When the school introduces and trains each child of society into membership within such a little community, saturating him with the spirit of service, and providing him with the instruments of effective self-direction, we shall have the deepest and best guarantee of the larger society which is worthy, lovely, and harmonious.

Much of Dewey's philosophy has been incorporated into American education. We *are* more cognizant of the learner as a child. We *do* stress reflective thinking. We *have* transformed our curricula from meaningless rote memory exercises to meaningful problem-solving situations. We *do* see education as a continuous process. Such recognition has not been easy. Both educational psychologists and educational philosophers made us more aware of the learner as a child, but some tipped the scales too far, and lost sight of the teacher in the classroom. Attempts have been made to eliminate memorization of the multiplication tables in favor of "discovering" and "understanding" multiplication facts, but, in the end, for practical purposes, the learner must still memorize "3 x 4" and "7 x 9." There is much greater awareness of the need to articulate subject-matter from one level of schooling to another. There is even recognition of the fact that adults continue to learn outside of the formal settings of education. Preparation for adulthood must be articulated with the life of the youth and the onset of maturity and its needs. Indeed, not only the American view of education has been affected by Dewey and his followers, but many of these principles and practices have been exported even to modern India, where they have been applied to an expanding program of basic education.[13]

Some disciples of the Pragmatists went even further in their applications of this philosophy to education. Although they extended Dewey's work, they also tended to exaggerate and in some cases distort some of the principles in the "child activity" movement of the 1930's and 1940's. One example of this activity by the Progressives was to try to implement Dewey's call for an "embryonic community life" in every school, but the result was to "throw the baby out with the bath water." Their conception of human nature being that men are inherently good, they had to advocate a child-centered curriculum. That the Progressives and later the Reconstructionists exaggerated Dewey's views can be seen also in the following passage.

clarence j. karier

Pragmatic Conceptions of Man and Society

In Dewey's theory of education means and end, freedom and responsibility, the child and the curriculum, and the school and society are viewed as fundamentally integrated. To separate one from the other results in all sorts of perversity and is

Karier, *op. cit.*, pp. 146–147.

destructive of the unity so necessary for the growth of the individual and society. To Dewey, the only single aim of education which could encompass all the diverse purposes of education was the idea of *growth*. In this context, the function of the teacher is to work himself out of a job. By using his psychological understanding of the child and his understanding of the way knowledge is created, the teacher would guide the child through a continuous, reflective learning experience which would culminate in an independent, creative, socially responsible thinker. Far from relieving the teacher from responsibility for what transpired in the classroom, Dewey challenged teachers with the Herculean task of not only understanding the child but also of understanding how knowledge was created in many diverse fields and then using those insights to enhance the intellectual, emotional, and social growth of the individual.

Unlike Robert Owen in the nineteenth century or G. S. Counts in the twentieth century, who saw the school as a vehicle for reforming society by blueprinting a new social order and then indoctrinating the young toward that end, Dewey saw the function of the school as a vehicle for reforming society by producing critical thinkers who as adults would make their own decisions. Dewey consistently refused to blueprint the new social order, not only because he knew any long-range blueprint in a society of rapid change would be fallacious but also because such a blueprint implied a control and direction of learning in conflict with his conception of free and continuous growth. Dewey's social reconstructionist ideas were, therefore, at odds with such reconstructionists as G. S. Counts and Theodore Brameld, who advocated more direct action on the part of the school.

Although Dewey's name is often associated with the Progressive Education Association and especially the child-centered wing of the movement, which advocated an extremely permissive approach to education, throughout his lifetime Dewey remained a severe critic of these excesses. Repeatedly he warned against a hit-or-miss impressionistic curriculum and suggested that unless progressive educators evolved an intellectually coherent curriculum, they would fail. In general, failing to heed his warning, progressive educators like William H. Kilpatrick and others used Dewey's criticism of the traditional school as a basis for advocating their own child-centered views. Dewey conceived human nature as plastic and learning as a rationally organized experience. Neither conception is compatible with the romantic, child-centered educator who generally assumed the child's nature to be innately good and thought of the learning process as unrestrained, real-life experience.

Perhaps the Progressives' most criticized proposition was that teachers were only to guide children's learning, not to direct it. The children themselves were to plan their development and activities in terms of their own interests. This method was used in many permissive schools, and was an integral part of the "core curriculum" developed in the 1930's. The concept of child-oriented activities led critics to question whether, if a child had no interest in reading until he was in the middle or upper grades, he need not learn to read until that time. Many non-educators as well as professionals complained that children were not learning the skills basic to our way of life, such as spelling and simple arithmetic, nor the information basic to it. The Progressives retorted that, following Dewey, the school should reflect life and not be merely a preparation for it.

The Progressive Education Association was disbanded in 1955, and the progressive movement condemned for our "technological lag" when Sputnik burst into the heavens in 1957. The picture is not all black, however. Progressives contributed much to our educational philosophy, curriculum development, and classroom practices.[14] Characteristics of the "good society" such as cooperation, consideration of the personal element, humaneness, and authentic experience were introduced into the classroom and will remain there. In recent years, the British have combined elements of progressive education with the learning theories of Jean Piaget, and have developed the "open classroom" and "integrated-day" approaches to primary-level education. These approaches have already had an impact in the United States, although with varying success. Wherever attempted, however, Dewey's idea of learning by doing is highly evident.

As one generation succeeds another, so the Reconstructionists claimed to be the true descendants of, or successors to, progressivism. The basic tenet of reconstructionist philosophy is ". . . that the chief purpose of education is to 'reconstruct' society in order to meet the cultural crisis of our time."[15] This was a social reform movement, as has already been indicated, aiming for a "genuinely democratic" social order in the context of political and economic upheavals in the world. Counts, Rugg, and Brameld were among its leaders. (A fuller discussion of their work may be found in Chapter 2 where the historical events of the 1920's and 1930's place reconstructionism more appropriately in perspective.) Kneller criticizes Brameld's orientation in particular, because it ". . . seems bound to lead to a collectivist utopia, in which men would believe anything to be true provided it was attained by scientific methods and met with informed social consensus when persuasively presented."[16] Of all the philosophical schools, reconstructionism is most strongly identified with the behavioral sciences. Its emphasis on "democratic" persuasion by the teacher to ensure student conformity to its doctrines does, however, a disservice to this identification. The view that education can take the lead in social reform, while it is itself reshaped by social and cultural forces, is in evidence today with the attempts to reduce or eliminate minority-group discrimination by restructuring administrative school districts, establishing educational parks, and redesigning curricula at all levels.

Essentialism

Of all the post-Sputnik (and pre-Sputnik) critics of American education, perhaps the most vocal and numerous have been the Essentialists—Bagley, Breed, Brickman, M. Smith, and the Council for Basic Education. They do not necessarily concur on all philosophical points, but do unite in seeking to reestablish matters in the classroom. They are not critical of all progressive innovations in education, but do favor the restoration of teacher authority to the classroom, more disciplined hard work and less problem-solving, more physical science and less social science in the curriculum. They are Traditionalists in a sense, but more flexible than the Classicists such as Adler and Hutchins. The Essentialists' concern is with the needs and values of society; that is, it is a "society-centered" rather than a "child-centered" philosophy.

Bagley, for example, a foremost Essentialist, strongly believed that literacy was necessary for democracy, as was discipline; that the mature should be responsible for the instruction and control of the immature; that the basic social arts, history, and science should be included in the curriculum, but in a systematic program of studies. Contrary to the reconstructionist and progressive view that cooperation, not competition, should be stressed in the classroom, Bagley stated that progress requires "struggle and competition, selection and rejection."[17] He may have been more correct in his point of view than the Progressives who urged group effort and cooperation as reflective of "real life."

Essentialists have long criticized contemporary education as unsatisfactory because of the "watering-down" of rigorous standards, the practice of "social promotion" in the schools, the discrediting of "exacting" subjects or those considered to be good for mental discipline in favor of an over-emphasis on "activity" movements and the social studies, and curriculum revisions which weaken a systematic program of studies. This philosophy leans heavily on the old and outdated "faculty psychology" of the nineteenth century. Faculty psychology held that the mind was a combination of a number of "faculties" which, like muscles, had to be exercised. Therefore, faculty psychologists urged the inclusion of difficult subjects in the curriculum, such as geometry, Latin, and Greek, as suitable "exercisers" for the "faculties" of the mind. This point of view had a long-lasting influence on secondary school curricula, and kept them primarily classical. This was also true at the university level. Proponents of this point of view have been particularly active in criticizing the inclusion of driver education, dancing, etiquette, home economics, and other non-academic courses in the curriculum.

Existentialism

No survey of the philosophical foundations of American education today would be complete without a consideration of the existentialist philosophy. This approach focuses on the person and his complete involvement with the real problems of life. It is a point of view stressing the actor, not the spectator. According to the Existentialists, "Since man is free, he 'makes himself.' Freedom being pure potentiality until it actualizes itself in deeds, man is 'nothing' until he acts."[18]

It is a philosophy which condemns conformity as inhibiting the individual. Combine the action aspect with the anti-conformity aspect and you have the student riots and insurgencies which have plagued France for the past few decades and which have created havoc on college and high school campuses in the United States for the past few years. Existentialism flourishes under conditions of social and economic disorder, and may, indeed, contribute to the utter collapse of these systems.

On one point, however, Existentialists might resemble the Essentialists. Existentialists believe that the family must exercise its educative force more and delegate less to the schools. This could agree with Essentialist demands for curriculum revision in accord with *their* views. Existentialists, for example, are also against the vocational emphasis current in the schools.

> Knowledge, properly conceived, brings freedom, since it delivers man from ignorance and prejudice and enables him to see himself as he really is. The school must, therefore, completely revise its conception of knowledge. It must cease to regard subject matter as an end in itself or as an instrument to prepare the student for his future career, and consider it instead as a means for the cultivation of self. Since authentic existence involves the whole

man, we should no longer regard learning primarily as mental discipline. On the contrary, the student should be urged to involve himself intellectually and emotionally in whatever he studies; he must appropriate to himself any exercise or problem or study he tackles. The whole emphasis of the curriculum must shift from the world of objects to the world of the person. Since the meaning of existence lies in man himself, the student should use his knowledge of external realities to come to terms more completely with his own nature.[19]

As you see, the means to be used—curriculum revision—is similar for both groups, but the ends or purposes are quite different.

At the extreme, the stress on freedom and individual choice and responsibility has led to a kind of nihilism in relation to education. The schools are perceived as threatening that individual self-determinism. They are also seen as impersonal and inhumane, not only by extremists, but also by the students who become enmeshed in bureaucratic institutions where their personal qualities and their efforts are summarized by the holes on a computer card. Illich (1971) called for the elimination of schools because they are barriers on the road to personal liberation. Other outspoken critics of contemporary education have called for modifications of the traditional curricula and setting of education, resulting in the development of free schools, alternative schools, and schools "without walls" or formal courses. Their emphases are on relevance and sensitivity. Existentialists in general would prefer that education stress the affective mode rather than the intellectual one, developing the individual's ability to appreciate his environment and to respond emotionally to whatever he encounters.

Summary

Each of the philosophies discussed has contributed in some way to American education something which is still apparent in some curricula. The classical college preparatory course reflects the influence of the Idealists, the Perennialists, and to some degree the Essentialists. The academic "talent search," which often stresses capability in the physical sciences, reflects realism. The classroom emphases on problem-solving techniques, reflective thinking, and meaningfulness stem from pragmatism and progressivism. "It is interesting that the key word which describes Kilpatrick's view of the good society is *cooperation*, while the key word for Conant's view is *competition*. One man seemed to walk on the child's side of the educational street, and the other on society's side. Neither man, however, went to the extreme."[20] (Conant's criticisms of American education, since they are quite specific, are included in several other chapters.)

Reconstructionism is seen in the attempts to have education upset the status quo with respect to inequalities and lack of opportunity for minority groups. And existentialism, as noted, is readily apparent in student action movements. The existentialist conception of the educated man, however, might be more acceptable than other aspects of this philosophy for its relevance to our present problems.

> . . . The educated man is characterized not only by what he *knows* but also, and perhaps even more, by what he is *capable of knowing and experiencing.* In a basic sense, then, the hallmark of an existentialist education is not knowledge as such but rather 'educability.'[21]

Truly, American education today is eclectic in its philosophy, for one can find evidences of each of the philosophies or variations of them in some school somewhere in this country. Eclecticism is not bad; it is vital to the contemporary scene. Badgered by the extremists, however, as never before, educators sometimes appear to be trying to respond to too many varying philosophies at one time. In so doing, they run the risk of satisfying no one as they lose any sense of philosophical direction.

Endnotes

1. Kneller, George F. *Introduction to the Philosophy of Education* (New York: John Wiley and Sons, 1964), p. 36.

2. Murphy, Charles Theophilus, Kevin Guinagh, and Whitney Jennings Oates. *Greek and Roman Classics in Translation* (London: Longmans, Green, and Co., 1949), p. 485.

3. *Ibid.*, p. 501.

4. Dewey, John. *Democracy and Education* (New York: The Macmillan Company, 1916).

5. Highet, Gilbert. *The Art of Teaching* (New York: Vintage Books, 1959), p. 162.

6. Kneller, *op. cit.*, p. 35.

7. Karier, Clarence J. *Man, Society, and Education* (Glenview, Ill.: Scott, Foresman, and Co., 1967), p. 7.

8. Highet, *op. cit.*, p. 163.

9. Kneller, *op. cit.*, pp. 41–42.

10. Cubberley, Ellwood P. *The History of Education* (Boston: Houghton-Mifflin Company, 1922), p. 391.

11. Whitehead, Alfred North. *The Aims of Education* (New York: Mentor Books, New American Library, 1958), p. 14.

12. *Ibid.*, pp. 18–19.

13. Kabir, Humayan. *Education in New India* (New York: Humanities Press, Inc., 1961).

14. For a detailed history of the progressive movement, see: Lawrence A. Cremin's *The Transformation of the School* (New York: Vintage Books, 1964).

15. Kneller, *op. cit.*, p. 119.

16. *Ibid.*, p. 127.

17. Bagley, William C. "An Essentialist's Platform for the Advancement of American Education," *Educ. Admin. and Super.*, 24, 1938, 244–256.

18. Kneller, *op. cit.*, p. 55.
19. *Ibid.*, pp. 64–65.
20. Karier, *op. cit.*, p. 252.
21. O'Neill, William F. "Existentialism and Education for Moral Choice," in *Social Foundations of Education*, ed. Dorothy Westby-Gibson. (New York: The Free Press, 1967), pp. 190–191.

For Further Reading

BAGLEY, WILLIAM C. "An Essentialist's Platform for the Advancement of American Education." *Educ. Admin. and Superv.*, 24, (April 1938), 244–256.

BAGLEY, WILLIAM C. *Education and Emergent Man* (New York: Thomas Nelson, 1934).

BRUBACHER, JOHN S. *Modern Philosophies of Education* (New York: McGraw-Hill Book Company, 1962).

CREMIN, LAWRENCE A. *The Transformation of the School* (New York: Vintage Books, 1964).

CUBBERLEY, ELLWOOD P. *The History of Education* (Boston: Houghton-Mifflin, 1922).

DEWEY, JOHN. *Democracy and Education* (New York: The Macmillan Company, 1916).

DUNKEL, HAROLD B. "W. T. Harris and Hegelianism in American Education." *School Review*, 81, 1973, 233–246.

FEINBERG, WALTER. "Progressive Education and Social Planning." *Teachers College Record*, 73, 1972, 485–505.

FROST, S. E., JR. *Historical and Philosophical Foundations of Western Education* (Columbus, Ohio: Charles E. Merrill, 1966).

GRENE, MARJORIE. *Introduction to Existentialism* (Chicago: University of Chicago Press, 1962).

HIGHET, GILBERT. *The Art of Teaching* (New York: Vintage Books, 1959).

HOWE, HAROLD, II. "Start with the Schools." *Saturday Review of Education*, (March) 1973, p. 20.

HUTCHINS, ROBERT MAYNARD. *The Conflict in Education* (New York: Harper and Row, 1953).

ILLICH, IVAN. *Deschooling Society* (New York: Harper and Row, 1971).

KARIER, CLARENCE J. *Man, Society, and Education* (Glenview, Ill.: Scott, Foresman, and Company, 1967).

KNELLER, GEORGE P. *Introduction to the Philosophy of Education* (New York: John Wiley and Sons, 1964).

KOZOL, JONATHAN. *Free Schools* (Boston: Houghton-Mifflin, 1972).

MARITAIN, JACQUES. *Education at the Crossroads* (New Haven: Yale University Press, 1943).

MORRIS, VAN CLEVE. *Existentialism in Education: What It Means* (New York: Harper and Row, 1966).

MORRIS, VAN CLEVE. *Modern Movements in Educational Philosophy* (Boston: Houghton Mifflin, 1969).

MURPHY, CHARLES THEOPHILUS, KEVIN GUINAGH, and WHITNEY JENNINGS OATES. *Greek and Roman Classics in Translation* (London: Longmans, Green, and Company, 1949).

PHENIX, PHILIP H. *Realms of Meaning: A Philosophy of the Curriculum for General Education* (New York: McGraw-Hill Book Company, 1964).

PRICE, KINGSLEY. *Education and Philosophical Thought* (Boston: Allyn and Bacon, Inc., 1962).

SAYERS, E. V., and WARD MADDEN. *Education and the Democratic Faith* (New York: Appleton-Century-Crofts, 1959).

SCHEFFLER, ISRAEL, ed., *Philosophy and Education: Modern Readings* (Boston: Allyn and Bacon, Inc., 1958).

TOWNSEND, HARVEY GATES. *Philosophic Ideas in the United States* (New York: American Book Company, 1934).

4

governmental responsibility for education

It is important to have a philosophy of education and to have educational goals, however changeable they may be. Someone, or some group, however, has to apply the philosophy and chart the course toward the goals. Whoever takes on the task of ministering to the educational needs of some or all of our 200 million people has in his grasp a mighty weapon.

Whoever controls education is in a position to mold if not control the minds of the next generation. In totalitarian societies, the issue of educational control is decided by centralized state power, behind which lies the power of the ruling party. . . .

Democratic societies, in comparison, depend upon a certain amount of free play of group interests, permitting diverse groups to organize and campaign for their own point of view. This characteristic of democratic societies holds whether the educational system is centralized, a national system such as found in France, or decentralized, a melange of discrete and local systems as in the United States. . . .[1]

By virtue of the Tenth Amendment to the Constitution, powers not specifically given to the federal government are reserved to the states. As a result, education is a state, and ultimately, a local function. It is this division of labor and power which we will now examine.

The National Level

Despite the constitutional abandonment of education to the states, there are formidable federal influences on education. The United States does not have a central ministry of education, as there is in most other countries, which establishes curricula and standards. The Office of Education is within the Department of Health, Education, and Welfare as a subsidiary body (despite the efforts of Senator Margaret Smith of Maine and others to establish it as a separate entity at the Cabinet level). The Office acts as a clearinghouse for information about educational activities, costs, etc., in the various states. It supports research programs at the several levels of education from nursery school through graduate school. It implements Congressional directives relevant to education. It publishes periodicals, such as *American Education.* But it does not officially set educational policies.

Much of the federal influence on education stems from legislated aid to education (see Chapter 6). Policy is established indirectly through Congressional approval of programs at the local level, or scholarship aid to college students working in specific fields of study, or grants for research in particular areas of endeavor. The primary areas of interest governing such aid are national defense and equality of educational and economic opportunity. Vocational education, the study of common and exotic foreign languages, educational programs for pre-schoolers, emphasis on scientific and mathematics studies, and other programs have all received their initial financial impetus from legislation and appropriations passed by Congress. Thus, in an indirect way, Congress says, "These are our educational goals; these are the things important to the nation." In reaching what amount to philosophical decisions in the field of education, congressmen are "aided" by lobbyists of all kinds. There are pressures from school teachers (National Education Association and American Association of University Professors), labor unions (American Federation of Teachers and others), chambers of commerce, taxpayers, management groups ad infinitum.

This surge of interest groups has been a relatively new phenomenon at the national level. Its:

"... existence is due to education's increasingly important role in our society and to its growth into a big enterprise. The growing contest over education in national politics is reflected in the attitudes of the two major political parties. Both the Democrats and the Republicans now see education as a rational issue, one in which there is political capital and on which positions must be taken. . . ."[2]

The increased political emphasis on education merely reflects the fact that education is now a matter of national defense concern. Further, the educational opportunities of a child cannot depend on the chance location of his birth or residence. The nation cannot be deprived of a citizen's potential talent because he happened to live in a "depressed" area and not an urban, industrial one. It is considered grossly unfair to the individual student who moves from one state to another to have the quality of his education vary from the first locale to the second.

Within the constraints of constitutional limitations on Federal action regarding education, there is obviously considerable influence exerted by Congress. Through Congressmen, the individual and the group at the local level can bring about needed changes, although this may take time.

thomas d. bailey

The Folklore of Local Control

Today, the need for many small independent school districts is being debated far and wide in our country. These small administrative units—relatively expensive and uneconomical—contribute to mediocrity in education by today's standards.

Bailey, Thomas D. "The Folklore of Local Control," NEA Journal, 50 (Dec. 1961), pp. 42–43.

When will we banish the folk-lore of absolute local control and forget the obsolescence of the past? How soon will we decide on local control of education supported by a more balanced financial effort that provides honest control of excellent education for all?

I like to think of myself as a middle-of-the-roader in a discussion of education, but I have rather frequent experiences with extremists. There are those who are recommending a national curriculum and a national testing program. I have heard it said a few times that the state and federal government should take over the responsibilities of operating public education in order to assure quality education for all. I do not agree with these people. Nor do I agree with those people at the other extreme who declare that localized foolishness would be preferable to centralized wisdom.

It is interesting to note that even citizens most in favor of traditional local controls seldom resist decisions made by a central authority if they agree with those decisions. To my knowledge, few citizens have raised objections to the state requirements for a minimum school term of at least 180 days; minimum qualifications for all teachers; mandated financial accounting for the handling of public funds; earmarking funds for certain purposes such as teachers' salaries, buildings, and transportation; or for prescribed procedures in appointing teachers.

Furthermore, even though absolute local control is a thing of the past, people in communities today can exercise very effective control over the decisions of state and federal agencies and even those of private organizations. Today, more than ever before, modern communications media, well-organized citizen groups, and increased leisure time make it possible for citizens to participate in local, state, and national meetings and to assist in formulating policies that deal with education.

Groups of citizens at the local level can wield such influence through legislators and administrators, not only in state government but also in federal legislation relating to education.

In my opinion, this extension of the influence on education by the citizens in each community is the new and modern approach to local control. Even financial assistance from state or federal agencies may be refused if the terms are contrary to the desires of local school officials.

The fact remains, however, that without a centralized office of education to set minimum standards for teacher certification, curricula, buildings, etc., the burden of responsibility for education rests on the states.

To put the roles of government at various levels in perspective, the first recommendation of the President's Commission on School Finance might be helpful:

We recommend that each State assume responsibility for determining and raising on a statewide basis, the amount of funds required for education; for the allocation of these funds among the school districts of the State, and for the evaluation of the effective use of these funds.

We also recommend that local boards of education be given wide latitude, within general State guidelines, to use resources provided by the State in ways that best meet their needs and demands. This should include choosing curriculums; employing, assigning, and dismissing staff; and defining local goals and objectives. Within this flexibility, local boards of education should be held accountable to local taxpayers, parents, students, and to the State.

The Commission recommends that the Federal role in elementary and secondary education embrace the following major functions: (a) providing leadership in educational reform through research, evaluation, and demonstration activities; (b) stimulating State and local public and private activity to meet national concerns and interest and, where necessary, providing continuing financial support; (c) providing incentives and mechanisms designed to more nearly equalize resources among the States for elementary and secondary education, and, (d) serving as a center for collection, evaluation and publication of educational data. In brief, the Commission sees the Federal Government performing a leadership and pioneering role in long-range educational policy, but only a supplementary role to the States in the financing of school capital and operating costs.[3]

This supplementary role in financial aid will be disputed, in the discussion of economics of education in Chapter 5, for there are those who would prefer that the Federal Government be the primary financier of education.

The State Level

In each of the fifty states there is a state department of education or public instruction created by the state legislature. This department is headed by a state superintendent who is elected in some states and appointed in others.

What are the responsibilities of the state with regard to education? Generally the state establishes minimum standards for school programs, sets certification requirements for teachers and administrators, appropriates and disburses state funds to local school districts for school construction and teacher salaries, and prescribes or guides local programs.

In Pennsylvania, for example, the state mandates a 180-day school year. At the local level, this means establishing a school calendar which provides for a minimum of 180 school days (a few extra are usually scheduled to allow for specific holidays and extreme weather conditions) and then keeping accurate attendance records to prove that the state requirement has been met. Standard curricula for the several grades are prescribed in state syllabi. That is, in fourth grade, for instance, Pennsylvania history and geography are to be taught as part of the social studies program. High school students must take three years of English, a course in world cultures, another in American history, and so on. The state, in consultation with appropriate professional personnel, orders that approved college programs with specific courses be taken by prospective teachers in order for them to earn a provisional teaching certificate, and that certain additional requirements (24 college credits under the supervision of a college or university, plus three years' experience) be met for the certification to be made permanent. Until 1968, for example, preparation for teaching had to include courses in audio-visual techniques and Pennsylvania history.

California has a slightly different set of standards and responsibilities. Regulations affecting education are contained in *The California Administrative Code*, Title 5. The state organizes its school districts by grade level rather than by community: elementary school districts (K-8), secondary school districts (9-12, 7-12, 10-12, or 7-14), junior college (13-14 and adult education), and unified or "city" school districts (K-12 or K-14). The Administrative Code details what *is* to be taught, what *may* be taught, and what is prohibited. Foreign languages, for example, *must* be taught in grade six. All schools *may* offer courses in outdoor science, conservation, and forestry. The chief prohibitions are those which would involve disparagement of any race or other group of people.[4]

Except for the elementary certificate, five years of education are required for teaching eligibility. Elementary teachers, to be fully certified, must earn their fifth year's credits within five years after beginning to teach. Examples of how these requirements affect teacher education curricula will be found in Chapter 10.

The state constitution guarantees state funds for education of not less than $180 per pupil in average daily attendance. Actually, this low figure does not approximate the current per-pupil expenditures of school districts, for it does not include local funds. Under the Administrative Code, too, the State mandates a school year of 175 days. In addition, "California is one of the few states which continues to adopt and distribute free textbooks for grades one through eight, and the only state which continues to print some of its own textbooks. The responsibility for selection is vested in the State Board of Education."[5] In grades nine through twelve, textbook selection, purchase, and distribution is the responsibility of the local board.

A statewide intelligence and achievement testing program was mandated beginning in 1961. The governing board of each school district, in accordance with rules and regulations established by the State Board of Education, selects one or more of the tests from an approved list and perhaps others not on the list, administers the testing program, and reports results to the State Department of Education. . . . The tests must be given at specified dates each fall in grades 5, 8, and 11. Local districts may test their students at other grade levels as well. Practice varies considerably on reporting the results of local district-sponsored tests to parents. Usually such information is given only on request.[6]

At one time, California had statewide Regents' examinations such as New York has, but they were discontinued a number of years ago.

California, like Pennsylvania, uses the county unit as an intermediate stage between the State Department of Education and the local district. It renders the following functions:

1. Instructional supervision and audio-visual services.
2. Psychological services.
3. In-service preparation (teacher institutes, extension courses, etc.).
4. Personnel services (including the registration and validation of teachers' credentials).
5. Fiscal and accounting services.
6. Transportation (for districts with fewer than 850 average daily attendance).
7. Coordination of regional use of educational television.
8. School operation (in three school districts).[7]

In Pennsylvania, counties or intermediate units may offer education programs in their own county schools, as well as give aid to small districts with such programs.

To summarize the activities of the state government in education,

. . . it may be said that each state legislature is responsible for establishing and maintaining an efficient system of public education. Most state constitutions use this language or words to the same effect. This has resulted in school codes, i.e., a body of laws setting up school districts, boards of education, detailing their powers, and duties. . . . The state creates school districts, delegates authority and responsibility to the voters and their school boards, and prescribes curriculum requirements for the operation of the public schools of the districts. . . .

The state departments of education vary in size, in organization, and in functions to a great extent. In general, their functions may be categorized as *coordination, leadership,* and *service.*[8]

There is increasing legislative pressure for control and co-ordination not only of elementary and secondary education, but also for higher education. Legislators in many states are greatly concerned about the rising costs of higher education, the expansion of facilities by individual institutions without regard to future needs (at least as some legislators see it), overlapping curricula among institutions, and professorial tenure. These matters are more and more becoming a responsibility of state departments of education.

The Local Level

Ultimately, as has been seen, the responsibility for setting and fulfilling educational goals rests with the local school board. This decentralization of power and responsibility is unique to the American educational pattern. Local autonomy in education is with the consent of the state and is limited by rulings of the state board of education and laws passed by the state legislature. ". . . both in practice and law, school communities in the United States are encouraged to exercise a high degree of local self-determination and to adapt their educational programs to the needs and peculiarities of their own communities."[9] In effect, there are as many statements of educational goals as there are school districts in the nation—about 10,000 in 1970. Although this is still a sizable number, consider the situation in comparison to these figures from 1933:

There is still approximately one school board member to every two teachers in the United States, according to a bulletin recently issued by the Office of Education. There are in round numbers 127,000 school districts for administrative purposes in the several States.

. . .

Of the 127,000 school districts, it is estimated that 100,000 are small common-school districts, 6,000 are town or township, 7,000 are independent or city school districts and the remaining 5,000 are consolidated, township, high, county, and other types.

. . .

It appears from the bulletin that some States have an excessive number of school districts in comparison with others. Just what size district is best suited for administrative purposes no one can say.[10]

Table 4.1 indicates the changes in the size of the school districts according to the most recent figures available. The number of very small school systems, those with fewer than 300 pupils, declined from 19,071 in 1961–62 to 5,096 in 1971–72. On the other hand, the number of very large systems, those with 10,000 or more students, increased from 467 to 742 in the same period. "The average operating school system had 1,200 pupils in the fall of 1961 and 2,750 pupils in the fall of 1971."[11] There were still wide differences among the states, however; Hawaii had one statewide system and Nebraska had over 1,400 school districts in 1970, according to figures published by the Department of Health, Education, and Welfare. In addition to this, there are moves both toward decentralization within large urban districts, such as the local area districts in New York City, and toward the consolidation of suburban school districts, as in the intermediate units, often based on county lines, in Pennsylvania.

Table 4.1   Number of local public school systems, by size of system: United States, fall 1971

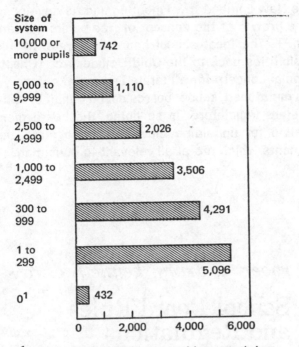

Size of system

Size of system	
10,000 or more pupils	742
5,000 to 9,999	1,110
2,500 to 4,999	2,026
1,000 to 2,499	3,506
300 to 999	4,291
1 to 299	5,096
0[1]	432

0   2,000   4,000   6,000

[1]These "nonoperating" systems either sent their pupils to a nearby school system or had no children enrolled in school.

Source: U.S. Department of Health, Education, and Welfare, Office of Education, Education Directory, Public School Systems, 1971–72.

The school board members act as the agents for the state and for the local population in operating the school system. Whether elected or appointed, chosen on a partisan or nonpartisan basis, they reflect their philosophical and social orientations in their appointments of school administrators, tolerance of academic freedom within the staff, willingness to permit or encourage innovation in the curriculum, attitude toward the building and design of new facilities, salary schedules, and so on.

". . . the American school board as an institution originated with the New England town meeting and its development paralleled the growth of the concept of free public education for all children."[12] The local school board can trace its history and responsibilities back to the Ould Deluder Act (Chapter 2) and the colonial concern for a literate and moral citizenry.

As mentioned, school boards act on behalf of and as agents of the state legislature. In so doing, the board members are responsible for upholding the laws of the state and Federal governments which are at all relevant to education.

robert l. drury, kenneth c. ray

School Board Rules and Regulations

In discharging duties imposed upon them by law, school boards have the power to make rules and regulations pertaining to the schools and pupils, which are considered administrative provisions. . . . In some jurisdictions the laws specifically empower a board of education to adopt such rules and regulations as are necessary for its government and the government of its employees and the pupils of the schools.

Such regulations must be suitably adapted to the purpose of the existence of the board and must be designed for the proper management and efficiency of the school system or the discipline and training of the children. Such rules and regula-

Drury, Robert L., and Ray, Kenneth C. *Essentials of School Law* (New York: Appleton-Century-Crofts, 1967), pp. 18–22.

tions must not be inconsistent with law, unreasonable, or oppressive, and must apply equally to all pupils regardless of race, color, or creed. The courts will not attempt to interfere with rules established by a board, revise them, or intervene to prevent their being made effective unless such rules are unreasonable, a clear abuse of discretion, or a violation of law. . . .

. . . It is recognized that no systems of rules, however carefully prepared, can provide for every emergency or meet every requirement. Consequently, much must necessarily be left to the administrative officers of a school system and to the teachers in the several schools. It follows that any reasonable rule adopted by a superintendent or a teacher, not inconsistent with some statute or some other rule prescribed by higher authority, is binding on the pupils.

In respect to pupils, a board of education may adopt rules regulating the dress and personal appearance of pupils, require pupils to pursue particular subjects, establish health regulations, require pupils to be vaccinated, and make such a condition of school attendance, require pupils to pay laboratory or breakage fees, describe reasons why a child may be disciplined or excused from school, forbid pupils to leave the school premises during the noon hour, regulate the use of automobiles and bicycles to and from school and while school is in session or during the noon hour, provide grounds for suspension or expulsion from school, provide rules as to absence or tardiness of pupils, provide rules for detention of pupils after school hours, adopt rules prohibiting pupils from wearing metal heel plates, adopt rules regarding pupils to wear caps and gowns at graduation exercises. A board of education may also adopt rules relating to the extracurricular, recreational, and social activities of pupils which are designed to promote proper discipline and training of the pupils and to direct the time and interest of pupils toward their schoolwork. A school board may also adopt regulations prohibiting a married or pregnant pupil from participating in athletics or extracurricular activities.

On the other hand, the courts will intervene to prevent the enforcement of a rule if the authority of the board of education has been illegally or unreasonably exercised, and the courts will interfere if the rule deprives a child of rights to which the law entitles him, or which tends to alienate the pupil from proper parental authority, or which exceeds the school board's powers, or its sphere of action, and in no way relates to the management or successful operation of the school. . . .

. . .

The authority of the school officials extends into the twilight zone between the school and the home and includes the enforcement of reasonable rules and requirements while the pupils are on their way home or on their way to school. The misconduct of pupils is properly within the scope of the power of the board of education, and the conduct of pupils outside school hours and school property which directly relates to and affects the management of the school and its efficiency is within the regulation of the board of education.

. . .

In recent years, the attention of the public has been drawn to some of these powers of school boards in cases involving very short skirts, excessively long hair on boys (the question being what is "excessively long"), and the presence of married or pregnant pupils in the schools. Court rulings in recent years have tended to support the students in these matters. Several cases dealing specifically with pregnant students have focused on the right of the student not to be excluded from the school, while also asking whether students' sexual activities are indeed the concern of the school board at all. Earlier decisions were resolved in favor of the school board's obligation to provide moral training and protect pupils from moral pollution, even at the expense of a pregnant student's right to equal educational opportunity. Since 1971, however, the emphasis has been on enabling the student to remain in school in order to prepare for a better future and to ". . . promote not social isolation but inclusiveness and affection for learning among students, even those who are pregnant and unmarried."[13]

More generally, the school board has several major functions. It must include in the local curriculum those courses required by the state, although it may also determine additional course offerings for its own district. School board members also consider the various funds available from Federal aid programs and, with the guidance of the professional staff, decide which funds to apply for and why they are needed. At the present time, such programs are principally organized under the Elementary and Secondary Education Act of 1965, with Title I financing approved projects for the education of educationally and economically deprived students, Title II funding library and audio-visual supplies purchases, etc.

The school board members appoint the local school superintendent or supervising principal. (Where the district is small enough to be included in the county school system, the chief local officer is usually a supervising principal under the office of the county superintendent of schools.) On the recommendation of this administrative head, the members then appoint other personnel (teachers, guidance counselors, psychologists, administrators) employed in the schools. The board members establish the salary schedules, keeping in mind both competitive salary scales and the revenue limitations imposed by the residents and the legislature. They determine when tenure shall be granted to instructional personnel. With the superintendent or supervising principal, the board members formulate the general policies of the school system.

School boards establish the local school budget, subject to the approval of the voters at public hearings, and adjust the local tax rate accordingly, within statutory limits, to raise the necessary revenues. The budget must incorporate personnel salaries, capital outlays for school equipment, and textbook and other instructional materials purchases, as well as any funds to retire indebtedness or payments on school bond issues.

Disputes between administrators and teachers, or teachers and students or their pupils are heard by the school board, which then rules in the dispute. The community relations aspect of the school board's task is also important in planning for future needs in terms of construction, faculty, course offerings, and budget.

john c. pittinger

School Board Most Harrowing Job in Education

The following is the text of Secretary Pittenger's remarks during the First General Session of PSBA's Summer Conference at the Indiana University of Pennsylvania, Friday, July 14, 1972.

If anybody asked me what I consider the most harrowing job in education today (outside of my own that is), I'd list at the top—being a school board member. Certainly it is the most thankless.

School boards across the nation are in a state of seige. They're caught in crossfires from educators, taxpayers, unions, parents, students—you name it.

. . .

First, there's a perennial problem—if it can be dismissed that easily—of money. Rocketing costs and soaring millages are triggering taxpayer rebellions—and the top of this beanstalk is nowhere in sight.

. . .

Pittinger, John C. "School Board Most Harrowing Job in Education." *Information Legislative Service* of the Pennsylvania School Boards Association, (July 28) 1972, vol. 10, pp. 5-7. Reprinted with permission from the Pennsylvania School Boards Association.

A second suggestion is to cut down the size of boards, and pay them salaries. Bills along those lines are pending in both houses of the [Penna.] General Assembly. I would oppose them. Paid boards would simply create another special interest in the educational establishment—and that we don't need.

A third solution—at least to the problem of school construction costs—is the referendum: "let the people decide." Well, that sounds attractive. But it erodes the authority of the board, and it would put an end to most school construction.

. . .

hire the right superintendent

I've now rejected three solutions to the crisis of the locally elected school board. Let me try to be more helpful. Let me suggest two ways in which you can come to grips with these very tough questions. First, develop a better understanding of your job. In fact, you have three distinct jobs. Perhaps most critical is the standards you set for hiring a superintendent. Nothing you do is more important. You only hire a new superintendent perhaps on the average of once every eight years. But he will make or break you.

What are you looking for? A popular football coach? The brother-in-law of the county chairman? Somebody who's in with the poker crowd at the Elks? Or do you want somebody who'll move your whole system ahead—dramatically. You can afford a first-rate person; but you won't get one unless you know what you're looking for. I'd suggest three qualities:

1. Ideas. A first-rate superintendent has to be an idea-man, not a glorified business manager. He can hire a business manager to buy supplies and balance the books. But he can't hire somebody to supply ideas and enthusiasms that he doesn't have.

2. A willingness to listen to other people. Other people have good ideas too. But you won't know who they are unless you're listening.

3. A willingness to delegate responsibility—including the right to make mistakes—to principals, teachers and, yes, to students.

When you have your man or woman (and it's an outrage that we have only one woman superintendent in 505 school districts), give that person the help he or she needs. For starters, financial support. And community support—be it a full-blown campaign for quality education or a word of praise at a cocktail party.

So hire the right superintendent. Drum up support. And ask tough questions. Not about the outfield grass, or the sophomore hop; but about the quality of teaching and the aims of education. Ask questions like, what is education? Do your responsibilities end when students learn the three R's, or do you provide people with motives for using these tools? Should your schools be open to the whole community? Should you be providing kids with a chance to earn and learn at the same time?

You can't ask your superintendent these questions—you won't have time—if you spend every school board meeting debating whether to buy a new wrestling mat or install vending machines in the cafeteria. It's the superintendent's interest to make you focus on things like that: it's yours to outwit him. So my first piece of advice is—think about the nature of your job. My second is—don't try to do it alone.

In your quests, use other people. Enlist advisory committees; open up schools to more citizen participation. Sure, you are the legally elected and responsible owners and operators of your schools—but you're not the only people in the community who are interested in public education.

Hold fewer executive sessions—the kind where all the decisions are hacked out—with a perfunctory formal meeting to ratify the deals you've made privately. Contrivance can almost never be disguised. Discuss your problems and ideas openly. The public confidence you gain will easily offset the discomfort of hearing yourselves criticized.

You ought, also, to involve the media. Too often, school boards relegate newsmen to the role of press agents, calling them with the good news, hiding from them the bad news. Most newsmen want to be genuinely dedicated public servants, just as you do. Give them a break—and they'll give you one.

Involve teachers. Their enthusiasm is crucial. In education, the kid in the classroom is central. What the rest of us do is unimportant except to the extent that it helps teachers teach and students learn. There's no way you can run a good school system without teacher support. And the way to get the support is to give them responsibility.

And finally, lest we forget why we're all here in the first place, I'd like to emphasize the urgent need to involve students themselves. They don't have to be the enemy. After all, students are the consumers of the system. They are not always right; but if they are bored or hostile, learning is really impossible. For that reason alone, they should be involved. Bring them to school board meetings. Encourage student forums, give them a bona fide say. Let them wear their hair the way they want to; worry more about what's inside their heads than what's on top. Let them help run the system because real responsibility is the best teacher of all.

There is considerable controversy over the question of who should be a school board member, including a sub-question of whether school board members should be required to have a child or children in the public schools of the district they serve. It has been suggested that this would be one way of ensuring involvement and serious commitment on the part of school board members in the quality and nature of education. Wallace and Schneider also call attention to the concept of "local control" and the provincialism that sometimes accompanies it. This problem has led to several proposals for inter-district and inter-state cooperation in educational efforts.

Consolidation and Cooperation

For the past forty years or more, there have been continuing efforts to consolidate school districts in order to provide more efficient and more effective instruction. As noted earlier, at one time there were over 127,000 local school districts; these have been reduced to almost one-tenth the number. Much of the effort has been inspired at the state level, and some of it has been the result of local desires. There is no question but that a single consolidated district composed of two, three, or four smaller districts can provide laboratories and special classes which any one of the smaller districts could not afford alone. Conant, too, has strongly recommended, at least at the high school level, that consolidation of several small high schools into a single larger comprehensive high school would improve the quality of education offered to the students affected.

A second type of cooperative effort is much newer. It stems from the civil rights activities of the 1960's and the Federal legislation affecting education passed in these years. In particular, there is the suggestion that educational parks and "magnet" schools be built which draw from several districts within large urban school districts (e.g., New York, Philadelphia, Chicago, Los Angeles). Educational parks consist of several school buildings for elementary and secondary pupils, clustered around a core facility which houses audio-visual instructional materials, an auditorium, art and music studios, central library (with smaller ones in each classroom for daily use), perhaps a cafeteria, and similar educational resource centers, as well as administrative offices for the entire complex. The centralization of these facilities is a move toward increasing use of them throughout the day, which, in turn, reduces costs and increases efficiency. Physical education facilities, too, would be in a central building, with the cost of building two pools in a single location (to permit two groups at a time to have swimming lessons), for example, much lower than if the pools were constructed in two separate locations a mile or more apart (see Figure 9.1, page 232).

Magnet schools, on the other hand, are designed to draw students from throughout a community to a single school with special courses in a particular field. An example of a "magnet" school might be any of the numerous vocational high schools in New York City which focus on a single trade, such as aviation, needle trade, etc. Boys attending the school of aviation trades, for instance, come from all over the city to learn the techniques needed for aircraft construction and maintenance. The magnet school plan is not restricted to vocational schools, however. The Bronx (New York) High School of Science, Hunter College High School (New York), Central High School (Philadelphia), Philadelphia High School for Girls, and Boston Latin School are examples of academically-oriented secondary schools which enroll pupils across school district lines. A prime advantage of such facilities, if planned properly, is that they are equipped with the best available instructional materials, too expensive to purchase for several schools but feasible for one.

Again it is believed that these innovations give more positive educational benefits than duplicating facilities at a lower level of quality in each sub-district. The *Report* of the National Advisory Commission on Civil Disorders even urges that such facilities be built on the borderline between urban and suburban school districts, with both units sharing the cost and use of them. In a conference on "The Unfinished American Revolution" in 1966, two of the speakers urged urban-suburban confrontation and cooperation. Richardson Dilworth, former mayor of Philadelphia and then president of its school board, recommended the formation of a regional school district, merging city and suburban school districts, in order, as he said, "to cut the white noose of the suburbs that is strangling our cities," and to help resolve some of the economic and racial difficulties of urban schools.[14] The then-superintendent of schools in Pittsburgh, Dr. Sidney Marland, Jr., was more concerned with ". . . direct competition and a direct confrontation with suburban schools and [the urban schools] must be so good that people

will want to move back into the city because of better educational opportunities."[15]

James B. Conant and others have urged that inter-state
cooperation might be effective in providing guidelines for better
education, even without enforcement authority. Some of the
concepts now included in such a cooperative effort are presented here.

compact for education

Preamble and Selected
Articles from the Constitution

preamble

WHEREAS, the proper education of all citizens is one of
the most important responsibilities of the State to preserve a
free and open society in the United States; and,

WHEREAS, the increasing demands of our whole national
life for improving and expanding educational services require
a broad exchange of research data and information concerning
the problems and practices of education; and,

WHEREAS, there is a vital need for strengthening the
voices of the States in the formulation of alternative nationwide educational policies,

The States affirm the need for close and continuing consultation among our several States on all matters of education,
and do hereby establish this Compact for Education.

"Preamble and Selected Articles from the Constitution," Compact
for Education. In *Social Foundations of Education*, ed. Dorothy Westby-
Gibson, (New York: The Free Press, 1967), pp. 217–219.

compact for education

Article I. Purpose and Policy

A. It is the purpose of this compact to:

1. Establish and maintain close cooperation and understanding among executive, legislative, professorial, educational and lay leadership on a nationwide basis at the state and local levels.

2. Provide a forum for the discussion, development, crystallization and recommendation of public policy alternatives in the field of education.

3. Provide a clearing house of information on matters relating to educational problems and how they are being met in different places throughout the Nation, so that the executive and legislative branches of State Government and of local communities may have ready access to the experience and record of the entire country, and so that both lay and professional groups in the field of education may have additional avenues for the sharing of experience and the interchange of ideas in the formation of public policy in education.

4. Facilitate the improvement of State and local educational systems so that all of them will be able to meet adequate and desirable goals in a society which requires continuous qualitative and quantitative advance in educational opportunities, methods and facilities.

B. It is the policy of this compact to encourage and promote local and State initiative in the development, maintenance, improvement and administration of educational systems and institutions in a manner which will accord with the needs and advantages of diversity among localities and States.

C. The party States recognize that each of them has an interest in the quality and quantity of education furnished in each of the other States, as well as in the excellence of its own educational systems and institutions, because of the highly mobile character of individuals within the Nation, and because the products and services contributing to the health, welfare and economic advancement of each State are supplied in significant part by persons educated in other States.

. . .

Article III. The Commission

A. The Educational Commission of the States, hereinafter called "the Commission," is hereby established. The Commission shall consist of seven members representing each party State. One of such members shall be the Governor; two shall be members of the State legislature selected by its respective houses and serving in such manner as the legislature may determine; and four shall be appointed by and serve at the pleasure of the Governor, unless the laws of the State otherwise provide.

Article IV. Powers

In addition to authority conferred on the Commission by other provisions of the compact, the Commission shall have authority to:

1. Collect, correlate, analyze and interpret information and data concerning educational needs and resources.

2. Encourage and foster research in all aspects of education, but with special reference to the desirable scope of instruction, organization, administration, and instructional methods and standards employed or suitable for employment in public educational systems.

3. Develop proposals for adequate financing of education as a whole and at each of its many levels . . .

. . .

5. Formulate suggested policies and plans for the improvement of public education as a whole, or for any segment thereof, and make recommendations with respect thereto available to the appropriate governmental units, agencies, and public officials . . .

There are difficulties in achieving maximum effectiveness in the work of the Commission, mostly because of political self-interest considerations. However, the fact that the Commission has advisory rather than legislative powers, and that it can perform many "clearinghouse" functions, have contributed to its present viability.

Problems and Issues Which Continue

The questions remain: Who should control American education? If local control is retained, following the traditional American pattern of decentralization, how can the most competent board of education be formed? Can and should the functions of the board and its appointed superintendent be sharply separated? In urban areas, should the board be integrated into the munici-pal administration or should it be a separate unit? Should school boards in large cities attempt to set policies for the entire city school system, or should their functions be de-centralized in smaller local boards? Should there be coopera-tive line-crossing between school districts as far as school operation is concerned, while retaining the autonomy of each district? At what point does school board policy intrude on personal privacy and on the right to education? These are some of the problems and issues still surrounding governmental responsibility in education.

Endnotes

1. Clark, Burton R. *Educating the Expert Society* (San Francisco: Chandler Publishing Co., 1962), pp. 122–123.
2. *Ibid.*
3. The President's Commission on School Finance. *Schools, People, and Money: The Need for Educational Reform.* Final Report. Washington, D.C.: Government Printing Office, 1972, xii.

4. Stone, James C., and Hempstead, R. Ross. *California Education Today* (New York: Thomas Y. Crowell Co. 1968), pp. 93–141.

5. *Ibid.*, p. 137.

6. *Ibid.*, p. 172.

7. *Ibid.*, pp. 99–104.

8. Hartford, *op. cit.*, pp. 152–153.

9. Thayer, V. T. *The Role of the School in American Society* (New York: Dodd, Mead, and Co., 1960), p. 62.

10. Diffenbaugh, W. S., and Covert, Timon. "School Administration Units," In Cubberley, *Readings, op. cit.*, p. 512.

11. Grant, W. Vance. "Statistics of the month: Trends in the Number and Size of Local Public School Systems," *American Education*, (June) 1972, 8, Back cover.

12. National School Board Association Information Service *Bulletin*, 5, Feb. 1967, p. 1.

13. Warren, Donald R. "Pregnant students/Public schools." *Phi Delta Kappan*, 1972, pp. 54, 114.

14. Corr, John P. "Dilworth Hits White Noose of Suburbs," *The Philadelphia Inquirer*, Oct. 26, 1966, p. 1.

15. *Ibid.*

For Further Reading

American Education, 8, 1972 (and previous volumes 1–7).

BAILEY, THOMAS D. "The Folklore of Local Control." *NEA Journal*, 50 (Dec. 1961), pp. 42–43.

BURCHILL, GEORGE W. *Work-Study Programs for Alienated Youth: A Casebook* (Chicago: Science Research Associates, 1962).

CAMPBELL, RONALD F., CUNNINGHAM, LUVERN L., and McPHEE, RODERICK F. *The Organization and Control of American Schools.* (Columbus, O.: Charles E. Merrill, 1965).

CLARK, BURTON R. "The Problem of Control." In *Students, School and Society*, ed. John A. Dahl, *et al*. (San Francisco: Chandler Publishing Company, 1964).

CUBBERLEY, ELLWOOD P. *Readings in Public Education in the United States* (Boston: Houghton-Mifflin Company, 1934).

DRURY, ROBERT L., and KENNETH C. RAY. *Essentials of School Law* (New York: Appleton-Century-Crofts, 1967).

EDWARDS, NEWTON, and HERMAN G. RICHEY. *The School in American Society*, second edition (Boston: Houghton-Mifflin Company, 1963).

GIBBONEY, RICHARD A. "The Role of the State Education Department in Education Change." In *Perspectives on Educational Change*, ed. Richard I. Miller, (New York: Appleton-Century-Crofts, 1967).

GRAHAM, GRACE. *The Public School in the American Community* (New York: Harper and Row, 1963).

GRAVES, FRANK P. *The Administration of American Education* (New York: The Macmillan Company, 1932).

HARTFORD, ELLIS FORD. *Education in These United States* (New York: The Macmillan Company, 1964).

KNEZEVICH, STEPHEN J. *Administration of Public Education* (New York: Harper and Row, 1962).

KNIGHT, EDGAR W. *Readings in Educational Administration* (New York: Henry Holt and Company, 1953).

LIEBERMAN, MYRON. *The Future of Public Education* (Chicago: University of Chicago Press, 1960).

MILES, JOHN R. *Government and Education; The Responsibility of State and Local Government* (Washington, D.C.: Chamber of Commerce of the United States, 1963).

MORPHET, EDGAR L., ROE L. JOHNS, and THEODORE L. RELLER. *Educational Administration: Concepts, Practices, and Issues* (Englewood Cliffs, N.J.: Prentice-Hall, 1959).

National School Board Association Information Service. *Bulletin*, 5, 1967 (and earlier volumes).

PASSOW, A. HARRY, ed. *Education in Depressed Areas* (New York: Bureau of Publications, Teachers College, Columbia University, 1963).

PSBA Bulletin, Penna. School Boards Association (bimonthly).

PETERSON, LEROY J., ROSSMILLER, RICHARD A., and VOLZ, MARLIN M. *The Law and Public School Operation.* (New York: Harper & Row, Publishers, 1969).

STONE, JAMES C., and R. ROSS HEMPSTEAD. *California Education Today* (New York: Thomas Y. Crowell Company, 1968).

THAYER, V. T. *The Role of the School in American Society* (New York: Dodd, Mead, and Company, 1960).

WALLACE, JOHN, and PHILLIP SCHNEIDER. "Do School Boards Take Education Seriously?" *Saturday Review*, Oct. 16, 1965, pp. 89–90, 103.

WESTBY-GIBSON, DOROTHY, ed. *Social Foundations of Education* (New York: The Free Press, 1967).

WILCOX, PRESTON R. "The School and the Community." *Teachers College Record*, 69, 1967, 133–142.

5

economics and education

Economics and education are forever entwined both with each other and with the several problems of poverty, segregation, Federal aid to education, quality in education, and professional preparation of teachers. The solution to each of these issues requires money as well as theory, hard cash as well as political or other philosophy.

Our concern here, however, is primarily with the mutual relations of economics and education. That is, we are concerned with how changes in the economy necessitate changes in the curriculum, and how quality and quantity of education affect the nation's economy. A single example will illuminate this thesis. For well over one hundred years of our history, the United States economy was dominated by agriculture. Within the past fifty years, however, both the wealth of the nation and the physical distribution of the population have shifted increasingly to non-agricultural areas. Since half or more than half of the children born in rural sections in recent years will ultimately leave the farm in pursuit of more rewarding occupations, the curriculum in rural schools must be changed to prepare these children for non-agricultural careers. While economics and mathematics may still be taught in terms of farm costs, prices, and subsidies, so as to be meaningful to the students, they will also need to be made aware of the financial facts of urban and industrial life. Greater preparation for college entrance is also needed, as more and more rural students seek higher education as a means of climbing the socio-economic ladder, on or off the farm. Both in terms of rising educational costs and of increasing academic demands, this has led to school district consolidation. With the joint or consolidated schools, more laboratory facilities and equipment can be provided, a greater variety of courses can be offered, and better teachers can be attracted to the rural areas. This represents a substantial sequence of modifications in rural education as a result of movement in the national economy.

In this chapter, we will explore not only this kind of situation, but also the problems of the poor in relation to education, of the migrant laborer's children and what has been done for them, the swelling mass of the "culturally different," and the problems of the "dropout." All of these problems are related to the national economy and to the spiraling costs of education, which will also be presented.

Poverty and Mobility

Because of the mobility of the population, resulting in part from the changes in the economy, the distance in quality of education between rural and urban, slum and suburban schools, keeps increasing. In general, slum schools have had the poorest physical plants, the least experienced teachers, and the most outdated texts and equipment, while the suburban schools, supported by ex-urbanites, have enjoyed the diametric opposite. Schools in economically depressed rural areas have suffered with antiquated one-room facilities (rapidly disappearing but leaving behind some nostalgic sentiments), underpaid and often undereducated teachers, and a lack of basic equipment. As Keppel says, "Control today over the quality of schools is . . . in good part a factor of residence, control over place of residence is dependent on money and on race."[1] It is for this reason that much recent Federal legislation, such as the Economic Opportunities Act of 1965, has been passed. The Elementary and Secondary Education Act of 1965 was also designed to remedy school weaknesses, and sections of the Civil Rights

Figure 5.1

Earl Palmer (Monkmeyer)

The one-room schoolhouse is rapidly disappearing through federal aid to education, but remnants of the past still exist. Wolfe Creek School, near Welch, West Virginia, is a one-room affair, typical of the poverty-ridden region in the heart of West Virginia's "Billion Dollar Coal Field."

Act of 1964 (and subsequent related legislation) contribute, too, to the remediation of educational inequities. Through Federal and private grants, there is now an intensive effort to upgrade rural and slum schools by providing funds for new school construction, the development of new and better textbooks, the creation of and expansion of school libraries, and the general alleviation of the distress engendered by unequal educational facilities. Again, according to Keppel, "One can start at either end—abolish poverty, segregation, oppression, the conditions on which neglect feeds, or ameliorate the conditions by improving the schools in the midst of poverty and prejudice."[2] Although attempting to do both, in a sense, simultaneously, the bulk of Federal efforts, and those at the state level, would seem to lie at this time with the second alternative.

What is it like in the inner city? What is it like to go to school there? And how do the schools compare with those in the suburban community?

james b. conant

Slums and Suburbs

Let me describe a slum that might be in any one of several of the large cities I have visited. The inhabitants are all Negroes and with few exceptions have entered the city from a state in the deep South anytime within the last month to the last three years. Often the composition of a school grade in such an area will alter so rapidly that a teacher will find at the end of a school year that she is teaching but few pupils who started with her in the fall. I recall the principal of one school stating that a teacher absent more than one week will have difficulty recognizing her class when she returns. This comes about because mothers move with their offspring from one rented room to another from month to month and in so doing often go

Conant, James Bryant. *Slums and Suburbs* (New York: McGraw-Hill Book Company, 1961), pp. 18–21, 36–38. By permission of the author.

from one elementary school district to another; I am told that resident tenements look more like transient hotels. I write "mothers" advisedly, since in one neighborhood, by no means the worst I have seen, a questionnaire sent out by the school authorities indicated that about a third of the pupils came from family units (one hesitates to use the word "home") which had no father, stepfather, or male guardian. This particular section was by no means homogeneous, of course. For while many moved about from room to room, a quarter of the parents reported that they owned their homes. Only 10 per cent of the parents had graduated from high school and only 33 per cent had completed the elementary school. Contrast the situation in which a third of the parents have completed elementary school with that in a high-income suburb where as many as 90 per cent of the parents have bachelor's degrees, if not graduate degrees from a university.

. . . to attempt to divorce the school from the community is to engage in unrealistic thinking, which might lead to policies that could wreak havoc with the school and the lives of children. The community and the school are inseparable. For example, I have walked through school corridors in slum areas and, looking into classrooms, have seen children asleep with their heads on their hands. Is this situation the result of poor teachers without either disciplinary control or teaching ability? No, the children asleep at their desks have been up all night with no place to sleep or else have been subject to incredibly violent family fights and horrors through the night. Checking into one case, a principal told one of my staff that after climbing six flights of a tenement he found the boy's home— one filthy room with a bed, a light bulb, and a sink. In the room live the boy's mother and her four children. I might add that it is not unusual for teachers in these schools to take home with them children with no place to go at night. The social attitudes found in this kind of slum neighborhood are bound to affect the atmosphere of the school. As one Negro teacher said to me, "We do quite well with these children in the lower grades. Each of us is, for the few hours of the school day, an acceptable substitute for the mother. But when they reach about

10, 11, or 12 years of age, we lose them. At that time the "street" takes over. In terms of schoolwork, progress ceases; indeed many pupils begin to go backward in their studies!"

. . .

The difference between the Negro slum of today and the slums of the Northern seaport cities of sixty years ago is a difference that deserves attention. The worries I have expressed about the continuation of present conditions may appear to be neutralized by contemplating the record of the past. Big cities have always had slums. In the United States in the past it was possible for people to raise themselves by their own bootstraps in the course of a generation. Why be alarmed about the present situation? Such a complacent projection of the past into the obscure future is fallacious for several reasons. First and foremost is the fact that in the past most of the inhabitants of slums were recently arrived white foreign immigrants. They knew that their predecessors for generations had worked their way out of poverty in the cities. They were convinced that they could do likewise. The almost complete lack of such conviction —a consequence of the tragic story of the Negro in the United States—is the outstanding characteristic of youth in the Negro slum. Secondly, a foreign immigrant came from an impoverished but stable society, for the most part a peasant society with its own ancient mores. The pride of family and often strong church connections were social cement that kept the slums from being complete social jungles in spite of the fact that the dwelling conditions were often as bad as they are today. Lastly, for most of the period of our history labor shortages rather than labor surpluses were characteristic of our economy. Particularly, unskilled laborers were in demand. When this was not so, namely, in the depression years, organized society had to step in on a large scale to bolster the tottering social structure. Today automation has affected the employment scene; there is much less demand for unskilled labor. Racial discrimination makes unemployment chronic for the Negro male, North and South. In short, neither in terms of the kinds of people involved nor in terms of the economic and social setting is there much resemblance between the poor city districts of 1900 and those which are the sore spots of our modern cities.

What was especially disturbing to me in my visits to the largest cities was the discovery that the employment of youth is literally nobody's affair. To be sure, there are groups concerned with various aspects of the problem, but no single agency in any of the cities has the data as to the unemployment picture in that city. There is little up-to-date information about youth unemployment even city-wide and only the estimate of school people about the slum neighborhoods. Seldom are figures available to distinguish between the unemployed who are high school graduates and those who have dropped out of school before completing the twelfth grade. Most important, it is not possible to say with any accuracy how the unemployed youth are distributed among various neighborhoods.

Information published in the past several years provides an answer to this last question raised by Conant. Youth unemployment frequently is as high as 4 times the national average unemployment rate.

The picture painted by Conant has not changed for the better in more than a decade. If anything, the negative aspects of the situation in inner-city schools have increased despite legislation and funds appropriated to improve learning, improve teaching, and to encourage the student to "stay in" rather than "drop out."

There is a vicious cycle in the slums from poverty to ignorance to poverty, perpetuating the problems of the unskilled and uneducated from generation to generation. Early in the school years, the slum children are often typed as "slow" or "dull" because of their poor home environment and relatively poor showing on standard verbal intelligence tests, and are shunted into curricula which do not offer them a way up and out of their situation. They become "dropouts" and pass on their dislike and distrust of the schools to succeeding generations, which then have the same unfortunate experiences. The teachers in these schools, too, often become "dropouts" because their idealism has been warped by the conditions under which they work.

Conant considered the problem both of the high school graduate and of the "dropout," and outlined his suggestions for ameliorating the problems incurred.

> . . . *guidance officers, especially in the large cities, ought to be given the responsibility for following the post-high school careers of youth from the time they leave school until they are twenty-one years of age.* Since compulsory attendance usually ends at age sixteen, this means responsibility for the guidance of youth ages sixteen to twenty-one who are out of school and either employed or unemployed. This expansion of the school's function will cost money and will mean additional staff—at least a doubling of the guidance staff in most of the large cities. But the expense is necessary, for vocational and educational guidance must be a continuing process to help assure a smooth transition from school to the world of work. The present abrupt break between the two is unfortunate.
> . . .
> Adult education courses, work-study programs of various sorts—these are all evidence of a continuing interest of the schools in furthering educational opportunities for out-of-school youth.[3]

Only in recent years have there been attempts to expand the horizons of slum children in an attempt to make them more academically-oriented and better-informed about the larger society around them.[4] The curricula in inner-city schools are being modified, including the teaching of English as a second language (TESL), because educators have become aware of the fact that many of the children in these schools speak a language markedly different from the "standard" English in which teachers normally teach.[5] Psychologists are desperately trying to devise "culture-free" or "culture-fair" tests which will evaluate the intelligence of the slum children more adequately and fairly. Compensatory education, pre-school programs, motivation programs at the junior and senior high school level, are all efforts to break the vicious cycle.

The same cyclical problem of poverty to ignorance to poverty is apparent among the children of the highly mobile migrant labor force.

> Each year, 150,000 children move with their parents across the croplands of this country, harvesting as they go. They are burdened by poverty and disease, deprived of education and legislation which could alleviate their condition. These are the migrants—rejected by communities and unwelcomed in schools. Temporary residence makes them ineligible for public assistance and other legal benefits. Many are illiterate; most are educationally retarded.
>
> Child labor and school attendance laws are inadequate and often ignored as children (at times as young as four years of age) work in the fields beside their parents. Deprived of cultural experiences which contribute much to success in schools, these children are frequently destined for failure in school and become misfits in adult living. They subsequently bear other generations of migrants. Thus the vicious cycle proliferates.[6]

What little schooling these children have ill-prepares them for anything better or different in life, since they usually attend schools in our most depressed areas for brief periods of time. Until quite recently, relatively little had been done to change this pattern for migrant children.

California is one of the states in which a large proportion of migrant families wander. As a result, the state board of education has formulated a philosophy and developed programs to help the children of these families. A California Master Plan for Migrant Children went into effect in the late 1960's. It established a central records center from which teachers could obtain the school records of newly-arrived migrant children, provided for interdistrict and interstate cooperation in the transfer of children and their records, and attempted to provide alternative skills for these children in the face of increasing automation.[7] This was the forerunner of the Uniform Migrant Student Record Transfer System that became a reality in 1969. With this system in operation:

> It was the first time there was even a hope of keeping track of the educational and health progress of children of migratory agricultural workers as they followed the crops across the country. In full operation today, the system maintains records of more than 293,000 migrant children and is itself producing "firsts." Perhaps the most important innovation is a monthly printout of information—the Nationwide Activity Summary—on the number of children being helped under federally financed education programs, their needs, and how these needs are being met. By way of illustration, a recent printout indicated, among other things, that 21,776 students were enrolled in public schools for the first time; 11,396 children had had physical, visual, audio, dental, or TB-screening examinations; 160 children had urgent health problems; 557 had taken the Stanford Achievement Test with 54 percent of them showing skill in math computations. Such hard data have never before been available to educators in migrant education. Moreover, the system breaks down the data by State to enable State and local officials to use it in planning more effective programs.[8]

The problem of educating migrant children is not unique to the Western states. Wherever large crops must be sown and harvested, in Florida, Georgia, New Jersey, Pennsylvania, and other states, this responsibility exists; attempts are being made on a statewide or local basis to provide opportunities for educating these children. Funds to support these efforts come from the Elementary and Secondary Education Act, Office of Economic Opportunity, and other Federal sources.

Frequently, the children are in one location only for a matter of four to eight weeks. Rapid data retrieval from the Transfer System reduces the time needed for placing the children at an appropriate instructional level. The level is usually quite low in all academic areas, but compounding the need for remedial work is the poor self-image and limited motivation for learning common to most of the children. Individual instruction techniques and a small teacher-to-pupil ratio appear to be vital to obtaining positive changes in all three areas. This *is* expensive, but obviously worth the expense and the effort if well-planned programs prove to be effective in bringing these children out of ignorance and poverty.

What is the significance of the problems of poverty and mobility to the nation's economy? It means that there is an incredible waste of human resources. It means that instead of investing in people's education as a basis for an expanding economy, we are allowing an irreplaceable asset—man's power to solve problems—to go down the same drain as many of our natural resources have done. In an era of increasing technology, the unskilled worker is a liability. When such an individual cannot find gainful employment because of his educational inadequacies, it costs the government, i.e., the taxpayer, more to keep him on the welfare payrolls than it would to keep him in school for twelve years. Under the various "War on Poverty" programs instituted during the Johnson Administration and continued since in varying intensity, attempts have been made to provide basic education and retraining for unskilled and unemployed (or presently unemployable) adults, but more of the people who need these courses must be motivated to attend them. In today's increasingly automated society, the emphasis in these programs, beyond the fundamentals of literacy and numerical competence, needs to be on the continuing desire and ability to learn—*not* on particular skills.

It used to be that a man who acquired a specific skill as a boy had learned what he needed to be able to do for the rest of his life. A skilled man was a man who had learned a traditional craft. Today, increasingly, craft skills as such become meaningless. In organizing the economic job as a "process" based on automation, that is, on the systematic flow of information and material, skills that never were together become one at a given place of work. And skills that formed a cohesive whole . . . become parceled out among a great many pieces of work in a great many different places. Worse still, skills that were apparently

eternal only yesterday, may overnight become obsolete—
and new skills, not yet visible, may become required overnight.[9]

This is, of course, valid also for all education. As is emphasized at several points in this book, we need to teach problem-
solving techniques as well as facts, means of coping with
change as well as traditional values.

The Problem of the "Dropout"

Many pupils leave school before graduation because of urgent
family financial needs. They can obtain jobs demanding little
in the way of skills—construction laborers, gasoline station
attendants, low-level service employment—and are generally
limited to such occupations for life. Others leave school because they are, or believe themselves to be, inadequate in the
face of learning, due to below average intellectual functioning,
and/or have insufficient motivation to keep on trying. In some
of these cases, pupils drop out because employment looks
more adult, *ergo*, more attractive, than the "childishness" of
continued schooling; or because the courses offered in the high
school bear no practical relation, in their thinking, to the type
of life they lead or wish to lead. In almost all of these cases,
the "dropout" is limited in his employment opportunities because he lacks a high school diploma. College "dropouts" may
also find themselves handicapped in finding employment in the
fields they consider desirable because their training is insufficient or inadequate and the fact that they dropped out of college, unless for urgent reasons, suggests a lack of persistence
and determination.

What are the characteristics of the dropout from high
school? Based on a survey of the literature, Schreiber reported
that the "typical dropout":

1) is just past the sixteenth birthday.
2) is more often a boy than a girl.
3) has average or slightly below average intelligence.

4) is an underachiever, i.e., is reading below grade level, and is in the lowest quartile of his class academically.

5) is over age for his grade placement due to retention in grade in either elementary or junior high school.

6) is not a delinquent, but is often a truant or discipline problem to the school authorities.

7) is seldom a participant in extra-curricular activities.

8) feels rejected by the school and in turn rejects the school.

9) has parents and older siblings who were dropouts.[10]

The dropout problem has become more acute in our society because of a variety of factors which are inherent in the school structure and peculiar to our time. The high rate of youth unemployment has already been cited. Delinquency and crime among youths continue to increase. The large-scale migration of population from rural and depressed areas to urban centers, previously mentioned, is another factor.

The population explosion—approximately 3.8 million youths are reaching age 18 each year. This is a million more than reached age 18 in 1964 and previous years.

The increase in the number of welfare families, especially in large cities, further heightened by a marked increase in the total cost of public assistance. . . .

The elimination of unskilled jobs through automation and the increased use of technology, resulting in unemployment.

The racial riots in the cities, in which the participants are overwhelmingly the unemployed, out-of-school youths of the area.[11]

As may be seen from Table 5.1, almost three out of every ten children in fifth grade in 1964 failed to graduate from high school in 1972. And at the college level, it is expected that only two of the four who entered college in the autumn of 1972 will graduate in 1976. Thus, it is really seen that this is a major problem, both from the point of view of school retention and of answering the problem of school dropouts.

Although minimum wage laws and union contracts guarantee an annual wage of around $4000, the dollar continues to shrink even as wages increase. Therefore, the purchasing power of the individual remains virtually static or decreases. To the dropout, this means continued near-poverty.

Table 5.1   School retention ratio (est.)

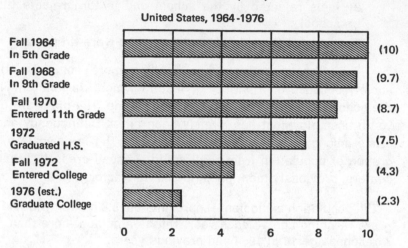

United States, 1964-1976

Fall 1964 In 5th Grade — (10)
Fall 1968 In 9th Grade — (9.7)
Fall 1970 Entered 11th Grade — (8.7)
1972 Graduated H.S. — (7.5)
Fall 1972 Entered College — (4.3)
1976 (est.) Graduate College — (2.3)

0   2   4   6   8   10

Source: U.S. Department of Health, Education, and Welfare; Office of Education. American Education, 9, July 1973, p.33.

Substantial differences in earning capacity cannot be ignored. Nor can the individual ex-pupil ignore the social stigma and diminished self-image he suffers as a dropout. None of this need happen, however. There *are* work-study programs which permit the student to earn as he learns, part-time jobs, and scholarships available even on the secondary level, which enable the financially-burdened pupil to continue his education *if he so desires*. There are also neighborhood tutoring projects without cost, and volunteer teachers without cost, available to help him overcome academic difficulties and deficiencies. It is simpler to correct economic inequities, however, than to arouse motivation. For the latter problem, other remedies, principally in the areas of curriculum revision and expansion, are needed.

> After considering all the available evidence in the literature, it appears that the outstanding dropout prevention programs of the future will contain at least eight basic program elements:
> The assurance of closer personal contact between students and significant adults. . . .
> A system for evaluating academic progress that does not destroy the student's self-esteem or stymie his critical, analytical, and divergent thought processes. . . .
> Allowance for flexible scheduling. . . . Traditional 8 A.M. to 4 P.M. schooldays and 50-minute periods may have to change.
> Gearing the educational program to personality and motivational aspects as well as intellectual capacity. . . . such as The Utah Instructional Systems Program . . .
> Provision of outlets for frustrations . . . Social and recreational programs should include all students, even if sometimes the program is very unusual. . . .
> Assurance of remedial work for students who need it, but with the "unsatisfactory" stigma removed. . . .
> Provision of inservice training for the school staff . . .
> Requirement and assurance of total community involvement. . . .[12]

The need for business, as part of the community, to become involved in this problem is also cited. The business people can sponsor training programs, work-study arrangements, job counseling, and even be used as resource personnel in the schools.

Massive publicity campaigns in the various media have urged youths to stay in school. It is a fact, though, that many who drop out do so because their needs and values are not met in the typical high school. To combat the apparent mismatching, the existence of which was confirmed in a study by the Institute for Social Research at the University of Michigan, it is suggested that both individuals and schools undergo some changes.

If greater emphasis is placed on preschool and early school intervention, then it is expected that individuals will have fewer problems as learners, thus reducing the frustrations that lead to becoming a dropout. Furthermore, "the range of educational options for young people aged 16 to 18 should be broadened, and serious consideration given to reducing the number of years necessary for attaining a high school diploma."[13] Both of these recommendations arouse controversy, although an awareness of the possible positive effects of early educational intervention is increasing. A third possibility exists that is unique to the state of California. Provision for continuing education has existed in that state since 1919, with all minors aged 6 to 18 years required to attend school until they have graduated from high school, except for those with severe mental or physical handicaps. Each school district must provide continuation education for minors who reside in the district and who need continuation education, under the threat of a reduction in their annual state apportionment.

> "Continuation education in California serves two main groups of students: those who drop out of the regular high school either because they want to or because they must work and those (a much larger group) who either cannot or will not adjust to the program of the regular full-time high school. The latter group includes an increasing number of youths for whom the large comprehensive high school has lost all meaning and relevance to life."[14]

The programs are more individualized than those in regular high schools, with short-term goals, greater flexibility and autonomy, and a strong counseling-guidance orientation built in. Most students must attend classes three hours per day. Those who are regularly employed attend at least four 60-minute hours per week.

Some of the alternative secondary school programs, such as the Parkway Program in Philadelphia and its offshoots, are also attempts to make education more relevant to disenchanted students. They tend to be soundly criticized or highly praised, depending on one's educational philosophy. In these programs, classes are held in hospitals, insurance company offices, and anywhere else where cooperation can be obtained and where students express an interest.

The Disadvantaged

Who are the disadvantaged? They come mainly from four sources. First, there are Negroes who have migrated from the rural South. Second, there are whites who have migrated from the hill lands of the South. Third, there is a significant group of Puerto Ricans, and fourth, a group of Spanish-speaking persons from the arid Southwest.[15]

Russell has omitted the American Indian here, but otherwise has indicated those groups which are an untapped human resource, a neglected reservoir of abilities which could be educated to the mutual profit of themselves and the nation.

The problems faced by Negroes in urban Northern slums have already been discussed. The Puerto Rican faces much the same situation as the Negro with the additional handicap of living in an alien culture and speaking a language other than English. New York and Philadelphia, two cities where the Puerto Rican population is sizable, have been attempting to minimize the cultural barrier by training Puerto Ricans as civil servants to work among their own people, by providing bilingual school personnel, and even by posting bilingual signs where necessary. Unlike earlier indigent and immigrant groups, however, Puerto Ricans come North with citizenship status already theirs, thus removing one incentive for acculturation and advancement. There is, also, among many of them, the attitude that if things do not go well in the North, it is an easy matter to return to their sunny native island. This, too, was not true of the earlier immigrants—they had no desire to return to their native lands. There are relatively few Puerto Ricans who have achieved at a high level in the States, with the result that there are too few heroes with whom the Puerto Rican child can identify as an incentive to remain in school. He becomes a school dropout and is added to the welfare rolls.

In Appalachia, the population is part of the white, Anglo-Saxon, Protestant majority, but bears little resemblance otherwise to the national population in economic or educational terms. As Peter Schrag noted in the *Saturday Review*,

> Despite its poverty, Appalachia remains perhaps the most typically American region; its people have not entirely shaken their frontier attitudes about the conservation of resources, about the value of education, and about relations with the outside world. Rivers are polluted with trash and garbage, refuse dumps foul scenic valleys, and the hulks of abandoned cars line many highways. While most of the nation has become more European, more cosmopolitan, Appalachia has changed but little, remaining behind its protective mountains. Thus there remains a suspicion of change, and of anything but the most conservative education.[16]

The combined forces of economic depression, due to closed mines and little industry, political conservatism, and social insularity have placed the children of the "mountain people" in the same educational (and economic) situation as the slum and migrant children. "Many of the mountaineers value education even though most never went beyond the eighth grade themselves. They want lives for their children that are better than they have had, but they do not know, and cannot know, what a good education is, or the kind of effort it requires."[17] The Teacher Corps and VISTA programs now operating in Appalachia are attempts to broaden the opportunities of these children. Federal funds are provided to stimulate new programs of enrichment and content in the schools. However, with still inadequate education and few occupational opportunities, these children drop out of school and soon, they, too, join the welfare rolls.

Another population group which has suffered educationally and economically, to the detriment of the national welfare and the national image, is the "native American"—the American Indian. Living on a government reservation, and governed ultimately by the Bureau of Indian Affairs (Department of the

Interior) in Washington, he has been sorely neglected and pitifully undereducated for our times. Some Indians have gone away from the reservation and attended the "white man's" boarding schools. For many of them, used to the cooperative atmosphere of the tribe, the competition and self-assertiveness expected at the schools have been emotionally disturbing to the extent that they have left school, and in some cases attempted suicide.

The Crossover Phenomenon

The academic-failure pattern of Indian students is so surprisingly uniform and well-documented that researchers have given it its own name: the crossover phenomenon. It works like this:

The Indian student enters schools and keeps pace with his white classmates for the first few grades. But between the fourth and seventh grades he starts falling behind both national achievement norms and his classmates. From there on, he falls further and further behind, thereby making him prime dropout material as he reaches high school. The overall dropout rate: nearly two out of three students.

The reasons for academic "crossover" from relative performance to clear-cut nonperformance are complex. But one major reason is that academic performance declines in the adolescent years when the Indian begins to feel the intense clash between the white, middle-class values of the classroom and the Indian values of his family.

One researcher, in a 1960 report, documented the testing of 657 elementary pupils—Indian, Spanish-American, and white—in five schools. All tested below national norms. But

"The Crossover Phenomenon," *Education News*, 2, (Apr. 8, 1968), p. 13.

whereas the white and Spanish students lagged behind the norms by about the same distance at all levels, the Indian pupils tested seven months below the norms in grade three, 11 months below in grade four, 14 months below in grade five and 15 months below in grade six. In other words, the longer they stayed in school the further behind they fell.

Similarly, Dr. Harry Saslow, a university psychologist in New Mexico, found in 1965 that high school seniors at the Albuquerque Indian School were an average of two-and-one-half years behind grade level—and that they had made "essentially no improvement" academically over where they were four years earlier.

Dr. Saslow contends that the pattern hangs on even into the college years. One Saslow statistic: Of 112 Indian students enrolled at Southern State Teachers College in South Dakota over a period of 35 years, more than half failed to last three quarters.

Table 5.2   Learning lag of Indian students, grades 3–6

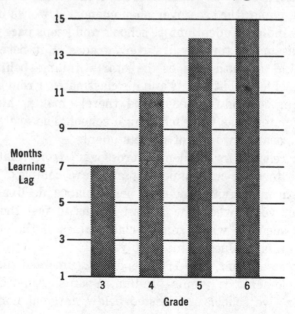

Source: *Education News, 2, April 8, 1968,* p. *13.*

A special United States Senate subcommittee, first chaired by the late Senator Robert F. Kennedy, found that education has failed the Indian. Evidence collected by these investigators and others indicates that ". . . the dropout rate is too high, achievement too low, and unemployment—perhaps the most valid test of all—too widespread (40 percent, 10 times the national average) . . ."[18] In what was supposed to be the first Presidential message ever on the Indian problem, partly as a result of the Senate investigation, President Johnson requested $500 million in fiscal 1969 for Indian programs. Specifically, the President recommended that in education: "Head Start programs be opened to 10,000 Indian pupils next year. Kindergartens be opened, for the first time, to 4,500 other Indian youngsters next year. All 4- and 5-year-old Indians be enrolled in preschool programs by 1971. . . ."[19] Also requested were funds to recruit and retain talented and dedicated teachers for the Indian schools, college scholarships for Indian students, the establishment of an "Upward Bound" program for the high school students, and the setting up of school boards made up of Indians.

Some Indians have achieved economic, though not educational success because of their skills which are useful to construction companies erecting skyscrapers. In the main, however, the American Indian has been less well treated in his native land than the Indians of India who visit here.

The Bureau of Indian Affairs has historically attempted to assimilate Indians into the dominant culture. Its current efforts to offer Indian parents greater opportunities for involvement with the Indian schools are met, therefore, with some distrust. A Senate bill in late 1972 would instead establish a National Board of Regents for Indian Education in the Department of the Interior (S 2724); because of its newness, this might have a better chance of creating rapport with the Indian community. Functions of the Board of Regents would include teacher education, funding programs designed to improve the education of Indian children, and school construction on or near Indian reservations (rather than at a distance). Kaltsounis advocated the major reform of staffing Indian schools with Indian teachers, a reform that would be possible if the Senate bill is enacted.[20] The foundation for a teacher education program exists in the Navajo Community College, which is attended by hundreds of Indians. Changes are also needed in the content of the curriculum in order to combine values and principles from the Indian culture with those of the dominant culture in a meaningful way for the children. As has been found to be true with other ethnic groups, and indeed with the young of the general population, relevancy is important. At this time, it appears to be crucial to retaining student interest and to promoting student learning.

Finally, one must consider the Spanish-Americans (Chicanos) living in the southwestern United States. Many of them have been more successful than the Puerto Ricans or the Indians, but the majority of this group must also be included among the disadvantaged. Like others in minority groups, Spanish-Americans are "last hired, first fired." They originally came to the Southwest as unskilled laborers, and remained seeking an escape from the intolerable economic conditions in their native soil. They did not find such relief. They live in the abject poverty of the slums, working in seasonal jobs (giving them some of the problems of the migrant laborers), and cling tenaciously to the culture and language of home— usually Mexico.

One means of reducing the prejudice of white classmates toward the Mexican children, thus hopefully causing them to find school more attractive, has been to make the Mexican culture more attractive. When the study of conversational Spanish was introduced in grades 4–6 of the San Diego schools in 1944–54, the teachers integrated the language study with social studies units on "Living in Mexico," and "Living in early California." Since the Mexican children were fluent in spoken Spanish and had artifacts and sometimes life experiences to contribute to the social studies units, they gained considerable status with their classmates. As a by-product of a foreign language experiment, it was found that "The study of Spanish leads to an increasing understanding of our Spanish-speaking children in San Diego and of our Latin-American neighbors."[21] This may not be a universally successful technique or by-product, but perhaps it is one way of making education sufficiently attractive to minority group members to keep them off the welfare rolls. A similar project could be undertaken in areas of high Puerto Rican and refugee Cuban population density.

For all of the disadvantaged, there is a common problem. They are undereducated and unskilled, and ill-equipped to meet their economic needs.

william g. mather

The Unskilled and Automation

Automation probably has had its greatest effect on the unskilled, the hand laborers whose only marketable assets are strong backs and willing minds. Machines that do the heavy digging and lifting already have taken their places, at least on the big jobs. Some more may be displaced by small machines for small jobs, as powered garden tools have replaced hand spading and raking; but the U.S. Bureau of Labor Statistics estimates that during the remaining years of the present decade, aside from a loss of 15% more of the farmers and farm workers, the need for unskilled non-farm labor will hold at about the same number it is now, in spite of the population growth of 28,000,000 people.

The problem here will come mainly with the children of the unskilled. The families of unskilled workers tend to be much larger than those of skilled workers. The old adage is in general true, that "the rich get richer and the poor get children." It is also true that the children of the poor do not receive much encouragement to stay in school and to learn a

Mather, William G. "When Men and Machines Work Together," In *Automation, Education, and Human Values*, ed. Brickman and Lehrer, (New York: School and Society Books, 1966), pp. 39–40.

trade, so that, even if unskilled jobs remain steady as they are, we will have more workers of this class than we need. The alternative, aside from population reduction by war, would appear to be a radically revised and expanded school system that will move the unskilled workers' children up and out of the unskilled group. If local school districts cannot do this, state and Federal powers must intervene, for we cannot afford the irresponsible flooding of the labor market with unfit citizens any longer. A real emergency exists in that automation is getting into its stride just as the biggest baby crop of all time hits our high schools and colleges.

Recognition of this emergency has finally come on the part of public officials. There is, at least, a growing awareness of the fact that the undereducated and unskilled—all the disadvantaged—are a large part of the problem of economics and education. Solving the problems of this segment of the population will be expensive.

At the opposite end of the spectrum, the early 1970's also had a problem of the overskilled and their unemployment. Thousands of engineers, for example, holding doctorate degrees and with years of industrial experience, found themselves overtrained for available jobs. Some turned to teaching, but even this was a shrinking labor market as financial support for educational programs faded, those with teaching jobs remained in the profession longer, and the number of entering students at the primary level decreased.

The Costs of Education

The costs of education to the nation and to the public can be measured in several ways. One method is to examine U. S. Office of Education statistics which show what percentage of the gross national product (GNP) is represented by the total national expenditures for education at all levels, in both public and private schools and colleges. For example, during the war years, 1941–45, education expenditures were 2% or less of the gross national product, while, following the initial space penetration of Sputnik in 1957, expenditures for education leaped to 6.4% of the GNP in 1964.[22] In the immediate post-Sputnik era, columnist Walter Lippman wrote in an article that this nation must acquire the will to put as much effort into meeting educational needs as we had, a few years earlier, into meeting wartime needs.

> If we compare our total effort—in public and private schools, and from kindergarten through college—with what it was 50 years ago, the quantitative increase is impressive. We are offering much more schooling of a more expensive kind to very many more pupils . . . The burden of living in America today and of governing America today is very much heavier than it was 50 years ago, and the crucial question is whether the increase of our effort in education is keeping up with the increase in the burden.
>
> When we use this standard of comparison, we must find . . . that the increase in our effort to educate ourselves is of a quite different—and of a very much smaller—order of magnitude than is the increase in what is demanded of us in this divided and dangerous world. Our educational effort and our educational needs are not now anywhere nearly in balance.[23]

He was a prophet without followers. In the 1970's, we still have not given education the priority it needs if it is to attempt to cope with the manifold problems of a complex and diverse society.

A second method of studying the costs of education is through per-pupil expenditures in public elementary and secondary schools. Despite having to make allowances for inflationary trends, this approach gives, perhaps, a more graphic and more meaningful view of educational costs. For example, where the percentage of the gross national product attributed to education doubled in the years 1929–64, the absolute costs per pupil multiplied over five times in the same period, and have continued to rise.[24]

It must be noted, however, that the national averages for per-pupil expenditures do not indicate the wide variation in expenditures both among the states and among school districts within each state (except for Hawaii, which has a single school district). Data compiled and published under the auspices of the Education Commission of the States reveal some startling and disheartening situations.

Table 5.3 **Per-pupil expenditures (district minimum and district maximum) for selected states, 1970–71.**[25]

State	District Minimum	District Maximum
Alabama	$294	$ 580
California	402	3,187
Delaware	633	1,081
Illinois	390	2,295
Massachusetts	454	4,243
Montana	467	8,515
New York	633	7,241
Oregon	431	4,941
Tennessee	315	774
Wyoming	617	14,554

Some of these differences defy reason. The magnitude of the differences and the variability in the quality of education provided within a state which is a result of these differences have led to court suits, notably the Serrano v. Priest (California) and Rodriguez v. San Antonio Independent School District (Texas) cases. These will be discussed more fully shortly.

In a longitudinal view, keeping in mind that instructional and staff personnel salaries increase from year to year, as do costs of materials, it might be helpful to compare the increases in per-pupil expenditures in three different school districts (urban, suburban, and rural) within a single state just through a recent five-year period.

Table 5.4   Per-pupil expenditures in Bald Eagle, Cheltenham, and Philadelphia (Pa.) school districts, 1966–67 through 1970–71

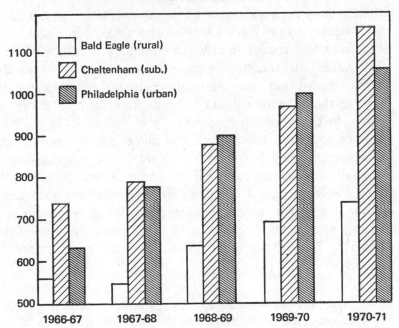

Source: Our Schools Today, Pennsylvania Dept. of Ed. (Dept. of Public Instruction), Bureau of (Educational) Statistics, Vols. 7–11 (1968–1972), per-pupil expenditure calculated from total current expenses data.

Although the rural district's expenditures are far lower than those for either the urban or suburban district, they did increase in this period to about 140% of the base year. The suburban district went to about 160% of the base year expenditures, and the Urban district to about 175% in the same period.

It must be recognized that teacher salaries, a major component of school district budgets, reflect several factors: geographic desirability of the school district or state, teacher qualifications demanded, willingness of the taxpayers to support quality in education, and unionization. In times of ample funds, school districts can afford and prefer to hire teachers who have both classroom experience and graduate credits, preferably a Master's degree. On the other hand, in the early 1970's, the combination of a surplus of available teachers and tight money resulted in the hiring of teachers just out of college because they were lower on the salary scale and willing to accept less money in order to obtain a job at all.

With the exception of the state of Hawaii, it is the local school board that establishes property tax rates for the support of the schools, subject to limitations set by state legislatures. In cases where a community of taxpayers is willing or able to pay only a small amount in taxes, salaries and per-pupil expenditures will necessarily be low. If the members of the school board try to exceed the implied or actual limitation, they may be voted out of office. Voters can similarly veto capital expenditures for school construction or other purposes by voting against bond issues, as has happened in many school districts. The disadvantaged character of rural and slum schools, however:

> ". . . cannot be demonstrated by financial statements alone; it is revealed even more urgently in the statistics of inferior educational performance of their children and the social consequences of poor education—unemployment, low income, broken and dependent families, delinquency, and crime."[26]

Dissatisfaction with this situation of disadvantage resulted in some forty court cases in 1971–72, the most prominent of which were Serrano v. Priest (California), Robinson v. Cahill (New Jersey), and Rodriguez v. San Antonio Independent School District (Texas), the last of which was appealed to the U.S. Supreme Court by the school district, and was accepted for hearing by that body. In March 1973, the Court ruled, in a 5–4 decision, that the financing of education in part by local property taxes was not unconstitutional, thus overruling a lower court decision. The minority opinions stressed the repressive and regressive effects of unequal educational opportunity on the very children who need the most opportunity, while in the opinion of the majority, the inequality of school expenditures and therefore educational opportunities was not seen as interfering with any fundamental right of Americans. Furthermore, since education is not even mentioned in the Constitution, it is not one of the rights specifically guaranteed by that document.

There was also, in 1972, a comprehensive study undertaken in New York State by the Fleischmann Commission, which was an attempt to find alternative methods of financing schools in order to reduce inequities and to provide equal opportunity for students in all parts of the state. The basic argument in the court cases, and an underlying premise of the Commission's study, is that the state must see that each of its citizens receives his fair share of the state's resources, and that this is impossible under present educational financing techniques. Background studies for the Fleischmann Commission report confirm that:

> "in a country where for more than fifty years a consistent goal of educational policy has been 'equalization' in financing public schools, communities rich in property tax base characteristically tax themselves at lower rates yet realize far greater yields per pupil than do less favored districts which tax themselves harder yet raise less proportionately and absolutely for their schools."[27]

What alternatives to the local property tax exist? What will be the effects of adopting one or more of these alternatives? Some suggested alternatives include:

1. a combination of income and sales taxes statewide
2. a statewide single uniform property tax
3. Federal-state revenue-sharing funds, earmarked for education
4. an increase in state subsidies to low-income districts (necessitating changes in state aid formulas).

The impact of balancing per-pupil expenditures and income for educational purposes, using one of the given alternatives or some other one, ". . . may go beyond education, for if revenue available for schools becomes independent of the assessable tax base of school districts, the desire to exclude low-income residents and to attract industry should diminish; and it may become easier to change the shape of local school districts for integration and other purposes."[28]

The Magnitude of the Problem

There are more than 60,000,000 Americans who are full-time participants in education as students, teachers, or administrators. Hundreds of thousands more are involved in education as non-professionals (on local or state boards of education, as trustees of institutions of higher education, or as non-teaching personnel), and on a part-time basis in formal or informal educational activities.

In contrast to the expansiveness of the 1960's, the fiscal limitations of the 1970's impose restrictions on meeting the demands of this major consumer area. We need more teachers in certain fields, such as education of exceptional children. With limited funds, class size for other teachers would have to be increased in order to reduce hiring and stay within the budget. Development funds are needed for extensive curriculum and textbook revisions in progress, as well as financial support for their implementation in the schools. In many school districts across the country, parochial and private schools are closing because of their financial hardships; their students will have to be absorbed by the public schools, again within restrictive budgets. Taxpayers, constantly confronted with rising taxes, more and more frequently are asking why, with all the increased expenditures for education in recent years, we are graduating less well educated students. Demands for accountability of the schools to the taxpayers are precipitating their own crisis in education. In some cases, legislative requirements for such accountability are at cross-purposes with movements to introduce innovations in instruction that might improve the quality of the end product. As an example, if the legislature mandates that behavioral objectives must be developed and that objective criteria are to be used as measures of the degree to which these objectives are being reached, then the whole effort of trying to get away from the regurgitation of textbook and lecture content is wasted. This is not to say that accountability is a poor or wrong concept in itself, but is a criticism of non-educators spelling out specific techniques.

A review of the problems presented in this chapter clearly shows four things: 1) in view of continuing inflation, the costs of education in absolute figures (dollars) must continue to rise; 2) in view of the number of substandard schools and disadvantaged children, the percentage of the Gross National Product devoted to education must continue to rise; 3) alternative means of financing education must be found; and 4) unquestionably, economics and education are mutually interdependent and intimately related to improvements in several areas of our national life.

Endnotes

1. Keppel, *op. cit.*, p. 39.
2. *Ibid.*, p. 41.
3. Conant, *Slums and Suburbs, op. cit.*, pp. 41–43.
4. See, for example, Birch, Richard M. "Upward Bound," *Penna. School Journal*, 116, (Feb.) 1968, 324–325.
5. Dillard, J. L. "The English Teacher and the Language of the Newly Integrated Student," *Teachers College Record*, 69, (Nov. 1967), pp. 115–120.
6. Frost, Joe L. "School and the Migrant Child," in *The Disadvantaged Child*, eds. Joe L. Frost and Glenn R. Hawkes (Boston: Houghton-Mifflin Co., 1966), pp. 248–249. By permission of the author.
7. Blubaugh, Ronald. "School Bells for Migrants," U.S. Office of Education: *American Education*, 4, (March 1968), pp. 6–7.

8. "Kaleidoscope: Migrant data," *American Education*, (June) 1972, 8, p. 23.

9. Drucker, Peter. "Education in the New Technology," In *Social Foundations of Education* ed. McLendon, (New York: The Macmillan Company, 1966), p. 159.

10. Schrieber, Daniel. "700,000 dropouts," *American Education*, 4, (June 1968), p. 6.

11. *Ibid.*, p. 6.

12. Russell, Kenneth. "Stay in School," U.S. Office of Education: *American Education*, 4, (June 1968), pp. 11–12.

13. Bachman, Jerald G. "Dropouts are losers, says who?" *Today's Education*, 61, (April) 1972, p. 30.

14. Weber, Edward J. "The Dropouts Who Go to School." *Phi Delta Kappan*, 53, 1972, p. 571.

15. Russell, James E. *Change and Challenge in American Education* (Boston: Houghton-Mifflin Company, 1965), p. 35.

16. Schrag, Peter. "The Schools of Appalachia." In Joe L. Frost and Glenn R. Hawkes, eds., *op. cit.*, p. 274. © 1965 *Saturday Review*, Inc.

17. *Ibid.*, p. 272.

18. *Education News*, 2, (Apr. 8, 1968), p. 14.

19. *Ibid.*, p. 2.

20. Kaltsounis, Theodore. "The need to Indianize Indian schools." *Phi Delta Kappan*, 53, 1972, 291–293.

21. MacRae, Margit. "Teaching a Second Language in the San Diego Elementary Schools," *Education*, 75, 1955, p. 511.

22. Keppel, *op. cit.*, p. 63.

23. Lippmann, Walter. "The Shortage of Education." In Carter, ed., *op. cit.*, pp. 240–241.

24. Keppel, *op. cit.*, p. 64.

25. "Public elementary and secondary school data." *PSBA Bulletin*, 36, (May–June) 1972, pp. 16–17.

26. Keppel, *op. cit.*, p. 80.

27. Berke, Joel S. "School Finance and Inequality of Educational Opportunity," in Berke, J. S., Campbell, A. K., and Goettel, R. J. (Editors), *Financing Equal Educational Opportunity: Alternatives for State Finance.* Berkeley, Calif.: McCutchan Publishing Corp., 1972, p. 1.

28. Preston, H. LeBaron. "The Supreme Court and school finance: some possibilities." *Phi Delta Kappan*, 54, 1972, p. 123.

For Further Reading

BACHMAN, JERALD G., *et al.* "Dropping Out—Problem or Symptom?" *Today's Education*, 61, (April) 1972, 26–30.

BEREITER, CARL, and SIEGFRIED ENGELMANN. *Teaching Disadvantaged Children* (Englewood Cliffs, N.J.: Prentice-Hall, 1966).

BENDINER, ROBERT. *The Politics of Schools: A Crisis in Self-Government* (New York: Harper and Row, 1969).

BERKE, J. S., A. K. CAMPBELL, and R. J. GOETTEL. *Financing Equal Educational Opportunity: Alternatives for State Finance* (Berkeley, Calif.: McCutchan Publishing Corp., 1972).

BIRCH, RICHARD M. "Upward Bound." *Pennsylvania School Journal*, 116, (Feb.) 1968, 324–325.

BLOOM, BENJAMIN S., *et al. Compensatory Education for Cultural Deprivation* (New York: Holt, Rinehart, and Winston, 1965).

BLUBAUGH, RONALD. "School bells for migrants." *American Education*, 4, (March) 1968, 5–7.

BRAZZIEL, WILLIAM F. "Quality Education for Minorities." *Phi Delta Kappan*, 53, 1972, 547–552.

BRICKMAN, WILLIAM W., and STANLEY LEHRER. *Automation, Education and Human Values* (New York: School and Society Books, 1966).

BROOKOVER, W. B., and D. GOTTLIEB. "Social Class and Education." *Readings in the Social Psychology of Education* (W. W. Charters, Jr. and N. L. Gage, eds.) (Boston: Allyn and Bacon, 1963).

CARLSON, KENNETH. "Equalizing Educational Opportunity." *Review of Educational Research*, 42, 1972, 453–475.

COCHRAN, LOTTIE H., and VIRGINIA FISCHER. "The rural deprived." *Pennsylvania School Journal*, 116, (Feb.) 1968, 330–331.

CONANT, JAMES B. *Slums and Suburbs* (New York: McGraw-Hill, 1961).

COOK, LLOYD ALLEN, and ELAINE FORSYTH COOK. *A Sociological Approach to Education* (New York: McGraw-Hill, 1950).

CORWIN, RONALD G. *A Sociology of Education* (New York: Appleton-Century-Crofts, 1965).

CRESSWELL, ANTHONY M. "Reforming Public School Finance: Proposals and Pitfalls." *Teachers College Record*, 73, 1972, 477–484.

CROW, LESTER D., WALTER I. MURRAY, and HUGH H. SMYTHE. *Educating the Culturally Disadvantaged Child* (New York: David McKay Company, 1966).

GLAZER, NATHAN, and DANIEL P. MOYNIHAN. *Beyond the Melting Pot: The Negroes, Puerto Ricans, Jews, Italians, and Irish of New York City* (Cambridge, Mass.: The MIT Press, 1963).

GUTHRIE, JAMES W., *et al. Schools and Inequality* (Cambridge, Mass.: MIT Press, 1971).

HAVIGHURST, ROBERT J. *Education in Metropolitan Areas* (Boston: Allyn and Bacon, Inc.), 1966.

JOHNS, R. L. "The Coming Revolution in School Finance." *Phi Delta Kappan*, 54, 1972, 18–22.

JOHNSON, HARRY A. "Multimedia and Innovative Techniques for Educating Teachers of the Disadvantaged." *Journal of Teacher Education*, 19, (Spring, 1968), 85–90.

KEPPEL, FRANCIS. *The Necessary Revolution in American Education* (New York: Harper and Row, 1966).

KERBER, AUGUST, and BARBARA BOMMARITO eds. *The Schools and the Urban Crisis* (New York: Holt, Rinehart, and Winston, 1965).

KOHL, JOHN W. "Cooperatives in Appalachia." *Pennsylvania School Journal*, 116, (March, 1968), 381.

MACREA, MARGIT. "Teaching a Second Language in San Diego Elementary Schools. *Education*, 75, 1955, 509–512.

MATHER, WILLIAM G. "When Men and Machines Work Together." In *Automation, Education, and Human Values*, eds. Brickman and Lehrer, (New York: School and Society Press, 1966, 37–49).

McGEOCH, DOROTHY M., CAROL R. BLOOMGARDEN, ELLEN O. FUREDI, LYNNE W. RANDOLPH, and EUGENE D. RUTH, JR. *Learning to Teach in Urban Schools* (New York: Teachers College Press, 1965).

McKENNA, WILLIAM J. "The Local Real Property Tax." *Pennsylvania School Journal*, 120, (April) 1972, 171–173, 198.

MILLER, HERMAN P. "Money Value of an Education." In *Intellectual Foundations of American Education* ed. Carter (New York: Pitman Publishing Company, 1965).

MOYNIHAN, DANIEL PATRICK. "Employment, Income, and the Ordeal of the Negro Family." *Daedalus*, 94, (Fall, 1965), 745–770.

The New York Times, March 22, 1973, p. 1.

PASSOW, A. HARRY, ed. *Education in Depressed Areas* (New York: Bureau of Publications, Teachers College, Columbia University, 1963).

PASSOW, A. HARRY, MIRIAM GOLDBERG, and ABRAHAM J. TANNENBAUM, eds. *Education of the Disadvantaged* (New York: Holt, Rinehart, and Winston, 1967).

PRESTON, H. LeBARON. "The Supreme Court and School Finance: Some Possibilities." *Phi Delta Kappan*, 54, 1972, 120–123.

ROUCEK, JOSEPH S. "The Most Oppressed Race in the United States: The Indian." In *Controversies in American Education*, ed. Full, (New York: The Macmillan Company, 1967), 244–252.

RUSSELL, JAMES E. *Change and Challenge in American Education* (Boston: Houghton-Mifflin Company, 1965).

RUSSELL, KENNETH, "Stay in School." *American Education*, 4, (June, 1968), 8–13.

SACKS, SEYMOUR. *City Schools/Suburban Schools: A History of Fiscal Conflict* (Syracuse: Syracuse University Press, 1972).

SCHRAG, PETER. "The Schools of Appalachia." In *The Disadvantaged Child*, ed. Frost and Hawkes (Boston Houghton-Mifflin Company, 1966), 269–274.

SCHREIBER, DANIEL. "700,000 Dropouts." *American Education,* 4, (June, 1968), 5–7.

SCHWARTZ, LITA L., ed. *Current Concerns in Educational Psychology* (New York: Associated Educational Services Corporation, 1968).

THOMAS, R. MURRAY. *Social Differences in the Classroom* (New York: David McKay Company, 1965).

U.S. Civil Rights Commission. *Racial Isolation in the Public Schools,* 1967.

U.S. Department of Health, Education, and Welfare; Office of Education. *Programs for the Educationally Disadvantaged* (Washington, D.C.: U.S. Government Printing Office, 1963).

WALKER, RONALD. "A School for Dropouts Only." *American Education,* 4, (June, 1968), 15–18.

WEBER, EDWARD J. "The Dropouts Who Go to School." *Phi Delta Kappan,* 53, 1972, 571–573.

6

federal aid to education

As in news reporting, we can pose certain basic questions to be answered in the "lead" of the story on federal aid to education. In providing historical background to the practice of Federal aid, we can ask "Who?," "What?," "Where?," "When?," and "Why?"

WHO receives federal financial aid? From 1785 to the 1940's, the recipients were principally institutions of higher learning, schools providing vocational and agricultural education programs, and so-called federally-affected communities. In addition, in more recent years, there have been federal subsidies to the school lunch program at all grade levels (below college), and the results of post-Sputnik legislation in the National Defense Education Act (1958), the Economic Opportunities Act (1964), and the Elementary and Secondary Education Act (1965).

WHAT has been the nature of the assistance? Perhaps the greatest initial contribution of the federal government to education was through land grants to the colleges and universities. Many of our largest universities started as colleges with lands granted to them by the government. There have also been, and there are today, numerous programs in which the government matches funds raised by the sponsoring institution. In other instances, specific grants for research and special programs are made through the Office of Education, the National Institutes of Health, and other federal agencies. Graduate fellowships supported by government agencies may also be subsumed under the heading of specific grants.

WHERE is the basis for federal aid to education? The "General Welfare" clause of the Constitution states that one reason for establishing the Constitution for this country was to "promote the general welfare." Before that, the Northwest Ordinances of 1785 and 1787 had laid the foundation for federal aid to education. This basis for financial assistance has been extended through practice as well as historical precedent, beginning with the Morrill Land Grant Act of 1862 and the establishment of the United States Office of Education in 1867.

WHEN does aid increase? Financial aid has usually been augmented during national emergencies, notably in wartime. The Morrill Land Grant Act was passed in 1862, early in the Civil War; the Smith-Hughes Act in 1917, World War I; assorted legislation in 1933 which directly or indirectly aided education, the Depression; Lanham Act of 1941 and Service Man's Readjustment Act of 1944, World War II; Federal Impact Laws in 1950, Korean War; and National Defense Education Act of 1958 and others subsequent to it, the "Cold War."

WHY is federal aid to education necessary? In general, one might say that local school districts need assistance, as was noted in Chapter 3, in meeting our national educational goals. More specifically, federal aid is often the result of reactions to evidences of inadequacies in our educational system. These include, today, the large number of illiterates rejected in the draft by the Armed Forces, lack of equality of educational and economic opportunity both in minority groups and in economically depressed areas, and the fear of many in the nation that we are lagging behind in the race to outer space.

The Development and Expansion of Federal Aid

The first national provisions for aid to education were in the Northwest Ordinances of 1785 and 1787, passed by the Continental Congress. These acts provided for the sale of public lands in the Northwest Territories. Under these laws, the lands were to be divided into townships having 36 sections of 640 acres each. The price of one section in each township was to be used for maintaining public schools. "Religion, morality, and knowledge being necessary to good government and the happiness of mankind, schools and the means of education shall forever be encouraged."[1]

Proponents of federal aid today, however, consider the aforementioned "General Welfare" clause in the Preamble to the U.S. Constitution as the actual basis for *federal* financial assistance to education. Education itself is not mentioned anywhere in the Constitution. However, the Tenth Amendment to that document states that powers not delegated to the federal government are reserved to the several states. This provision serves as the foundation for arguments by the opponents to federal aid, and also is the root from which local and state systems of education have ultimately grown. It might be added that state systems of education were greatly abetted by the Enabling Acts, providing land grants to schools, which were part of each Statehood Act from Ohio's in 1802, through those of Alaska and Hawaii in the 1950's.

The expansion of federal involvement in education really began with the passage of the Morrill Act of 1862. In this major legislative step, lands were donated to states and territories for the establishment of colleges. The land grants were made for several reasons: 1) the growing need for scientific, agricultural, and industrial training in an age when most of the colleges were classically-oriented; 2) too much public land falling into private hands, frequently for speculative purposes; and 3) regional inequalities in the ability to support public education. The third problem we have with us still. As a result of the Morrill Act and subsequent laws derived from it, some sixty-eight colleges and universities exist today with twenty percent of the nation's undergraduates enrolled in them. Together, the land-grant colleges award about forty percent of the doctoral degrees annually. These include institutions of prestige and high national repute such as the Massachusetts Institute of Technology, The Pennsylvania State University, the University of California, Ohio State University, and others.

In 1867, the Department of Education was established for the purpose of collecting and diffusing information about education, and to encourage education through various programs and research funds. After almost a century of changing status, the United States Office of Education is now part of the Department of Health, Education, and Welfare. A recent former secretary, Dr. John W. Gardner, was particularly well-qualified to administer federal programs related to education, having been a college professor, and from 1955 until his appointment to the Cabinet, president of the Carnegie Foundation for the Advancement of Teaching.

There were numerous other attempts to establish general educational funds and systems in the late nineteenth century, but these were not enacted into law by the Congress. Two bills which did become laws, however, were the Hatch Act (1887), which added funds for agricultural experiment stations to the land-grant colleges, and the Morrill Act of 1890 which introduced the principle of specific federal grants for instruction. The grants in this case aided the expansion of agricultural and mechanical schools, such as the Texas Agricultural and Mechanical College (Texas A. and M.).

As the economy of the nation changed, so did the nature of laws providing aid to education. The Smith-Hughes Act of 1917 was designed to encourage vocational training and home economics education below the college level. This was in an era of almost nationwide compulsory education (Mississippi was the last state to pass such a law, in 1918), stricter child labor laws, growing industrialization, and the beginning of an awareness that not all pupils could cope with the classic academic curriculum. This awareness stemmed in part from the new "intelligence" tests, designed in France by Binet and adapted in the United States by Terman, which permitted evaluation of children in terms of their intellectual functioning.

During the Depression of the 1930's, much federal legislation, aimed at relieving the victims of the nation's economic breakdown, also supported education. In the Public Works Administration Act (PWA) of 1933, aid was given for the construction of school and college buildings, more to reduce unemployment it must be admitted, than to benefit educational institutions. The Civilian Conservation Corps (C.C.C.), also established in 1933, offered employment and vocational training for older unemployed young men through the development of natural resources. This program was extended by the National

Youth Administration (1935), which provided relief and employment for the 16–25 year age group. The C.C.C. was thus a direct ancestor of today's Job Corps, at least in philosophy. A wide variety of projects, many of which were related to education, were begun under the Works Progress Administration (W.P.A.), to provide relief and employment funds without charity. In this period, too, the school lunch program was started, in which schools were reimbursed with federal funds for using surplus foods in their lunch menus. The subsidies enabled school districts to charge the students less money for a nutritious meal which was probably the main one of the day for many Depression era schoolchildren. Even today, the subsidized school lunch program can charge as little as 50¢ (in the Philadelphia area) for a menu including a hot main dish, bread and butter, juice or a relish, fruit or baked goods for dessert, and milk. These provisions for school lunches were extended from the original ones by subsequent legislation such as the Child Nutrition Act of 1966, amended in 1968 [and later years] to provide food services for poor preschool children in daycare centers, settlement houses, and recreation houses.[2]

With the rise of defense industries and military bases before and after our entrance into World War II, many school districts suddenly had many more pupils but no increase in tax revenues or resources. The Lanham Act (1941) and the Federal Impact Laws (1950) attempted to ease the hardships caused by the rise of defense establishments near small communities, particularly, throughout the country. Funds were provided for school building maintenance, nursery schools for the children of women working in defense and later, war, industries, and, under the later laws, general operating funds were supplied for the school districts in impacted areas. In 1973, President Nixon recommended a change in the distribution of funds to impacted areas that narrowed both the concept and the benefits received by the school district.

Concern for civilians was not the only one during the war years. As victory in World War II came closer, there was great public concern about what the returning service personnel would do in civilian life. The Service Man's Readjustment Act of 1944, more familiarly known as the "G. I. Bill," offered tuition and subsistence funds to servicemen and women with which they could acquire education and training, without financial hardships, in order to aid their transition to civilian careers. Without the funds provided, most of the veterans would not have been able to attend post-high school educational institutions. Without the additional education, many of today's professional men and women would not be employed as doctors, lawyers, teachers, and engineers. Not all of the "ex-GIs" went to college. Many went to technical institutes, acquiring the training needed to make them self-supporting and self-respecting. This siphoning off of several million veterans to educational facilities also aided the economy, in that the labor market was not flooded at a time when industries were re-trenching, re-tooling, or trying to convert from wartime needs to peacetime desires. Later legislation has extended the same educational tuition and subsistence privileges, with somewhat modified arrangements, to veterans of the Korean War and to those who have served over six months on active duty in the Cold War since mid-1955. The influx of almost eight million veterans of the Second World War and the Korean action boosted enrollments in the educational institutions tremendously. Their arrival caused rapid expansion of colleges, universities, and technical training schools in a wide variety of fields. In the immediate post-World War II period, even some women's colleges opened their doors to male veterans on a non-resident basis. As of this writing, more than an additional half-million "Cold War" and Viet Nam veterans have been helped by the extended legislation.

The next major federal legislation aiding education followed the shocked public reaction to Russia's launching of Sputnik I in October, 1957. Great consternation was in the air. Incredulity that our scientists were "behind" the Russians reigned. Harsh criticisms of American education, with invidious comparisons to European education, were common. The designer of our atomic submarines, Admiral H. G. Rickover, became particularly vocal.

. . . I am neither a writer nor an orator. I should, therefore, not have spoken out if the obstacles to progress merely delayed the time when we can profit by the benefits of higher technical competence. What induced me to voice my concern was the threat of Russia which, as any engineer would, I noticed many years ago when the first bad news came trickling from behind the iron curtain—bad news of astonishing scientific and engineering achievements; of a revolutionary reform in Russian education; of Russian success in combining mass education with highest-quality education for large numbers of her children. Most disturbing to me was the clear evidence that we were losing momentum at the very moment when Russia was increasing hers.

. . . It was difficult, before Sputnik, to present the full picture of Russian successes in the realm of the intellect. There was little patience then in this country with anyone who told of areas where we were no longer supreme. Unpleasant facts were so unwelcome that it was actually risky to mention them.

. . . This book, then, is based on my conviction that Russia's technological progress forces us forthwith to revise certain attitudes, assumptions, and ways of going about our business . . . I began by wanting to remove obstacles hindering my work. My interest was simply to build nuclear reactors . . . Anything that interfered with building them as fast as possible was bad. But, as with Plato when he asked "What is Justice?" my investigations led me from the particular to the general and resulted in this present inquiry into the delays which lengthen our lead time so dangerously. Not only in production of things, but in production of well-qualified professional people as well, we now need more time than does Russia or, for that matter, Europe. I believe we must put first things first. This means, above all else, that we must bring excellence to American education. Let us stop fooling ourselves by counting school desks without considering what the children sitting at these desks are being taught. Many of our children are merely parked in the schools. They merely have a good time there. Few get a twentieth-century education.[3]

Table 6.1   Major federal legislation affecting education (Colonial Period to 1973)

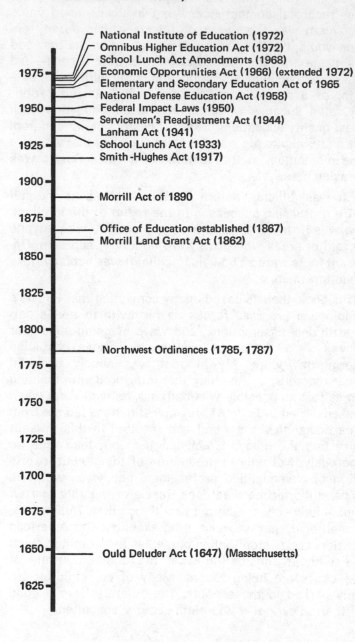

The ultimate result of this statement and others was the passage of the National Defense Education Act of 1958 (N.D.E.A.), which was designed to stimulate our educational programs and institutions particularly in the fields of science, foreign languages, and mathematics. Under the N.D.E.A., federal funds were offered for loans to students studying in the specified fields, for graduate fellowships for majors in these areas, for guidance and counseling programs, foreign language institutes, audio-visual research, and vocational education programs. Other laws later followed which supplemented these programs and enabled them to be continued.

Among the more significant legislation enacted, as part of the result of messages by Presidents Kennedy and Johnson to Congress, was the Elementary and Secondary Education Act of 1965. Sections of this law provided $775 million for the education of children from low income families, to be handled in part by the Office of Economic Opportunities; funds for a five-year program to expand school library resources and provide additional textbooks; the development of supplementary educational centers and services, such as "magnet" schools, model schools, pilot programs, etc.; funds for educational research and training under the Cooperative Research Act; and for State Departments of Education," . . . a program of grants . . . to provide consultative and technical assistance for local school districts and local school leadership. Formulate long-range plans. Expand educational research and development. . . . Conduct periodic evaluation of educational programs. Promote teacher improvement courses."[4] President Johnson proposed, and the Congress passed in 1966, other bills to encourage international teacher exchanges and institutes of international education. As part of the "War on Poverty," under the Economic Opportunities Act, federal funds and legislation have effected the creation of "Operation Headstart" and "Operation Get Set" programs for children of pre-school ages, and projects have been designed to fill the needs of children from low-income families in local school districts (e.g., reading improvement). Most of these programs have been extended and given additional funding during the Nixon administration.

Arguments Advocating Federal Aid

The advocates of federal aid to education include Presidents Eisenhower, Kennedy, and Johnson; the AFL-CIO; the National Farmers' Union; and the National Education Association. Their individual statements of reasons for favoring federal aid vary, but can be condensed essentially into several major arguments.

One principal point is that the distribution of federal funds will reduce state-to-state, sometimes district-to-district, inequalities, and will tend to equalize educational opportunities for all. Annual published figures showing teachers' salaries paid, percentage of state income spent on schools, and expenditures per pupil, reveal wide discrepancies from state to state. Obviously, states which offer higher salaries will attract more teachers and can be more selective in their hiring. States which spend more money per pupil usually provide more opportunities for laboratory work, libraries, audio-visual supplements, and other learning aids, as well as the financial and fringe benefits to the teacher. The affluent states have a fairly difficult time trying to provide these funds within a tax burden limit which the people impose in the voting booth. In the economically depressed states, education suffers even more acutely. Therefore, one argument in favor of federal aid to education is that federal funds can be used to aid the poorer states substantially, and the wealthier states to the degree needed by them.

The inequality of educational opportunity is closely related to the problem of high population mobility. As families move, the children must adjust not only to the new school, but also to an academic program which differs from that of the former school to a greater or lesser degree in terms of requirements and standards. Correction of the financial and educational factors via Federal aid, it is alleged, could alleviate the effects both of varying standards of education among the state and of mass migrations.

Since local taxation is the major source of revenue for educational purposes, advocates of federal aid point out that use of the federal tax apparatus would broaden the tax base (personal and corporate income taxes in addition to local property taxes), and would be a more efficient and economical method of collecting taxes. At present, the local government collects approximately 16 percent of the tax dollar, but pays about 56 percent of the educational expenses. Abraham Ribicoff, testifying in 1961 as Secretary of Health, Education, and Welfare, stated:

> While Federal tax dollars have increased 85 percent in the post-war years, State and local communities have had to increase their tax revenues by 221 percent. From 1946 to 1959, while the Federal debt increased by 6 percent, State and local debt soared by more than 300 percent. Property taxes, the traditional source of revenue for education, are in many areas rapidly approaching the limits of reasonableness.[5]

At the same time, Edgar Fuller, executive secretary, Council of Chief State School Officers, said that: "The broader and more effective federal tax system dominates the local and State tax systems, and impinges strongly on local and State tax sources. . . . State and local funds are increasingly difficult to obtain. A more equitable allocation of responsibility for the support of public education among the three levels of government is needed."[6]

Fears that a change in tax collection policy will result in federal control of education at the local level are countered by the fact that most current legislation expressly forbids federal control of local school district policies. Some years ago a proposal was made by Robert Heller, an economist, that instead of merging local, state, and federal taxes, or simply increasing outright federal grants, "The Federal Government should recognize future increase in local and state taxes used for education by giving full credit for such increases against personal and corporate taxes."[7] This would relieve the taxpayer of the mounting costs of taxes on his federal tax return, while the local government would still receive the additional revenue required.

Advocates of federal aid further emphasize that there is great national concern about education. It is felt that there is a direct relationship between the national welfare and educational welfare, as seen in the use of education to rectify "inadequacies" of training which handicap us in the "Cold War," and in attempts to use education as a means of correcting or modifying social problems. Concomitant with these applications of education, it is widely recognized that school construction, the quality of teacher training, and teacher salaries must all be increased.

Proponents of federal aid to education believe that local governments cannot raise the necessary funds, and therefore need help from the central government. Precedents for federal financial aid abound since, as a result of 200 or more laws passed since 1785, as seen earlier in this chapter, more than forty federal agencies now disburse funds in excess of $2 billion per year to educational institutions or for educational purposes.

Arguments against Federal Aid

Those who oppose federal aid to education include the United States Chamber of Commerce, the National Association of Manufacturers, the Farm Bureau Federation, the National Grange, the Daughters of the American Revolution, and the American Legion. Some of their arguments are direct opposites of the claims of the advocates; others stem from other sources, such as philosophical orientation.

The opponents believe that it is impossible to equalize educational opportunity because the educational level would be dragged down to the minimum acceptable standards rather than raised. Opponents of national educational standards, often the same groups or individuals, feel the same way. It is feared that if minimum standards are set, many local school districts presently operating above such standards would decrease their educational expenditures to a point closer to the minimums set.

They further emphasize that federal aid is unconstitutional since there is no provision in the Constitution for education, and powers not reserved to the federal government are reserved to the states in the Tenth Amendment. There is great anxiety on the part of these opponents, too, that, "Aid to education is simply the opening wedge for an all encompassing move on the part of the federal government to enslave the American people and to seize control in all areas of endeavor."[8]

Along with many other critics of American education, the opponents of federal aid to education believe that the elimination of "frills" and the improvement of the curriculum, often a return to so-called "basic education," will enhance education in themselves, and will reduce expenditures accordingly so that federal assistance will be unnecessary. Certainly the elimination of music, art, driver-training, speech, journalism, and similar courses would reduce the number of teachers and classrooms needed for each school district, thereby permitting budget reductions. In addition, the opponents say that the size of the national debt is now so large that federal income taxes cannot be increased to aid education without endangering individual initiative. According to Tiedt, federal aid is unpopular with the people, partly because of the potential increase in tax burden.

There is much consternation expressed about the diminution and discouragement of individual initiative, as well as the infringement on individual freedom which federal assistance would bring: scholarships would offer unfair competition to commercial loan agencies; emphasis would be placed on research rather than teaching by professors able to obtain research grants; some professions would be preferred to others because grants-in-aid were available, rather than because of interest or aptitude for the work involved; local pride and participation in education would be reduced; and the importance of the family as a basic socio-economic unit would likewise be diminished. Many individuals feel that "working one's way" through college is a character-building exercise which would be sorely neglected if higher education, in particular, were free or nearly so. (Note: This has not been the case with students and graduates of the free city colleges in New York City. To the contrary, without the opportunity provided by city-subsidized education, most of our professional fields would have lost many of their finest men.)

There is, finally, the argument that federal aid to education lacks the historical precedent claimed by its advocates. The opponents aver that so-called education laws have been passed to solve non-educational problems primarily, such as the encouragement of land settlement as the nation moved westward, to reduce our stocks of surplus foods and thereby aid the agricultural branch of our economy, as a substitute for taxes, to improve our position in the space-race, and so on. There is some validity in this particular position since our social, economic, and educational problems are inter-related.

Although the debates on Federal aid to education continue unabated, they are really exercises in futility to some extent. Federal aid to education has been and is a fact. In the early 1970's, Federal financial aid amounted to about 7% of educational expenditures. Many economists and educators believe that this should be increased to 25–30%, a belief that is an outcome of the difficulties in obtaining adequate revenues at the local and state levels, as discussed earlier. Apart from monetary aid, legislation in the past several years has provided a kind of "moral" aid to education as it provided for new programs and new directions in this field.

The Kennedy-Johnson Administrations

Several bills were proposed to the Congress by Presidents Kennedy and Johnson to aid education, but not all were passed. The School Assistance Bill of 1961 was designed to grant money to the states for either school construction or teachers' salaries, to be determined by each state; to aid underprivileged children in depressed areas; to aid higher education; and to increase adult literacy. Controversies developed in the Congress about whether non-public, i.e., private and parochial, schools should be included, and because aid would be denied to segregated schools in the interests of the civil rights program. The strong opposition to these possibilities doomed the bill to failure. Similar sources of controversy also resulted in the non-passage of the National Education Improvement bill of 1963, which covered all areas and levels of education, and was an attempt to expand education both in quantity and in quality.

Some bills were enacted, however, which directly or indirectly aided education. The Vocational Education Act of 1963 established a permanent program ". . . to strengthen and improve the quality of vocational education opportunities in the nation . . ." The National Defense Education Act of 1958 was amended in 1963 and 1964 to extend the fields of effort included and to provide additional loan funds. The Higher Education Facilities Act of 1963 provided funds for classroom construction from junior colleges to graduate centers. Church-supported and private colleges were included as long as the construction was not used for religious purposes. The Higher Education Act of 1965 offered further financial assistance to the colleges, as well as to students and teachers. The Elementary and Secondary Act of 1965, discussed earlier, was probably the crowning achievement in this area for President Johnson. Legislation passed in 1966 furnished additional support to education at all levels. It should be obvious from this summary, that it was easier to obtain Congressional passage of restricted bills, in the sense of limited areas of coverage, than to have the omnibus-type bills proposed in 1961 and 1963 passed.

Indirect aid to education has come through the Economic Opportunities Act of 1964, which established the Job Corps, VISTA, and other community action programs, as well as college work-study programs which offer needy students the opportunity to earn up to $500 per year in on-campus jobs. The Civil Rights Act of 1964 has sections which encourage school desegregation. The provisions in this act which permit denial of federal aid funds to segregated schools have caused great debate in the Congress, and are being questioned under the equal rights clauses of the Fourteenth Amendment. The National Foundation for the Arts and Humanities, established in 1965, provides educational grants in these fields. In addition, numerous specific laws were enacted in the period 1961–66 which gave financial assistance to trainees in nursing and other health professions, to programs aiding the mentally retarded, to anti-juvenile delinquency projects, and for the expansion of library services in schools and colleges. Extensions of the laws passed in this period have provided continuing funding and expansion into other specific educational areas as the needs arose.

The Nixon Years

Looking back on the 1969–73 administration of Richard Nixon, we find mixed support for education. Although every President voices his support for education (like apple pie and motherhood), implementation of support varies from one holder of the office to another. Faced with a Congress dominated by the opposition, President Nixon often submitted proposals for educational programs which were perceived by the legislators as "too little and too late." They would pass enabling legislation, but increase the budgets to a level higher than those the President had recommended. This often led to a presidential veto and therefore to no program.

On the other hand, President Nixon did establish a number of commissions to study educational problems and make recommendations. These included the President's Urban Education Task Force (1969) and the President's Commission on School Finance (1970–72). During this administration, the Department of Health, Education, and Welfare began investigating hiring practices, including those at institutions of higher education, resulting in the enforcement of a policy of "affirmative action" (i.e., more proportionate hiring of women and members of minority groups at all levels within institutions). The National Institute of Education was established. The White House Conference on Children and Youth, held every ten years, took place in 1970. Many recommendations were made by the commissions and conferences, and many Congressional bills were passed, but despite verbal support on all sides, many educational programs either were lost between Congress and the President, were never funded, or were not operable long enough with sufficient resources to create the desired effects. The apparent failure of "performance contracting," under the auspices of the Office of Economic Opportunity, was one example of insufficient resources.

Urban education, recognized by everyone as being in a state of fiscal and academic disaster, continued to move downhill on both fronts. The Federal-state revenue-sharing act of 1972 provided for state use of funds for educational purposes (if desired) but did not permit the local government the same option. Redefinition of the term "handicapped" in legislation and practice led to an extension of special services to more children in this category, but without adequate funding to do the job needed. The Mondale Child Development Act, which would have provided early childhood development programs in day care centers staffed by trained personnel, was vetoed. In a period of inflation and "tight money," education too often lost out, at least in the minds of many, to defense priorities. In 1973, many of the OEO programs were phased out or placed under state funding plans despite the inadequate financial resources and attitude of benign neglect toward the poor at this level of government.

The Federal Government, in its executive, legislative, and judicial aspects, was deeply involved in continuing segregation issues, which will be reviewed in the appropriate chapter. Similarly, President Nixon's commitment to aid to non-public schools, as well as Supreme Court rulings on state legislation in this area, will be discussed in the chapter on religion and education.

Apart from the laws establishing programs for education in general, it should be remembered that the federal government also operates schools and disseminates educational information. It is responsible for the several military service academies which award Bachelor's degrees as well as commissions; for schools on Indian reservations (see Chapter 4), in trusteeship areas such as Samoa and Guam, and in federal districts such as Washington, D.C.; and finally, for the schools at military bases overseas for service personnel's dependent children. Several Departments represented in the Cabinet have the function of providing information to farmers (Agriculture), businessmen, large and small (Commerce), parents (U.S. Children's Bureau; Health, Education, and Welfare), *et al.* As was noted earlier, there is also an Office of Education with a commissioner as its executive officer. There is no question that, approve or not, the federal government is deeply involved in education.

An Estimate of the Future

The expansion of federal aid to education here and abroad is almost a certainty, despite strong opposition in some quarters. The responsibilities of the Office of Education will doubtless be multiplied. In fact, some people in public and professional life have urged that a separate Department of Education be created, of Cabinet rank, to permit a more authoritative voice to be heard on behalf of education. Also recommended, notably by Conant, is the creation of a National Advisory Council on Education, designed to achieve greater coordination of educational efforts on a national scale.

We are already sending teachers to underdeveloped nations and have some foreign exchange student scholarship programs. Professors, too, teach and live in foreign countries under the aegis of the Fulbright Act.

Education and other national problems are inextricably intertwined, with the growing prospect that attempts to remedy our socio-economic problems and technological puzzles will depend to an ever greater extent on our educational institutions. National efforts to reach the moon by 1969 stirred educators at all levels to improve science and mathematics curricula, and existing legislation provides funds for the exploration and development of new techniques, as well as the revision, of academic courses. Because of national needs in technology, in the "War on Poverty," in civil rights, and in the military establishment, and because programs in these areas are so expensive, one hardly needs a crystal ball to predict ever-increasing federal aid, financially, to education. The "strings" attached to this particular balloon can be foreseen as greater emphasis on innovation and on quality—all for the general welfare of the nation and its people. One can hardly debate any longer the question of whether or not there should be federal aid to education. Such aid is a *fait accompli.* The questions which now arise are: To whom should aid be given? For what purposes should aid be given? How much aid should be given?

Endnotes

1. Tiedt, Sidney W. *The Role of the Federal Government in Education,* (New York: Oxford Univ. Press, 1966), pp. 15–16.
2. *Education News,* 2, May 27, 1968, p. 17.
3. Rickover, H. G. *op. cit.,* 1960, pp. 35–38.
4. Johnson, Lyndon B. Message to the Congress, Jan. 12, 1965, II. E.
5. Rich, William B. "Federal Aid to Education: Issues Before Congress." In Carter (ed.), *op. cit.,* p. 185.
6. *Ibid.,* p. 187.
7. Heller, Robert. "A Proposal for Financing Tax-Supported Education." In Carter ed., *Ibid.,* p. 305.
8. Tiedt, Sidney W. *op. cit.,* p. 74.

For Further Reading

ATKIN, J. MYRON. "The Federal Government, Big Business, and Colleges of Education." *The Individual and Education: Some Controversial Issues,* eds. Frederick M. Raubinger and Harold G. Rowe, (New York: Macmillan Company, 1968), 261–272.

Education News, 2, (May 27, 1968).

FINN, CHESTER E., JR. "What the NIE Can Be." *Phi Delta Kappan*, 1972, 53, 347–351.

GOLDWATER, BARRY. "In Place of Federal Aid." In *American Education Today* eds. Paul Woodring and John Scanlon, (New York: McGraw-Hill Book Company, 1963).

HELLER, ROBERT. "A Proposal for Financing Tax-Supported Education." In *Intellectual Foundations of Education*, ed. Harold J. Carter, (New York: Pitman Publishing Corporation, 1965).

HILLWAY, TYRUS. "Historical Perspectives." In *American Education: An Introduction through Readings*, ed. Hillway, (Boston: Houghton-Mifflin Company, 1964), pp. 13–74.

JENCKS, CHRISTOPHER, *et al. Inequality: A Reassessment of the Effect of Family and Schooling in America* (New York: Basic Books, 1972.)

JOHNSON, LYNDON B. *Message to the Congress* (January 12, 1965).

LAMBERT, SAM M. "The Case for Federal Support of Education." *Readings in American Education*, eds. Clifton L. Hall, Samuel M. Holton, Frederick D. Kershner, and William W. Savage (Chicago: Scott, Foresman, and Company, 1963), pp. 313–325.

REED, WAYNE O. "The Federal Government and Education." *Controversy in American Education: An Anthology of Crucial Issues*, ed. Harold Full, (New York: The Macmillan Company, 1967), pp. 277–282.

RICH, WILLIAM B. "Federal Aid to Education: Issues Before Congress." In *Intellectual Foundations of Education* ed. Harold J. Carter. (New York: Pitman Publishing Corporation, 1965).

RICKOVER, H. G. *Education and Freedom* (New York: E. P. Dutton Company, 1960).

SARETSKY, GARY. "The OEO P.C. Experiment and the John Henry Effect." *Phi Delta Kappan*, 1972, 53, 579–581.

Saturday Review, August 20, 1966.

SAYLOR, GALEN. "The Federal Colossus in Education: Threat or Promise?" In *Controversy in American Education: An Anthology of Crucial Issues*, ed. Harold Full (New York: The Macmillan Company, 1967), pp. 282–290.

SHERMIS, SHERWIN S. "The Semantic of Federal Aid and Federal Control." In *Contemporary American Education,* eds. Stan Dropkin, Harold Full, and Ernest Schwarcz (New York: The Macmillan Company, 1966), pp. 484–488.

TIEDT, SIDNEY W. *The Role of the Federal Government in Education* (New York: Oxford University Press, 1966).

7

religion and education

The controversies in the area of religion and education focus on two specific questions. One is intimately connected to the entire matter of federal aid to education (Ch. 6, *supra*). Should there be federal, or state, aid to non-public, i.e., private and parochial, schools? Secondly, to what extent, if at all, should religion be included in the school day?

Historical Background

The statement of the First Amendment to the Constitution that "Congress shall make no law respecting an establishment of religion or the free exercise thereof" has governed church-state relationships throughout our history as a nation. Prior to 1787, however, schools were created in the service of religion, usually a particular denomination supported by a colony, and were publicly-supported—thus *establishing* a state religion. The colleges of colonial times were largely oriented to the education of clergy-to-be.

The theocratic society of Massachusetts which fused the functions of Church and State also, almost from its inception, accepted the idea that education was a public responsibility. This attitude was a by-product of the theocratic society which assumed strict social controls over the lives of adults as well as of the young.[1]

193

For some years after we gained national independence, the emphasis on the religious benefits of education continued, as was seen in earlier chapters. The gradual change in that point of view, plus the arrival of thousands of Irish Catholics as immigrants in the mid-nineteenth century led ultimately to a separate parochial school system which was oriented to Catholic rather than Protestant values.

The Catholic school system arose at that time both because Catholic children were not welcomed in the public schools and because their religious views were not respected.

It is not beyond the realm of possibility that had the Catholic child in the nineteenth century received the same cordial welcome from the public school given the Jewish child in the twentieth, and that had the religious conscience of the Catholic child been respected as was the Jewish child's, the Catholic community might have adjusted to the American school system. . . . The transition from Protestant to secular public education, moreover, took place during a period when anti-Catholic bigotry was strong and extensive, when Nativism and Know-Nothingism flourished over a large part of the country. The child of the Jewish immigrant from Russia and Poland came from a background of persecution, discrimination, and bigotry to a public school of acceptance and equality. The child of the Catholic immigrant from Ireland came from a climate of equality to a public school of persecution, discrimination, and bigotry. The difference in attitudes toward the public school on the part of the Catholic and Jewish communities hardly needs any other explanation. . . .[2]

Even the Jewish immigrants of the nineteenth century had found public education congenial. The majority of American rabbis of the time had learned that in the absence of public schools, Jewish children were educated in private Christian schools. (There were few Jewish parochial schools then, as there are relatively few today.) The rabbis therefore preferred public education. In addition, they felt that denominational education was a ". . . deterrent to the urgent need for the social integration of diverse stocks of immigrants in a cosmopolitan city. . . . For Jews to continue their separateness in education was to spurn the gift of equality, a gift offered uniquely by America to *all* its citizens."[3]

Today, the parochial schools of different faiths exist parallel to the public schools, but largely without the financial resources with which they could improve their faculties, facilities, and curricula. The Catholic schools, specifically, have a severe problem because of too many pupils and too few teachers. The religious obligation placed on Catholic parents to send their children to parochial schools is partly responsible for the still too-common practice of having fifty to eighty elementary pupils in a single classroom. Although the educational preparation of nuns for teaching has improved greatly in recent years, there are still too many poorly-qualified lay teachers at the elementary level. The latter are underpaid in terms of their responsibilities. They are generally required to continue their professional preparation while they teach, but far too many are still years away from a Bachelor's degree. At the secondary level, parochial school teachers are, on the whole, much better prepared to teach their specialties, and the teacher-pupil ratio is not as large.

In the Jewish and Protestant-oriented day schools, enrollment is more a matter of parental choice than obligation, with the result that many parents do not choose to have their children in a private or parochial school atmosphere, especially at a tuition fee usually in excess of $500 per year (as against about $100 for Catholic parish schools). The Protestant and Jewish schools are more often in the category of private college preparatory schools, academically speaking.

The Protestant schools, as was noted earlier, began in colonial times. The Jewish schools were established at various times in the past 100 years. There are comparatively few of these, partly because of inadequate financial support, and partly because synagogues established afternoon and week-end programs for religious instruction.[4] Both of these major denominations have, on the whole, supported public education for secular instruction.

The problem of church-state relations with respect to education is, therefore, primarily involved with the large Catholic parochial system. Even within the Catholic Church there are several points of view as to what the final solution to parochial school problems might be. Dean Francis M. Crowley, of the Fordham University School of Education, urged that a separate school system be continued so that religion may be ". . . the foundation and crown of the youth's entire training at every level of instruction."[5] In a way this is similar to the conservative and orthodox Jewish viewpoint which also prefers to see religious values permeating the child's ongoing daily experience rather than being limited to a few hours after public school and on the Sabbath.

A second approach to the problem is called "shared time." Here, parochial school students study technical, non-religious courses at a nearby public school for half a day, and religion, social studies, and English at the parochial school for the other half-day. Such programs are being practiced in several communities. In some such programs, classroom facilities are shared; in others, specialist teachers (e.g., in art and music) from the public school system act as "visiting" teachers in parochial schools.

There are both merits and faults to this approach. Critics of it say that it is in violation of the First Amendment because permitting parochial school pupils to use public, tax-supported facilities releases funds for the Church which can thus be used for religious, not educational purposes. This is, say the critics, an unconstitutional establishment of state-supported religion. Those in favor of the "shared time" plan believe that it avoids wasteful duplication of facilities, permits greater and more natural social interaction among all the young people in a community, and supports the goal of excellence. It is presumed, on this last point, that the public school can attract teachers of higher caliber than can the parochial system.

Another alternative suggested has been to abandon the parochial elementary schools and maintain separation at the high school level only. As Msgr. George W. Casey, a parish priest, has averred, children rarely lose their faith in the elementary years, but need the support of religion in the teen years when they become more involved in community and social activities.[6] If this program were to be carried out, the public elementary schools would be inundated with more pupils than they are presently equipped to handle. There would not be enough physical space, or teachers, or textbooks to take care of the additional pupils.

The most radical Catholic approach is to abandon the parochial system entirely because of inadequate resources and segregation from the larger community.[7] The financial problems would then fall more heavily on all the taxpayers if state aid to non-public schools is not allowed, as it would in Msgr. Casey's proposal. Integrating Catholic and non-Catholic pupils would, however, reflect the ecumenical spirit of our times.

A fifth possibility has also developed. Following the lead of public school district consolidation, some parishes in smaller communities or in large cities with changing neighborhood populations, have consolidated their facilities and faculties to avoid operational inefficiency, inadequate teaching resources, and wasteful duplication.

These are the problems and possibilities which underlie the question of federal aid to non-public, principally parochial, schools. It is appropriate here to give equal time to the proponents and opponents on the question, in order to place in perspective the Supreme Court decisions which bear on it.

The Federal Aid Controversy—Pro

Those who favor federal assistance to non-public schools stress five factors in their arguments:
1) freedom; 2) justice; 3) size and growth; 4) pluralism; and 5) precedent.

Some Catholics feel that lack of federal aid actually is a form of discrimination. Since they are morally obligated to send their children to parochial schools, lack of government funds to support those schools is, in their eyes, impinging on their freedom of religion.

The point of "justice" is closely related to some of the alternatives just presented. These proponents point out that the parochial schools are performing a public function in educating thousands of children, and are actually saving taxpayers money. This is quite true. If there were no parochial schools, taxpayers would have to provide greater financial support for the public schools. Catholic parents also are taxpayers, and some resent the fact that their tax monies do not provide education for their children.

carl n. degler

Why Not Federal Aid to Parochial Schools?

. . . As a non-Catholic I am not directly interested in whether the parochial schools continue or not; but as a citizen interested in the future of my country and the preservation of its social amity, the Catholic's concern for his religious schools is of great moment. In what sense, then, does the Catholic argument for a share in public funds for education recommend itself to non-Catholics?

For decades Catholic leaders have asserted that those parents who send their children to parochial schools are being taxed doubly; once, when they pay school taxes for the public schools and again when they pay to support their own parochial schools. Logically and legally, of course, this argument carries little weight. No law requires that the Catholic parent support

Degler, Carl N. "Why Not Federal Aid to Parochial Schools?" *Vassar Alumnae Magazine*, 48 (Feb., 1963), pp. 2–7.

two school systems; his children are welcome at the public school. To call the arrangement double taxation is to mislead if not to provoke. Such has usually been the traditional and, I might say, Protestant, answer to the Catholic complaint. But from the Catholic standpoint is there not a real injustice, even if there is no legal basis for complaint? Is it not a fact that Catholics do indeed pay for two school systems and, more to the point, in doing so relieve many non-Catholics of the obligation to pay millions of dollars in taxes? For the Catholic children educated in parochial schools do not have to be supported by public taxes. Thus non-Catholics actually benefit, in a definite and material fashion, from the parochial schools at the same time that Catholics themselves have to contribute to the support of an educational system they do not use. In view of such solid advantages, the Catholic of average income cannot be too harshly criticized if he sometimes doubts the disinteredness of his non-Catholic neighbor's commitment to separation of church and state.

. . .

The fact is that American society, long simply Protestant, no longer is so. Now that Catholic influence is growing, non-Catholics will have to face the fact that the traditional view of separation of church and state as it applies to education will seem increasingly unsatisfactory to a large and influential portion of the population. After all, as Americans, Catholics are as free to judge and interpret our traditions as are Protestants. Nor should it be thought, as is sometimes said, that criticisms of the present arrangement emanate only from the hierarchy. In one recent study of Catholic lay opinion, 90 per cent of those who sent their children to parochial schools thought the failure to provide *some* government aid was unjust. A Gallup poll in 1949 found 79 per cent of all Catholics favoring *federal* aid to parochial schools on an equal basis with public schools.

Similar polls among non-Catholics always show just the opposite response. What are the sources of Protestant opposition to public aid to parochial schools and how valid are the objections? Much of the opposition undoubtedly stems from the quite inconsistent conceptions of the Roman Catholic Church held by Catholics and Protestants. To many Protestants their conception of the Church always stands, ominously, like some gray eminence, behind any otherwise rational discussion of government aid to private schools. For such Protestants the Catholic Church is only incidentally the embodiment of a religion; first and foremost it represents power, a power which appears so great that it is held under secular control only by the greatest effort.

. . .

But only a part of the objections to any aid to parochial schools stems from a simple fear of Catholic power. Another part arises out of a traditional and quite justified American pride in the virtues of the public school. For a good part of our history the common school has been the great Americanizer of the immigrant, the institution which has probably done more than any other to weld a nation out of a loose bundle of nationalities. (Another, though admittedly not as important an Americanizing influence, has been the Catholic Church.) But this historic function of the public schools is now apparently over. . . . Moreover, the public school, once a place where all classes and nationalities might meet, today often fails to fit that description. . . .

. . .

But it will be asked, "Suppose anti-Catholic prejudices are honestly examined and abandoned and the alleged threat to national unity put into its proper perspective, are we still not faced with constitutional obstacles to government aid to religious schools? There are two ways of answering this question. One is to suggest that constitutional interpretations are never static. . . . But the constitutional basis for government aid to parochial schools at the present time suggests that another avenue would be more immediately fruitful. . . .

. . .

The child-benefit conception of aid to private schools not only makes constitutional sense, it also makes social sense. The fact of the matter is that parochial schools are educating large numbers of children. In some localities, particularly in cities like Pittsburgh, New York, and Chicago, the proportion reaches as high as thirty and forty per cent of the school population. With such numbers, the parochial schools are public schools, performing a service to the community. Nor does it meet the practical issue to reply that this service need not be performed by private schools, that the public school system is perfectly capable of doing it.

There is another, and more important, reason to think that parochial schools function as quasi-public institutions. Since Catholics will continue to send their children to religious schools—and the Constitution seems to guarantee this right to all Americans—it seems very short-sighted from a social point of view to deny assistance to schools which educate such a large proportion of our children. Without some kind of public assistance these schools will cease to be first-rate institutions, and those which are not will never become first-rate. Yet from these inferior institutions in time will emerge millions of citizens who will have been provided with only a second and perhaps a third-rate education. Regardless of the merit of religious education as such, that stark social factor should give all Americans pause. It raises in concrete fashion the question of whether adamant refusal to grant some governmental support to denominational schools is worth such a high social price. It is here not a question of social justice but one of social intelligence.

Although the child-benefit approach seems to offer an avenue whereby some states could constitutionally take cognizance of the double educational burden assumed by many Catholic citizens, it is not an avenue open to all states. Most of the states, in fact, in their constitutions have explicit prohibitions against payment of public funds to sectarian schools. No such denial, though, rules the federal government. (Of course, no direct aid intended to support religious institutions is permissible.) As a matter of historical fact, the child-benefit conception has been applied by the federal government for a long time. Right after the Second World War the G.I. Bill of Rights provided tuition to attend religious schools, even for

training in the ministry or priesthood, without any objection
that the money involved was helping to support religion. The
practice, it is true, has never been tested in the courts, but it
continues today. . . .

It would seem then, from the standpoint of both the theory
and the practice of the child-benefit conception that some form
of federal aid to non-public schools would be consistent with
both the Constitution and historic American practice. . . .

Proponents of federal aid point to the changes in enrollment
as well as escalating costs as another reason for federal
financial assistance. Since many of the families involved have
limited economic resources, it is unlikely that they can be
called upon to pay increased tuition fees or book costs.

As Degler indicated, there is an abundance of precedent
for federal aid. Under now-existing legislation, supported in
most instances by court rulings, there are federal subsidies to
the school lunch program, to projects under the National Defense Education Act of 1958 and extensions of it, to church-run
hospitals, to the chaplaincy service of the armed forces, and
directly via tax exemptions at several governmental levels to
religious institutions themselves. In addition, Supreme Court
rulings in the past two decades have permitted substantial aid
to parochial schools in the areas of transportation and textbooks.

The final argument on behalf of federal aid to parochial
schools is the opinion that the support of this parallel system
of education contributes to and maintains diversity in our society. There is no question that parochial schools provide an
alternative to public education, which is a contribution to
diversity. Whether it is a desirable alternative depends on
one's point of view.

The Federal Aid Controversy—Con

Opponents of public aid to private schools maintain that the dual concepts of church-state separation and non-sectarian schools are in keeping with American tradition. They also stress that public support would be contrary to the spirit and letter of the First Amendment and would therefore be unconstitutional.

r. freeman butts

Public Funds Should Not Support Parochial Schools

. . . As we face the problem of public and private schools, we all know that the really controversial element in it for over a century has had to do with religion. As Americans sought to create a republican form of society to replace their colonial status, and as they built a public school system to be the main support for a free society, they had to face the religious problem.

During the century of political and religious conflict from 1830 to 1930, the public school idea was hammered out. As we know it and cherish it, the idea involves five basic principles: 1) Universal free education must be available for all in common public schools supported by taxation on everyone. 2) Public schools should be maintained under the authority of the state and administered by local public authorities. 3) In order to

Butts, R. Freeman. By permission. "Public Funds Should not Support Parochial Schools." In Ehlers and Lee, *op. cit.*, pp. 101–104.

protect freedom of conscience, the public schools should not engage in religious instruction. 4) In order to keep church separated from state, public funds cannot be given to religious schools. Finally, 5) the state can compel all children to attend some school, but children cannot be compelled to attend a public school. This idea of public education gave enormous strength, vitality, and unity to American society. It made possible, within a relatively short time, the creation of a democratic American nation out of diverse peoples. . . . The results in economic and technological progress, in political stability, and in strength of loyalty to the processes of a free society have been incalculable.

Now, the question is, "Shall we modify or possibly reverse this general pattern of public education?" An increasing number of voices in recent decades has begun to argue, to plead, to cajole, and to demand that we do so. One of the most dynamic forces in this process has been the Roman Catholic Church. . . . Catholic schools enrolled about 5 percent of the elementary and secondary school total in 1900, and still only 6 or 7 percent in 1940. But during the past twenty years, the rise has been spectacular. While public school enrollments increased 36 percent, nonpublic enrollments increased 118 percent. Today, about 14 percent of all school children are in Catholic schools, perhaps as much as 16 percent in all nonpublic schools. . . .

For one hundred years, the public school idea was on the march throughout America, but since 1930 or so it has been on the defensive. Piecemeal exceptions to the basic idea began to be made, such as the provision of free textbooks, bus rides, and lunches to parochial school children. "All we want," said the Catholic bishops in 1948, "is cooperation between church and state in education." "All we want," said Cardinal Spellman in 1949, " is public aid for auxiliary services, including health and welfare services." These services will benefit the child, they said, not aid the school; therefore, they are quite within the constitutional and legal limitations of the public school idea.

But since 1950 the character of the campaign has changed radically. The argument for benefits to the child and for the right of the parents to choose the school they desire had been extended to a full-blown theory of private rights in education. In 1955 the Catholic bishops spoke of the *partnership* of private and public schools, each having equal rights to public aid because they both perform a public service. Since that time we have heard more and more of the argument that the rights of parents in the education of their children are prior to the rights of the state. Similarly, the rights of the Church in education are presented as superior to those of the state. . . .

We hear the argument that the only real purpose of taxation for education is merely to subsidize parents and thus aid them to get the kind of education they wish for their children. . . . What this means is that the earlier demand for indirect aid for peripheral welfare services in justice to children has become a demand for direct financial subsidy by government or for a least tax credit as a constitutional right of parents. The *principle* of liberty and of civil rights *requires* the state to subsidize parents by full government support for the education of their children, and if the state refuses such aid, it will be infringing their rights of freedom of conscience under the First Amendment. . . .

If you accept the principle that the state should subsidize parents rather than maintain a common public school system, why not call on the principle to justify parents' choices on economic, political, social status, or intellectual grounds as well as on religious or racial grounds?

A proper course between voluntarism, or privatism, on the one hand, and totalitarianism, or state monopoly of education on the other, must be based on the right *and the obligation* of a free people, through its free government, to establish and maintain public schools devoted to the promotion of freedom. The people of a free state cannot rightfully create a monopoly for public education by interfering with or destroying private schools, nor can they rightfully create a monopoly for private schools by undermining or destroying their public schools.

A system of free public education is the chief means by which a free society continually regenerates itself. Public education is therefore an integral responsibility of a free and republican form of government. It is a kind of fourth branch of government, as essential to freedom as are responsible executives, elected legislatures, and independent courts. In this sense, the rights of the free people in public education are prior to the rights of individual churches or of individual parents in private education. This is the individual's guarantee that he will have any educational rights to exercise at all.

In the economic sphere, opponents of federal aid point out that parents may choose or not to send their children to public tax-supported schools. If they choose not to take advantage of public education, any resulting costs are voluntary and self-imposed, and cannot be considered, as they are by some Catholic parents, double taxation. The Dickman Case ruling (Oregon, 1961) stated that payments to non-public schools are tuition, not taxation, since the church has no power to tax.

Part of the freedom enjoyed by private and parochial school is their relative independence in bookkeeping. Opponents of federal aid to these schools, like those at the local level who oppose any federal aid to education, indicate that this freedom would be reduced. Public officials could demand a fiscal accounting of expenditures, and might even gain a measure of control over admissions and curriculum.

To those who claim that the parallel systems of education will maintain the pluralism inherent in our society's "melting pot," the opponents retort that public support of religious school systems would encourage fragmentation and division in the population.

Louis R. Gary, a consultant to both Nixon's Commission on School Finance and the Fleischmann Commission in New York State, wrote that:

"Increasingly, Catholic families moving to the suburbs are choosing public schools, which often have attractive physical facilities, gymns, learning labs, and other niceties that Catholic schools can't afford. . . . Catholic schools also are caught in ideological conflicts in the Church itself. Liberal parents believe that teaching in Catholic schools can be too restrictive; conservative parents are dissatisfied with the new permissiveness and lack of fidelity to Roman Catholic dogma. . . .

Along with falling enrollments, the decline in numbers of teaching brothers and nuns is the most serious economic problem for Catholic schools. In dollar terms, the presence of the religious-order teacher represents a great subsidy to the school."[8] This economic problem stems from two sources: fewer people entering religious orders and the rising salaries, partly due to unionization, of lay teachers.

For each argument for federal aid to non-public schools, there is a rebuttal by those against it. Much of the controversy over not only federal aid but also the very existence of non-public schools has boiled over from citizen discussions to the courts.

The Court Decides

An early decision in the area of governmental expenditures concerned the use of Indians' tribal funds for parochial schools. This was the case of Quick Bear v. Leupp (1908), with the majority opinion delivered by Justice Fuller.

Charles E. Leupp, Commissioner of Indian Affairs on the Rosebud Agency in South Dakota, made a contract with the Bureau of Catholic Indian Missions in Washington, D.C. for the purpose of educating a number of Indian pupils. Payment for this was to be made from the Sioux treaty fund, trust fund, or both. Some of the Indians protested any use of funds for sectarian education. They declared that the Commissioner's action, in behalf of the Indians, violated the policy of the government to make no appropriation for education in any sectarian school.

The Commissioner declared that appropriations of public moneys were not involved, but that money belonging to the Indians as a matter of right was being used. The Court upheld the action and view of the Commissioner. The United States had entered into treaties with the Indians, under which the Indians gave up certain lands and other rights when promised aid from the government. The trust funds and treaty funds belonged to the Indians as a result of such treaties. Thus they were not the same as a congressional appropriation. A portion of the Court's opinion stated that it is ". . . the moral right of the Indians to have this 'trust fund' applied to the education of the Indians in schools of their choice, . . ." This was the only money which the Indians could claim as theirs, and even though it wasn't delivered directly to them, they have the privilege of directing its expenditure for their benefit.[9]

It is easy to see from this example how "hair-splitting" the Court decisions may be.

In the rash of post-World War I nationalism, the state of Oregon enacted a law in 1922 (effective 1926) stating that all students, with very few exceptions, must attend public schools between the ages of 8 and 16 years. The Society of Sisters (of the Holy Names of Jesus and Mary) appealed to the courts for relief, with the case reaching the Supreme Court as Pierce v. The Society of Sisters in 1925. The Court ruled that Oregon had no right to make this requirement as long as a non-public school developed intelligent and competent citizens for the state. This case established the legal precedent for the existence of private and parochial schools, although they had, in fact, existed for decades before.

Having ruled that parochial schools were legal, the Supreme Court in the ensuing forty-odd years, has had to deal with a number of cases which evolved from that decision. In 1930, for example, the Court ruled, in the case of Cochran v. Louisiana State Board of Education, that the state of Louisiana could provide all of its children, whether in public or non-public schools, with non-religious textbooks. The Court stated that the school children and the state were the beneficiaries of this action, not the schools (or by implication, the Catholic Church). As recently as June 10, 1968, the Court again upheld the constitutionality of this practice.

The U.S. Supreme Court . . . affirmed the constitutionality of a New York law requiring school boards to provide non-sectarian textbooks to parochial school pupils. The vote was 6 to 3.

Justice Byron W. White, speaking for the majority, said the law did not violate the Bill of Right's prohibition of State aid to religion because the measure was secular in purpose and, in primary effect, neither helped nor hindered religion.[10]

That attempts to provide aid to non-public schools continue to be a source of controversy, despite recent Court decisions, is apparent. It *is* politically popular to support this type of aid, but the mechanics of doing so are complex. In April 1972, for example, President Nixon told the National Catholic Education Association that he would help ". . . preserve the non-public school system in the United States," but offered no specific details.[11]

William B. Ball, counsel to the New York parents in the Allen or Textbook Loan Act case, before the Supreme Court, pointed out that Justice White, writing for the majority, stated

. . . that the Court had long recognized that "religious schools pursue two goals, religious instruction and secular education." By this recognition, the Court discountenanced the main argument which the plaintiffs had raised in their briefs, namely, that "there is no such thing as secular education in a parochial school." This argument has been the bedrock presumption in all litigations, legislative arguments and propaganda against parochial school aid. The presumption is now judicially deflated in favor of the next chief point established by the majority opinion—namely, that the *secular*, or public, function of church-related education may, under due safeguards, be publicly aided without violation of the First Amendment.[12]

Ball wrote, also, that in handing down the two decisions on the right to sue (Flast case) and the right of the State to loan textbooks to parochial schools (Allen case), the Supreme Court recognized religious liberty in the first, and public need in the second.

Hechinger referred to the Court decision in the matter of supplying free bus transportation to parochial school children. The New Jersey legislature passed a law in 1941 authorizing payments to parents for money spent on transportation of their children to their choice of school, public or private. In 1947, the Supreme Court heard the case of Everson v. Board of Education (330 U.S. 1), and upheld the New Jersey law as being beneficial to the general welfare, to children, and consistent with the state's obligation to provide education without respect to religion. Justice Jackson, in a dissenting opinion, wrote, however.

It is of no importance in this situation whether the beneficiary of this expenditure of tax-raised funds is primarily the parochial school and incidentally the pupil, or whether the aid is directly bestowed on the pupil with indirect benefits to the school. The state cannot maintain a Church and it can no more tax its citizens to furnish free carriage to those who attend a Church. The prohibition against establishment of religion cannot be circumvented by a subsidy, bonus or reimbursement of expense to individuals for receiving religious instruction and indoctrination.[13]

Here, too, controversy continues. A Pennsylvania law providing reimbursement to non-public schools for the cost of teachers' salaries, textbooks, and instructional materials in specified non-religious subjects was ruled unconstitutional in June 1971. At the same time, a Rhode Island statute which provided for direct payment of 15% of teachers' salaries to teachers in non-public schools was similarly declared unconstitutional. In April 1972, a three-judge Federal court declared another attempt to support non-public education in Pennsylvania unconstitutional. In this instance, parents were to receive partial reimbursement for tuition paid to non-public schools. The decision stated that such repayment constituted direct support of religious education, since it was assumed that parents sent their children to religious schools in order to secure a religiously-oriented education for them.

New York and Pennsylvania both have laws that permit non-public school children to ride public school buses on standard school bus routes. These laws have not been upset to date.

How Much Religion in the Schools?

In view of the theocratic basis of American education, it is surprising in some respects how bitter is the battle about church-state relations in this sphere. When does educational practice impinge on religious freedom? When does religion enter too much into education?

The answer to the first question may be found in two cases in the early 1940's involving members of the Jehovah's Witnesses sect and what was then a compulsory flag salute in the schools, and later in the Engel v. Vitale and Abington Township School District v. Schempp cases of the 1960's. In the earlier case, it was claimed that a compulsory flag salute violated individual religious freedom, for members of Jehovah's Witnesses do not recognize any "graven image," in this case, the symbolic national flag. The Mihersville (Pa.) School District required students to participate in a patriotic ceremony including the flag salute. In 1940, the Supreme Court ruled that the school district could expel a child for not obeying this law on the grounds that he was acting contrary to national unity. This was a period of high nationalism and isolationism in this country.[14] Three years later, in wartime, the Court reversed itself in a similar case known as West Virginia State Board of Education, *et al.*, v. Barnette, *et al.*, holding that the compulsory flag salute was a violation of the First and Fourteenth Amendments.[15]

Some differences do exist in the two cases. Here the ruling was made by the state rather than the local board. Also, and probably more significant, is the fact that parents could be held accountable for refusal to comply, whereas in the earlier case the child was expelled but no further action was designated. The Court felt that an "affirmation of belief and an attitude of mind" could not be regulated or enforced against an individual or a group. Refusal to perform the act in question did not interfere with the rights and privileges of any other person.

The Court also pointed out that the Congress of the United States had dealt with similar questions concerning conscientious objectors and made such acts voluntary. Concerning national unity, the Court held that persuasion and example, but not force or coercion, were permissible. The use of compulsion to promote nationalism has proven throughout history to be futile.

Thus, according to the Court's decision, schools could include, and even require, patriotic exercises in their programs as long as those with true conscientious objections were excused from the exercises.[16]

The later cases questioned the validity of having required prayers read or recited in the schools. In Engel v. Vitale (1962), the Court declared that required reading of the non-denominational "Regents' Prayer" was unconstitutional, since it was in conflict with the First Amendment. This, despite the statement in the majority opinion written by Justice Black that "It is true that New York's establishment of its Regents' prayer as an officially approved religious doctrine of that State does not amount to a total establishment of one particular religious sect to the exclusion of all others— . . ."[17] In School District of Abington Township (Pa.) v. Schempp and in Murray v. Curlett (Md.), both 1963 decisions, the Court outlawed Bible reading because of its required nature, and recitation of the Lord's Prayer from the public schools. In both cases, it was found that the exercises which included the prayers went against the petitioners' freedom of religion, and constituted State support of religion. It was possible for the children involved to be excused from the Bible reading and recitation, but the parents (petitioners) believed that this unfairly drew attention to their non-conformity. Justice Brennan brought out the point, in his opinion, that in the Barnette decision, *supra*, "The Court held that the State must make participation in the exercise voluntary for all students and not alone for those who found participation obnoxious on religious grounds."[18] It was judicially recognized, then, that some children do tease, condemn, or otherwise make life difficult for children who do not conform to the usual pattern.

The question of religious interference with education was treated in a different series of cases. In McCollum v. Board of Education (Illinois, 1948), the problem concerned permission granted by the school board in Champaign, Ill., for religious instruction to be offered on public school property during school hours to children of the three major religious faiths whose parents signed "request cards" for the instruction. The Supreme Court found the released time arrangement in this situation to be unconstitutional because,

> Here not only are the State's tax-supported public school buildings used for the dissemination of religious doctrines. The State also affords sectarian groups an invaluable aid in that it helps to provide pupils for their religious classes through use of the State's compulsory public school machinery. This is not separation of Church and State.[19]

New York also had a State law allowing religious instruction during school hours, called "released time." However, religious school classes were held at sites other than the public school buildings, and school authorities had less involvement with the program than had been true in Illinois. In Zorach v. Clausen (1952), therefore, the Court ruled that the New York program was constitutional as long as the classes did not involve coercion, meeting on school property, or support by public tax money.[20] Opponents of the decision maintained that the state was supporting religion by pressuring children to attend the classes, but the Court declared that no such pressure existed. In practice, under the "released time" program in New York,

Table 7.1   Major supreme court decisions affecting religion and education, 1920–1972

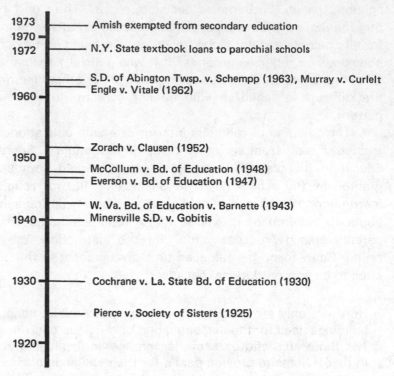

children whose parents requested that they be excused, simply left public school classrooms an hour earlier once a week than the other children—much to the chagrin of their classmates!

In another facet of the religion and education problem, one minority group, the Amish, has steadfastly fought to have its children exempted from state compulsory education laws on the grounds that school attendance after the eighth grade would violate their religious principles. Finally, in May 1972, after years of battles in the courts, the Supreme Court declared that Amish children cannot be forced to attend school beyond the eighth grade.

"The Old Order Amish have always maintained that their children do not need a high school education. They believe that excessive contact with modern education will spoil

Amish youth for farm life. They oppose the modern 'worldly' curriculum of the new consolidated schools, contending that, according to the Bible, their children belong to them and thus are not to be educated by the state nor for the benefit of the state."[21]

The Amish, who have developed prosperous farming communities in Pennsylvania, Iowa, and Wisconsin, among other states, are a quiet, peace-loving, hard-working people. Their long fight to maintain their religious beliefs, which include a strong opposition to all that is "worldly" and therefore sinful, is but another example of their tenacity. Their legal victory is a testament to the promise of religious freedom in the First Amendment.

Conclusions

The whole problem of religion and education is obviously quite complicated. Our historic alliance with God as evidenced in oaths of office, oaths in the courts, in the Pledge of Allegiance, and on our coins, has been questioned at the local level and again in the federal courts. Many school districts have added a study of comparative religions to the curriculum in an attempt to incorporate the moral and ethical values of past generations into today's teaching. Still to come, no doubt, are cases involving the quasi-religious classroom observances of Christmas and Chanukah, Easter and Passover.

It is equally obvious that it is difficult to reconcile our devotion to the church-state separation principle with our desire to ensure every child a good education, whether in the interests of the nation or just for his own well-being. The intra-parochial school consolidations will help the parochial system to provide better education than they have before. There is a need to provide certain services in the cause of humanity, no doubt, so that all the children in the nation will have equality of educational opportunity. However, like women, the Supreme Court reserves the right to change its mind. Recent decisions favoring some state aid and services to parochial (and private) schools may yet be reversed. It is difficult for the average citizen to say whether or not they should be, because it is easier to see the points of view of both sides of this situation than to decide whether one is right and the other wrong.

The Court has contributed in some ways to the maintenance of religious pluralism in the nation. It has

> ... expanded freedom in two principal ways. It has insisted upon a policy of neutrality that forbids government promotion or sponsorship of religious beliefs. By this insistence, the Court has not merely protected the freedom of those who hold different beliefs; it has protected the freedom of commitment to favored beliefs from being compromised by government sponsorship. In the second place, the Court has also expanded religious freedom by permitting, and sometimes requiring, special provisions to be made for religion where this is necessary to neutralize the otherwise restrictive effects of government's expanding activities.[22]

Endnotes

1. Karier, *op. cit.,* p. 11.
2. Pfeffer, Leo. *"Creeds in Competition,"* (New York: Harper, 1958), pp. 75–76. By permission of Harper and Row, Publishers.
3. Davis, Moshe. *The Emergence of Conservative Judaism* (Phila.: Jewish Publication Society of America, 1965), p. 40.
4. Grayzel, Solomon. *A History of the Contemporary Jews* (New York: Harper Torchbooks, Harper and Row, 1965), pp. 35–38.
5. Crowley, Francis M. "A Separate School System." In Ehlers, Henry and Gordon C. Lee, eds., *Crucial Issues in Education*, Third Edition, (New York: Holt, Rinehart, and Winston, 1964), p. 94.

6. Casey, George W. "Separation in High School Only," In Ehlers and Lee, *ibid.*, pp. 96–97.

7. O'Connor, William F. "Abandonment of the Catholic School System." In Ehlers and Lee, *op. cit.*, pp. 97–99.

8. Gary, Louis R., and K. C. Cole. "The Politics of Aid—and a Proposal for Reform," *Saturday Review*, (July 22) 1972, p. 32.

9. Quick Bear v. Leupp, 210 U.S. 50, In *Essentials of School Law* ed. Robert L. Drury and Kenneth C. Ray, (New York: Appleton-Century-Crofts, 1967), p. 144.

10.

11. O'Rourke, Lawrence J. "President Ties Funding to Fate of Cities." *The Evening Bulletin* (Philadelphia), (April 6) 1972, p. 1.

12. Ball, William G. "The School Aid Decisions," *Commonweal*, 88, (June 28, 1968), p. 432.

13. Everson v. Board of Education of the Township of Ewing, *et al.*, 330 U.S. 1 (1947), p. 24.

14. Minersville School District v. Gobitis, 310 U.S. 586 (1940).

15. West Virginia Board of Education v. Barnette, 319 U.S. 624 (1943), pp. 624–642.

16. Drury and Ray, *op. cit.*, p. 148.

17. Engel v. Vitale, 370 U.S. 421 (1962), p. 436.

18. Abington School District v. Schempp, 374 U.S. 203–320 (1963), p. 252.

19. McCollum v. Board of Education, 333 U.S. 203 (1948), p. 212.

20. Zorach v. Clausen, 343 U.S. 306 (1952).

21. Wittmer, Joe. "The Amish and the Supreme Court." *Phi Delta Kappan*, 1972, 54, p. 52.

22. Katz, Wilber G., and Harold P. Southerland. "Religious Pluralism and the Supreme Court," *Daedalus*, 96, (Winter, 1967), 180–192.

For Further Reading

American Jewish Committee. *Religion in Public Education* (New York: American Jewish Committee, 1969).

BALL, WILLIAM B. "The School Aid Decisions," *Commonweal*, 88. (June 28, 1968), 431–432.

BLUM, VIRGIL C., S.J. Freedom in Education: *Federal Aid for All Children* (New York: Doubleday and Company, 1965).

BOLES, DONALD EDWARDS. *The Bible, Religion, and the Public Schools* (Ames, Iowa: Iowa University Press, 1963).

BUTTS, R. FREEMAN. *The American Tradition in Religion and Education* (Boston: Beacon Press, Inc., 1950).

DAVIS, MOSHE. *The Emergence of Conservative Judaism*. Phila.: Jewish Publication Society of America, 1965.

DRINAN, ROBERT F., S.J. *Religion, the Courts, and the Public Policy* (New York: McGraw-Hill Book Company, 1963).

DRURY, ROBERT L., and KENNETH C. RAY, eds., *Essentials of School Law* (New York: Appleton-Century-Crofts, 1967).

DUKER, SAM. *The Public Schools and Religion: The Legal Context* (New York: Harper and Row, 1966).

Education News, May 27, 1968.

Educational Policies Commission. *Moral and Spiritual Values in the Public School* (Washington, D.C.: National Education Association, 1952).

EHLERS, HENRY, and GORDON C. LEE, eds. *Crucial Issues in Education* (New York: Holt, Rinehart, and Winston, 1964).

FREUND, PAUL A., and ROBERT ULICH. *Religion and the Public Schools* (Cambridge, Mass.: Harvard University Press, 1965).

GARY, LOUIS R., and K. C. COLE. "The Politics of Aid - and a Proposal for Reform." *Saturday Review*, (July 22) 1972, 31–33.

GRAHAM, FRED P. "High Court, 8 to 1, Forbids States to Reimburse Parochial Schools, But Backs Help at College Level." *New York Times*, (June 29) 1971, pp. 1, 18.

GRAYZEL, SOLOMON. *A History of the Contemporary Jews* (New York: Harper Torchbooks (Harper and Row), 1965).

HEALEY, ROBERT M. *Jefferson on Religion in Public Education* (New Haven: Yale University Press, 1962).

HERBERG, WILL. *Protestant-Catholic-Jew* (Garden City, N.Y.: Doubleday and Company, 1956).

KARIER, CLARENCE J. *Man, Society, and Education* (Glenview, Ill.: Scott, Foresman, and Company, 1967).

KATZ, WILBER G., and HAROLD P. SOUTHERLAND. "Religious Pluralism and the Supreme Court." *Daedalus*, 96, (Winter 1967), 180–192.

LA NOUE, GEORGE R. "Religious Schools and Secular Subjects." *Harvard Educational Review*, (February 1961), 91–95.

MADAUS, GEORGE F., and ROGER LINNAN. "The Outcome of Catholic Education?" *School Review*, 81, (February 1973), 207–232.

MADDEN, WARD. *Religious Values in Education* (New York: Harper and Brothers, 1951).

"School Aid Upset in Pennsylvania." *New York Times*, (April 7) 1972, p. 14.

SHAW, RUSSELL, and RICHARD J. HURLEY (eds.). *Trends and Issues in Catholic Education* (New York: Citation Press, 1969).

THAYER, V. T. *The Attack upon the American Secular School* (Boston: Beacon Press, 1951).

The New York Times, June 16, 1968.

The Philadelphia Inquirer, June 11, 1968.

TIEDT, SIDNEY W. *The Role of the Federal Government in Education* (New York: Oxford University Press, 1966).

Vassar Alumnae Magazine, 48 (February 1963).

8

segregation and education

The battles over civil rights which are reported daily by the communications media are the source of a national "black eye" on the international scene. Visitors from other countries frequently have a distorted picture of race relations here, and the stories of police brutality, inferior housing, picketing at schools, and bloody riots do little to dispel this image. In the field of education, the conflict is complicated by the concept of neighborhood schools, which in turn depends upon population dispersion and mobility. The problem is not one new to the scene, however; segregation in education has a long and checkered history.

Historical Background

Before the Civil War, many slaves were given Christian religious instruction. A comparative few were taught how to read and calculate by more liberal-minded slave-owners. There were relatively few schools in the colonial South, at least as compared with New England in the same period, and these were often restricted to the wealthy white children, which automatically excluded the slaves. In the early nineteenth century, the split between the industrial North and the agrarian South was reflected in their respective attitudes toward public education as well. Slavery and a rigid class system in the South, as well as the geographical separation of plantations, negated enthusiasm for public school systems there in favor of private tutors or private schools. Indeed, after the Nat Turner Insurrection of 1831, fear of "educated" slaves was so great that the slave-owning states prohibited the education of Negroes. It was feared that literacy would lead to further uprisings.

> In Northern cities, benevolent societies and churches established segregated schools for Negroes, as did free Negroes also . . . Early responses to the demand of public aid for Negro education differed from state to state, and integration and admission of Negroes to public schools came slowly and gradually. New Jersey (1844), Massachusetts (1855), Rhode Island (1866), and Connecticut (1868) legalized integration in public schools, separation being previously the official policy. . . . There was much opposition in the North and Middle West to efforts to educate Negroes. White workers saw Negroes threatening their jobs, and the education of Negro paupers an obstacle to the education of their own children.[1]

After the collapse of slavery, the right of Negroes to be educated as free men was established. Several Negro schools and colleges were founded with religious and Northern philanthropic support during and after the Reconstruction period. Among the church-supported schools were Lincoln University (founded in 1853 and later renamed) and Wilberforce University (1855). Hampton Institute (1870) and the world-famous Tuskegee Institute (1881) were designed to provide higher education for Negroes. Most of the Negro colleges founded in the Reconstruction period, however, actually functioned at a secondary school level. There are now over 100 Negro colleges, most still in the Southern or border states, and, until recent years, providing an inferior quality of education due to lack of funds for teachers, books, and equipment. Howard University has been a notable exception. Part of the blame for the inadequate education provided can be placed on the basic conflict among Negro educators as to the types of curricula to be offered—vocational or teacher training. The emphasis at Booker T. Washington's Tuskegee Institute was on vocational education, while several other colleges specialized in training teachers for the segregated schools of the South. An interesting note in the current segregation situation is that reverse integration is taking place at some formerly all-Negro colleges (e.g., in West Virginia).

The segregated school system which arose in the South after the Civil War resulted in the duplication of facilities in the states which could least afford the double expense. The practice was maintained under a "separate but equal" policy until the Supreme Court decision of 1954.

The "separate but equal" doctrine stemmed from the Plessy v. Ferguson decision in 1896, when the Supreme Court sustained a Louisiana law requiring separate but equal railroad accommodations. It was reaffirmed in the case of Berea College v. Commonwealth of Kentucky (1908) which supported a 1904 Kentucky law prohibiting mixed schools. Further support of the "separate but equal" doctrine is seen in the "Gaines" or "Missouri" case (1938) in which the Supreme Court stated that the state of Missouri must provide within its borders professional educational facilities for Negroes equal to those enjoyed by whites, or be in violation of the Fourteenth Amendment.

> The basic consideration here is not as to what sort of opportunities other States provide, or whether they are as good as those in Missouri, but as to what opportunities Missouri itself furnishes to white students and denies to Negroes solely upon the ground of color. . . . The white resident is afforded legal education within the State; the Negro resident having the same qualifications is refused it there and must go outside the State to obtain it. That is a denial of the equality of the legal right to the enjoyment of the privilege which the State has set up, and the provision for the payment of tuition fees in another State does not remove the discrimination.[2]

Although the Gaines decision upheld segregated education, it was also the first of a series of Court decisions leading the declaration that "separate but equal" schools were, in fact, unequal and unconstitutional. In 1950, the Supreme Court, in Sweatt v. Painter, ruled that the University of Texas must admit

Negroes to its Law School because the newly established law school at the Texas State University for Negroes (established as a result of legal suit) did not furnish equal educational opportunities to white and Negro law students in terms of faculty, library resources, accreditation, available courses, or standing in the community. At the same session of the Court, in the McLaurin case, it was held that the University of Oklahoma must not segregate white and Negro students when Negroes were finally admitted to that institution because separate but equal facilities were not available. McLaurin was seeking a doctorate degree in education. He was admitted to the University of Oklahoma as a student, but restricted under state law from eating with white students, and was assigned to specific classroom and library locations in order to maintain aspects of segregation. In the Court's decision, an interesting argument was stated:

> It may be argued that appellant will be in no better position when these restrictions are removed, for he may still be set apart by his fellow students. This we think irrelevant. There is a vast difference—a Constitutional difference—between restrictions imposed by the state which prohibit the intellectual commingling of students, and the refusal of individuals to commingle where the state presents no such bar . . .[3]

The final blow to legal school segregation came in Brown v. Topeka Board of Education (1954). In this case, the Supreme Court outlawed separate but equal schools in favor of school integration on the grounds that segregation in the public schools deprives some citizens of the equal protection of the laws of the Fourteenth Amendment.

> Today, education is perhaps the most important function of state and local governments. . . . In these days, it is doubtful that any child may reasonably be expected to succeed in life if he is denied the opportunity of an education. Such an opportunity, where the state has undertaken to provide it, is a right which must be made available to all on equal terms.

We come then to the question presented: Does segregation of children in public schools solely on the basis of race, even though the physical facilities and other "tangible" factors may be equal, deprive the children of the minority group of equal educational opportunities? We believe that it does.[4]

Table 8.1   **Sequence of major supreme court decisions affecting segregation in education, 1895–1972**

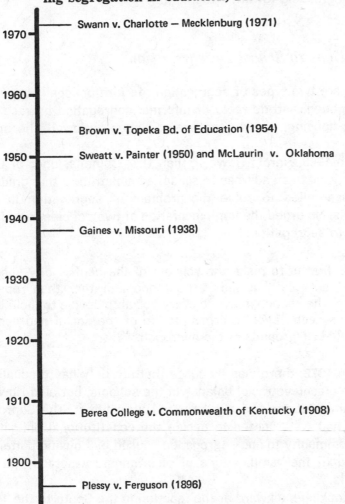

The reaction to this decision was strong on the part of both partisans and opponents of school segregation. In terms of historical background, however, let us just conclude this portion of the chapter by mentioning that the Civil Rights Act of 1964 enforced and assisted desegregation in the schools. Under Title IV of this Act, and through subsequent legislation, there have been attempts to enforce the 1954 decision by prohibiting Federal aid grants to segregated schools which are not progressing toward integration.

Reactions to School Desegregation

There are two types of segregation: *de jure* or legally-imposed segregation, and *de facto* or informal segregation by race, income, housing, etc. As the one has been outlawed, the other has increased.

In 1966, Harold Howe II, then U.S. Commissioner of Education, said in an address to school administrators that gradualism had failed to solve the problem of segregation in the schools. He urged the implementation of two policies to reduce *de facto* segregation:

"The first is to make the schools of the central city such good schools that they attract people rather than repel them. The second is to use every possible device to include within each school a cross-section of the social and economic backgrounds of the metropolis."[5]

In 1972, there was evidence that not only had gradualism failed to achieve racial balance in the schools, but also Howe's recommendations had similarly had little effect. The Supreme Court had ". . . agreed to decide the constitutional obligation of a community to end segregation caused by housing patterns. . . . [and] the ramifications of discriminatory acts by public officials."[6]

Looking backward at the reaction in the South to the 1954 desegregation decision, one recalls explosive incidents in many communities, with occasional outbursts occurring even two decades later. Violence and disorder were so great in Little Rock, Ark., that President Eisenhower had to send troops to that city both to keep the peace and to permit a handful of young Negroes to integrate the high school there. In New Orleans, families were bombed in their homes and pickets strongly attempted to discourage the few white parents willing to allow their children to attend school with Negroes. In Oxford, Miss., the National Guard was called out by President Kennedy to ensure James Meredith's admission to the University of Mississippi. In Prince Edward County, Va., public schools were abolished for over four years to avoid having to support non-segregated schools. Propaganda was spread about the dire effects of desegregation, and the relationship of this policy to Communism. Legal and economic pressures were put upon citizens—the whites not to send their children to school with Negroes and the Negroes not to send their children to white schools at all. Several Negro families who thought that what was said in the law was meant found themselves out of jobs, cut off from credit at local stores, or at the mercy of mob action.

In some areas there were attempts to forbid support of non-segregated schools while all-white schools were being supported. This move was declared unconstitutional in 1960. Pupil-assignment laws were passed in other communities, so that school placements were based on admissions tests. Due to the nature of the test and the often inadequate prior schooling of the young Negroes, few passed high enough to be placed in the all-white schools.

Against this shoddy show of democracy in action, however, can be placed the record of those school systems which complied with the Supreme Court ruling almost immediately. Washington, D.C., effected school integration very quickly. Louisville, Ky., a "border" city, desegregated its schools in one year. St. Louis, Mo., also moved to eliminate segregation shortly after the Court's decision. The Board of Education of Nashville, Tenn., began desegregation at the rate of one grade per year in 1956. Although these schools were integrated successfully, as were others during the middle and late 1950's, the unhappy fact is that *de jure* segregation has been replaced in the 1960's by *de facto* segregation as more and more white families move to suburban areas and leave behind a Negro ghetto that is almost city-wide. Those families which have not moved have often transferred their children to private schools. With the Negro residents becoming a larger proportion of both the city and the school populations, as Howe pointed out, it is virtually impossible in some sections of the cities to avoid *de facto* segregated schools.

In the remainder of the country, where *de facto* segregation has existed for years because of the neighborhood school concept, the picketing and protests have come from both Negroes and whites. Negro opposition to neighborhood, therefore segregated, schools has led to policies of "busing" white and Negro children to schools at a distance from their homes, a move vigorously protested by white parents. They had selected their residences with regard to school locations so that their children could walk back and forth, receive the benefits of better teaching, and perhaps to avoid integration in schools.

> The continued migration of white parents from the old central cities and the immigration of additional nonwhites to take their place is the single most persistent cause of greater segregation . . . in all big Northern cities. Since there is no reason to believe that a Supreme Court interpretation of the law will prevent change of residence by either race, no immediate solution to this problem can be seen. The best long-term resolution of the situation appears to lie in the provision of better schools for *all* children and in the assurance that the real purpose of any school desegregation is not solely racial balance but quality education.[7]

Should entire school systems be desegregated at one time in the South or should desegregation take place grade-by-grade? If the latter method is chosen, at which grade should desegregation begin? Since many Southern communities have been reluctant to obey the 1954 ruling at all, they have usually chosen the second and slower method rather than total simultaneous desegregation. The pattern of Supreme Court decisions has often caused this to be done from the top down, since the pre-1954 rulings involved higher education levels. Attempting desegregation initially at the high school level, as was done in Little Rock and elsewhere, was psychologically poor. In high school, adolescents are dating and thinking of marriage, so that integration begun at this level is emotionally threatening to them and their parents. A great fear of the segregationist white, particularly, is that of miscegenation, and he sees it as the ultimate result of school desegregation. In addition, prejudice against non-whites, or indeed against anyone who is "different," has congealed at this age, making the possibility of normal interpersonal relationships among integrated schoolmates even more difficult. On the other hand, if desegregation were started in the lowest grades first, even grade-by-grade, as was done in Nashville, the friendly relations established at a more impressionable and flexible age would do much to combat home-taught prejudices. In the normal course of children's social development, there is a natural segregation by sex, socio-economic background, and ethnic groups, to forestall the interracial dating of which the parents are so afraid.

In the other areas of the nation, the major question is whether the neighborhood concept is bad. Is it completely wrong for white parents to want their children in schools close to home among children of similar backgrounds? Is it wrong for them to object to transportation of their children to schools where the facilities for learning are less adequate and the classmates less well-prepared? And is it wrong for Negro parents to want their children to share the advantages of schools in more privileged neighborhoods? Since some means of satisfying all or most of the parents must be found, large city school boards have been forced to consider busing and open enrollment plans as alternatives to the status quo. Then they must choose which of these alternatives would be the more effective *and* more acceptable solution.

Figure 9.1

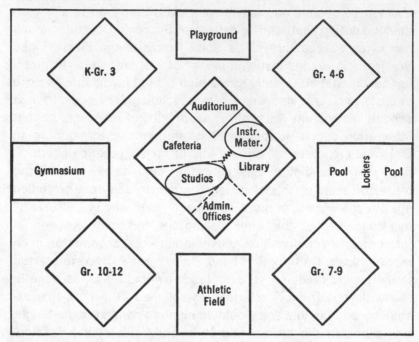

The educational park complex, as illustrated in the diagram above, is one measure that has been suggested to relieve racial imbalance in urban school systems. Housing from 2000 to 4000 students in grades K-12, the parks draw students from a wide geographic area. The central unit offers common facilities for all schools in the complex.

Busing seems to evoke nothing but controversy politically. On the one hand, it appears to be the most feasible alternative to apartheid in education. On the other hand, President Nixon himself expressed his support of the neighborhood school concept and his opposition to busing to rectify racial imbalance in the schools.[8] A temporary moratorium on court-ordered busing was imposed by him, and Congressional legislation similarly supported the anti-busing movement.

Redistricting of school boundaries, another attempt to increase school integration, was declared a permissible means of implementing desegregation plans in the Swann v. Charlotte-

Mecklenburg (N. C.) decision (1971).[9] This practice has led to some rather odd gerrymandered school districts in large cities, and has aroused only a little less hostility on the part of affected citizens.

Generally speaking, the white schools are less crowded than those in the ghettos, so that permitting Negro parents to enroll their children in a white school with pupil vacancies seems defensible. However, this is not true of busing for the sake of busing, or for the sake of changing numerical balances of white and Negro pupils (and teachers) in a school. As opponents of national educational standards have stated, acceptance of minimum standards alone leads to mediocrity. If white children are transported to Negro schools just to change the enrollment figures, they are being forced in most cases to accept a reduced quality of education, simply because the ghetto schools have been treated up to now as "step-children." Such a "share and share alike" policy is unfair to both parties. All of the children involved are being cheated of their right to a quality education. Raising the quality level of education in Negro schools is a means of attracting white pupils where vacancies exist—and few do in the ghetto schools, but, as in the case of I.S. 201 in New York, initially busing by fiat would have to be used to convince the Negro parents that the improvements were not just a means of mollifying their hostility toward continued school segregation. Magnet schools and educational parks, proposed in past Congressional legislation and endorsed by the National Advisory Commission on Civil Disorders, can do more to attract white pupils and Negro pupils to an integrated setting for a positive purpose, than all of the busing and balancing plans combined. It is imperative that efforts and funds be committed to improving the quality of education in urban schools, to making them more attractive as schools to pupils, teachers, and parents.

There has been widespread recognition and intellectual acceptance of the fact that most schools in the Negro-Puerto Rican areas of the cities are woefully and wholly inadequate from the physical plant to the faculty qualifications. A noted minister in the Philadelphia area said one evening that if he had children and lived in the district served by one particular center city school, he would not send them there because by the end of three years they would be two years behind the children in other parts of the city. Textbooks are outdated and torn, young and inexperienced teachers on their first assignment make up the faculty, supplies are missing, and buildings are poorly maintained—these are the problems that have plagued and characterized slum schools in many Northern cities for years. Yet, when a brand-new, well-equipped Intermediate School 201 was to be opened in New York's Harlem in September, 1966, staffed with superior teachers to provide Negro students with a quality education, Negroes protested loudly and violently because the school had been located in the ghetto and would be segregated. They also objected to the white principal assigned to the school, but the faculty voted to strike unless he remained in the position.[10] Parents and others in the neighborhood of I.S. 201 demanded, in effect, that they have the powers of the city board of education regarding their school, and that white children be bused to the school to achieve some air of racial balance. They sought justice, although their methods may have been too direct and forceful.

The conclusion of the National Advisory Commission on Civil Disorders, in March, 1968, stressed the dismal record of ghetto schools as one factor in the civil riots of the summer before. Several remedial measures were suggested, including:

1) increased efforts to eliminate *de facto* school segregation.

2) Federal aid as reinforcement for school systems developing desegration programs.

3) development of educational parks and magnet schools (as provided for in Title IV of the Civil Rights Act of 1964).

4) year-round innovative school programs.

5) expansion of preschool programs.

6) a strong literacy drive among ghetto residents.

7) major efforts to attract and retain qualified teachers for ghetto schools. Many specific programs were put forth,

a number of which could be effected under the existing Elementary and Secondary Education Act of 1965, Education Professions Development Act, Civil Rights Act, and Economic Opportunities Act.[11]

In the opinion of the Commission, remediation of the segregation in education problems involved more than simply changing the racial balance of the schools. Included in their recommendations are ideas relating to economics, governmental responsibility at all three levels, Federal aid to education, teacher preparation, and quality in education. Thus, this one problem area seems to circumscribe several of the problem areas discussed in this text.

Particularly in the light of the Commission's recommendations, it is worth looking at a number of attempted solutions to the segregation problem across the country. Because of the size of New York City's population, remedies tried there are often used as guides by other cities. Several of the trial solutions will be briefly examined here. New York has transported pupils from their home school districts under an open-enrollment plan, but the number of pupils involved is less than one percent of the total school enrollment. Special projects such as "Operation Headstart" and "Higher Horizons," one of several cultural enrichment programs at the secondary level, were instituted to modify the effects of ghettto life and impoverished schooling. The results of these older programs have been good, reducing the drop-out rate and encouraging capable students to continue on to higher education. They are not effective in desegregating the schools, however, nor were they intended to do so. In addition, a number of private colleges have conducted and are presently conducting intensive summer academic programs to prepare talented Negro youths for entrance into Ivy League-level schools. This is an effort to integrate these institutions more thoroughly, as well as to equalize educational opportunities for these students. Scholarship help is given to those students accepted by the colleges.

New Rochelle, N.Y., a suburb of New York City, and San Francisco have tried to reduce *de facto* segregation through rezoning school boundaries. In Princeton, N.J., all children in the first five grades are in neighborhood schools, but pupils from grade six on attend the same school. The divisions of city schools into a 4-4-4 plan would accomplish much the same kind of integration. In Los Angeles, voluntary, limited busing has been proposed, with students from overcrowded minority area schools being transported from their schools to white schools with available classroom space and seats, and possibly busing children from white elementary schools to a minority area school. Here, too, redistricting might be necessary to make the most effective use of available classrooms.[12] Following the National Advisory Commission *Report*, Chicago decided to initiate a busing program involving eight white elementary schools, and less than 600 Negro children.[13] In Boston, the neighborhood school concept has been the source of bitter political contests, the result of a state law passed in 1965 which fixed penalties for failure to reduce racial imbalance in the schools by rezoning or busing.

In a study by University of Michigan researchers, the reactions of white and Negro fifth-grade children were studied before and after busing for a school year. Attitudes of the children before the integration experience (September, 1966) reflected skepticism, doubt, and some anxiety. Mutual antagonism and mistrust were reported, but also some nondiscriminatory attitudes were expressed. The research team recognized, on the basis of earlier research reports,

> . . . that we cannot automatically assume that brotherhood and harmony will always accompany racial mixing. In fact, desegregation that is not carefully planned may heighten pre-existing tendencies for racial separation and hostility. In this context one of the vital questions yet to be answered is, what happens after youngsters from different races are placed together in the classroom?[14]

Re-interviews with the children at the end of the year did not indicate massive changes in attitudes on the part of the white students toward Negroes in general or their Negro classmates.

There was no specific curriculum emphasis on racial questions to help each group to become better acquainted with the other, nor was there any real encouragement for the children to get to know each other as individuals. The white students gave responses, at the end of the year, ranging from strongly anti-Negro to an acceptance of greater integration.

> Negro youngsters had markedly different perspectives on racial matters. Already accustomed to living in a white world, almost all accepted the new schooling patterns and channeled their attention to facilitating adjustment to the pattern. When asked what advice they would give to others of their own race entering newly desegregated schools the following year, their answers revealed that they had worked out means of coping with stresses involved. They had concrete advice to offer based on their own experiences with teachers and peers.[15]

Their advice focused on three areas: 1) obey the teacher's requests and orders without an argument; 2) try to understand white behavior and attitudes; and 3) avoid fights. These were eminently sensible children, without regard to their race. The researchers were also aware that it might be, and probably is, too late to change parental attitudes toward other races, but asked if it would be possible to alter or modify the attitudes of the children without help from the parents. "What kinds of curricula, instructional media, interaction settings, or school structures will be most helpful in working with either group of these youngsters?"[16] So far, educators, psychologists, and sociologists are still trying to answer this question.

Other techniques are also being used in different parts of the country. Compensatory education represents a major effort to increase and enrich the instructional program for children from "culturally deprived" homes. The program provides, usually, some combination of: smaller class size, individual or small group tutoring, extra periods of English, and the aid of psychologists, social workers, and other allied personnel. In some cases the tutors are prospective teachers doing field work with or without credit. Textbooks, too, are being changed to present reading material more meaningful to Negro children than the usual white, middle-class illustrations so familiar in primary-level readers.

The cause of school integration has not been aided by the reintroduction to public and professional controversy of the role of heredity in determining intelligence. Jensen (1969 and later) and Shockley (1972 and earlier) maintained that all the efforts of compensatory education could not overcome the handicap of innate inferior intelligence in blacks. Gage (1972) was one among many educators and psychologists who refuted the bases for this theory in print and in lectures.

Human relations in-service programs for educational personnel are another attempt to minimize friction as desegregation continues. Such positive actions are offset, however, by the withdrawal or reduction in amounts granted of federal funds from ongoing successful programs. Inadequate follow-up of "Head Start" programs in the primary grades also deflates the benefits which might have been gained from them.

Action in the North and Middle West has not generally been as violent as that experienced in the South, but there have been street marches, sit-ins, bus bombings, and attempts to revamp the entire school administration by the Negro population. Benjamin Willis in Chicago, John Whittier and Mark Shedd in Philadelphia, and Bernard Donovan in New York, among others, found their positions as superintendents of schools under fire from all sides during desegregation crises. No matter what remedies they attempted, one group of citizens or another protested loudly. Unfortunately, too, many routine occurrences in the schools have been interpreted in terms of racial factors rather than on a more objective basis. Teacher criticisms of students' work or behavior, school elections, and other normal school happenings are still being subjected to racial and racist interpretations, much to the discredit of those involved.

Attempts to meet community protests with administrative decentralization of school districts in large urban areas have encountered mixed receptions. Where local school boards have been established, as in the Ocean Hill-Brownsville section of

Brooklyn (New York), there has been potential or actual disruption of the educative process. The desire to exercise hiring/firing power over school personnel led to city-wide strikes in 1968 by teachers in this case, because the community leaders would not permit a number of white teachers assigned to the schools in the district to teach there. In other instances, decentralization, which is supported by many school administrators, has simply degenerated into a black power vs. white power struggle, with serious damage to both children's education and inter-group relations as a consequence. It is apparent that the details and limitations of any decentralization program must be clearly worked out in advance by school district personnel and involved members of the lay community. This also means reconciling the viewpoints of integrationists and black separatists in the Negro community.

Arguments for integrated schools stress the educational benefits to the culturally different learners and the social benefits to all children. Loving wrote, for example, that one goal of education is a society free of racism (1972). In practice, however, while many schools are integrated, their classrooms are not, due to homogeneous grouping. Arguments for separate, segregated schools reflect the growing consciousness of ethnic identity and the desire for a voice and power in decision making in many minority groups. With community control of school boards, the separatist minority elements can dominate hiring of teachers, curriculum content, and the destiny of the group's children.

Findings of the Coleman Report and the Jencks' rebuttal to it lead inescapably to the conclusion that, although education has long been perceived as a prime means of reducing the negative effects of segregation and poverty, integration in education cannot do the job alone. As the minority population increases in large urban school systems, annual achievement test results show more students further behind in reading achievement despite large injections of public and private funds and a host of special programs. The persistence of inequality in the schools reflects the continuing inequality in society at large. Jencks' conclusions about the relative ineffectiveness of education in eradicating equality are seen as contributing to the decline in funding compensatory programs and other Federal aid to education.

Summary

In this chapter, the history and present status of segregation in education have been discussed, with particular emphasis on the alternatives to segregation. Although the principal court rulings have been concerned with the rights of black students to equal educational opportunity, their problems are also faced by the Mexican-Americans (Serrano v. Priest, California, 1971), Indians, Puerto Ricans, and other minority groups. Busing and redistricting are the prime techniques for achieving racial balance in the schools. Compensatory education and early childhood intervention approaches have their supporters and detractors. The educational voucher system, to be discussed in a future chapter, offers yet another alternative.

Since it is doubtful that unanimous agreement will be obtained on any plan of school integration, within localities and across the nation, we must consider this the current phase of the American dilemma. The desegregation or integration plans, as you will, which have been adopted successfully, do leave one with hope that the dilemma will be resolved peacefully.

Endnotes

1. Mulhern, James. *A History of Education* (New York: The Ronald Press Co., 1959), p. 624.

2. 305 U.S. 348. In Knight, Edgar W. *Readings in Educational Administration* (New York: Henry Holt and Co., 1953), p. 491.

3. 339 U.S. 637–42. In Knight, *Ibid.*, p. 523.

4. Brown v. Board of Education, 347 U.S. 483. In Hillway, Tyrus. *American Education: An Introduction Through Readings* (Boston: Houghton-Mifflin Co., 1964), p. 118.

5. Howe, Harold, II. "The Time Is Now." *Saturday Review,* (July 16) 1966, p. 58.

6. Editorial: "Time to Eliminate the Distinction Between De Jure and De Facto." *Phi Delta Kappan,* 1972, 53, p. 402.

7. Hill, Henry H. "School Desegregation North and South." *Saturday Review,* July 16, 1966, p. 55.

8. *The New York Times:* "The Week in Review," Mar. 19, 1972, p. 1.

9. 402 U.S. 1 (April 20, 1972).

10. Buck, Jerry, and Hollie I. West. "Harlem's Showcase School Becomes a Bitter Battleground for Black Power," *The Philadelphia Inquirer,* Sept. 26, 1966, p. 6.

11. *Report of the National Advisory Commission on Civil Disorders* (New York: Bantam Books, 1968), particularly pp. 424–456.

12. "Busing Conflicts Threaten Racial Progress in Three Cities," *Education News,* 2, Mar. 18, 1968, p. 3.

13. *Ibid.,* p. 3.

14. Chesler, Mark, Wittes, Simon, and Norman Radin. "When Northern Schools Desegregated," *American Education,* 4, (June, 1968), p. 2.

15. *Ibid.,* p. 4.

16. *Ibid.,* p. 4.

For Further Reading

CHESLER, MARK, SIMON WITTES, and NORMAN RADIN. "When Northern Schools Desegregated." *American Education,* 4, (June, 1968), 2–4.

CLIFT, VIRGIL A., ARCHIBALD ANDERSON, and H. GORDON HULL-FISH. *Negro Education in America* (New York: Harper and Row, 1962).

COLEMAN, JAMES S., *et al.*, *Equality of Educational Opportunity* Washington, D.C.: Department of Health, Education, and Welfare, 1966.

CRONIN, JOSEPH M. "The Centralization of the Boston Public Schools." Paper presented at the American Educational Research Association, New York, February 1971.

DENTLER, ROBERT A. "Barriers to Northern School Desegregation." *Daedalus*, 95, (Winter, 1966), 45–63.

Education News, March 18, 1968.

FAMIGHETTI, BOB. "Major Court Decisions in Education." In The Education Yearbook, *1972–73* (Johnston, B., Randall, P.B., and Paradise, J., eds.). (New York: Macmillan and Free Press, 1972, 113–120).

FISCHER, JOHN H. "Race and Reconciliation: the Role of the School." *Daedalus*, 95, (Winter, 1966), 24–44.

FOSTER, MARCUS A. *Making Schools Work: Strategies for Changing Education* (Philadelphia: Westminster Press, 1971).

FUCHS, ESTELLE. "The Navajos Build a College." *Saturday Review*, (March 4) 1972, 58–62.

GAGE, N. L. "I.Q. Heritability, Race Differences, and Educational Research." *Phi Delta Kappan*, 1972, 53, 308–312.

GINZBERG, ELI, and ALFRED S. EICHNER. *The Troublesome Presence: American Democracy and the Negro* (New York: The Free Press, 1964).

HAMILTON, CHARLES V. "Race and Education: A Search for Legitimacy." *Harvard Educational Review*, 1968, 38, 669–684.

HARRINGTON, JOHNS. "The College Dream for Inner-City Youngsters." *Phi Delta Kappan*, 1972, 54, 53–55.

HARVEY, JAMES C., and CHARLES H. HOLMES. "Busing and School Desegregation." *Phi Delta Kappan*, 1972, 53, 540–542.

HILLWAY, TYRUS. *American Education: An Introduction through Readings* (Boston: Houghton-Mifflin Company, 1964).

HUMPHREY, HUBERT H., ed. *Integration vs. Segregation* (New York: Thomas Y. Crowell Company, 1964).

JENSEN, ARTHUR R. "How Much Can We Boost I.Q. and Scholastic Achievement?" *Harvard Educational Review*, 1969, 39, 1–123.

KING, MARTIN LUTHER, JR. *Why We Can't Wait* (New York: New American Library, 1964).

KLOPF, GORDON J., and ISRAEL LESTER, eds. *Integrating the Urban School* (New York: Teachers College, Columbia University, 1963).

KNIGHT, EDGAR W. *Readings in Educational Administration* (New York: Henry Holt and Company, 1953).

LOVING, ALVIN D., SR. "A Case for Multi-Ethnic Schools." *Phi Delta Kappan*, 1972, 53, 279–280.

MULHERN, JAMES. *A History of Education* (New York: Ronald Press, 1959).

The Philadelphia Inquirer, September 26, 1966.

Report of the National Advisory Commission on Civil Disorders (New York: Bantam Books, 1968).

Saturday Review, July 16, 1966.

SHOCKLEY, WILLIAM, "Dysgenics, Geneticity, Raceology: A Challenge to the Intellectual Responsibility of Educators." *Phi Delta Kappan*, 1972, 53, 297–307.

SILBERMAN, CHARLES E. *Crisis in Black and White* (New York: Random House, 1964).

SIZEMORE, BARBARA A. "Is There a Case for Separate Schools?" *Phi Delta Kappan*, 1972, 53, 281–284.

Southern School News, Nashville, Tenn. (monthly).

Transaction, III, 6, 1966.

9

excellence and education

Excellence: a single word which implies the highest level of quality in any field of endeavor. It does not matter whether we speak of the work of a skilled craftsman, or a student's academic performance, or the talent of an artist. Excellence, perfection, is the goal for those who have pride in themselves and what they do, and who have the potential for reaching it. It is this goal toward which, Keppel wrote, the third revolution in American education is aimed.

The Quality of Education

We have moved far along the road to victory in Keppel's first two revolutions in American education—quantity and equality—although much needs yet to be done as earlier chapters have shown. Now we seek to increase quality in education for the benefit of the individual and the nation. In the early stages of this third revolution, John W. Gardner wrote of the importance of the drive toward excellence.

john w. gardner

Toning Up the Whole Society

A conception which embraces many kinds of excellence at many levels is the only one which fully accords with the richly varied potentialities of mankind; it is the only one which will permit high morale throughout the society.

Our society cannot achieve greatness unless individuals at many levels of ability accept the need for high standards of performance and strive to achieve those standards within the limits possible for them. We want the highest conceivable excellence, of course, in the activities crucial to our effectiveness and creativity as a society; but that isn't enough. If the man in the street says, "Those fellows at the top have to be good, but I'm just a slob and can act like one"—then our days of greatness are behind us. We must foster a conception of excellence which may be applied to every degree of ability and to every socially acceptable activity. A missile may blow up on its launching pad because the designer was incompetent or because the mechanic who adjusted the last valve was incompetent. [note: Gardner's prediction unfortunately was accurate. The tragic loss of three American astronauts in January, 1967, was attributed in part to just such human failure.] The same is true of everything else in our society. We need excellent physicists and excellent mechanics. We need excellent cabinet members and excellent first-grade teachers. The tone and fiber of our society depend upon a persuasive and almost universal striving for good performance.

Gardner, John W. *Excellence* (New York: Harper and Brothers, 1961, pp. 131–134).

And we are not going to get that kind of striving, that kind of alert and proud attention to performance, unless we can instruct the whole society in a conception of excellence that leaves room for everybody who is willing to strive—a conception of excellence which means that whoever I am or whatever I am doing, provided that I am engaged in a socially acceptable activity, some kind of excellence is within my reach. . . .

We cannot meet the challenge facing our free society unless we can achieve and maintain a high level of morale and drive throughout the society. . . . Men must have goals which, in their eyes, merit effort and commitment; and they must believe that their efforts will win them self-respect and the respect of others.

This is the condition of society we must work toward. Then, unhampered by popular attitudes disparaging excellence, we can dedicate ourselves to the cultivation of distinction and a sense of quality. We can demand the best of our most gifted, most talented, most spirited youngsters. And we can render appropriate honor to that striving for excellence which has produced so many of mankind's greatest achievements.

It is important to bear in mind that we are now talking about an approach to excellence and a conception of excellence that will bring a whole society to the peak of performance. The gifted individual absorbed in his own problems of creativity and workmanship may wish to set himself much narrower and very much more severe standards of excellence. The critic concerned with a particular development in art, let us say, may wish to impose a far narrower and more specialized criterion of excellence. This is understandable. But we are concerned with the broader objective of toning up a whole society.

This broader objective is critically important, even for those who have set themselves far loftier (and narrower) personal standards of excellence. We cannot have islands of excellence in a sea of slovenly indifference to standards. In an era when the masses of people were mute and powerless it may have been possible for a tiny minority to maintain high standards regardless of their surroundings. But today the masses of people are neither mute nor powerless. As consumers, as voters, as the source of Public Opinion, they heavily influence levels of taste and performance. They can create a climate supremely inimical to standards of any sort.

I am not saying that we can expect every man to be excellent. It would please me if this were possible: I am not one of those who believe that a goal is somehow unworthy if everyone can achieve it. But those who achieve excellence will be few at best. All too many lack the qualities of mind or spirit which would allow them to conceive excellence as a goal, or to achieve it if they conceived it.

But many more can achieve it than now do. Many, many more can *try* to achieve it than now do. *And the society is bettered not only by those who achieve it but by those who are trying.*

The broad conception of excellence we have outlined must be built on two foundation stones—and both of them exist in our society:

1. *A pluralistic approach to values.* American society has always leaned toward such pluralism. We need only be true to our deepest inclinations to honor the many facets and depths and dimensions of human experiment and to seek the many kinds of excellence of which the human spirit is capable.

2. *A universally honored philosophy of individual fulfillment.* We have such a philosophy, deeply embedded in our tradition. Whether we have given it the prominence it deserves is the question which we must now explore.

Gardner's message hit a responsive chord in the American nervous system. It was a broader conception than that in the National Defense Education Act of 1958, and it was unlimited in its appeal to all the people, for Gardner considered even the effort toward excellence important.

To achieve this highly desirable goal in American education, we must look to different aspects of the educational system: 1) the teachers; 2) the curriculum; and 3) research and development. These are the areas in which the quality of education is determined.

Teacher Recruitment and Retention

Some years ago a professor from the University of Zagreb, Yugoslavia, visited us. We were very interested in his views of teaching under Communism in his country as compared with teaching under Communism in Russia, for Russian professors enjoyed great prestige and Yugoslavian professors seemed to have less prestige. He agreed that the prestige was highly desirable, but said that he would take less of that and more of the personal freedom he had in Zagreb. There is, perhaps, a moral for us in this incident. Prestige is indeed an incentive for good teaching and for continuing in the profession, but a teacher also needs the freedom of non-professional citizens and the freedom to think in ways that do not necessarily conform to the ideas of a few citizens or a few administrators.

A generation and more ago, the local American school teacher was held in high esteem by the community. Part of the respect for her (his) position no doubt stemmed from the fact that she had had more education than most of the population. However, many restrictions were placed on the teacher's personal life, not the least of which was one which obliged female teachers to resign their position if they married. In the 1860's and 1870's,

> Male teachers were not immune from social supervision. A young bachelor named Abel Samson created a near scandal when he was observed walking with a female companion. But Abel fought back. In a letter to the editor of the *New York Teacher*, he said: "I do not intend, for $35 per month, to resign all the privileges guaranteed to me by the social compact. I am a citizen, and I shall exercise the immunities

of citizenship as I deem proper, the whole town of L_____ notwithstanding." If the young lady in question had designs on Abel, she got an assist from the editor, who advised him to take one last walk with her—down the aisle to the minister.[1]

Today, teachers may marry and even teach while pregnant in most communities. They have more personal freedom in urban areas than they did thirty years ago, and most rural areas have also relaxed their restrictions on teachers. They are no longer, however, on "pedestals." Suburban parents are often better educated than the teachers, and some have no hesitation in telling the teacher so. Pupils brought up in a permissive atmosphere frequently tell the teacher what to do, at least after the first few grades. Disorderly and delinquent youths threaten the teacher's very life. Under these conditions, who would want to teach? On the other hand, there are many who enter the teaching profession on a temporary basis while they wait for the right husband, or until their first child is born, or as a step on the ladder to some other goal. Who would want some of these as teachers? "At one time the teacher had a single major professional responsibility: to impart knowledge to the young. Now she is expected to be a knowledge specialist, a counselor, a co-ordinator of instruction, and a surrogate parent."[2] The burdens mount.

The question then becomes, if we desire to have excellent teachers, how can we attract *and* retain good teachers? One answer involves the restoration of respect for teachers. There must be a change from the attitude that "Those who can, do; those who can't, teach." If, via vastly improved teacher preparation programs, we can see a better-qualified teacher, community and parental respect will increase. If the teacher is herself (or himself) a better model for identification as an adult and as a representative of society and authority, student respect will grow. If a teacher can respect herself or himself as a member of a fine profession, she is more likely to remain in teaching or to return to it after child-bearing, and he is also more likely to remain in the classroom.

Figure 9.1

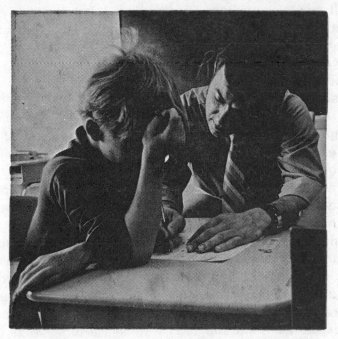

Norman Hurst (Stock, Boston)

Today's teachers work under more advantageous conditions than ever before. Like this elementary school teacher, they teach with tools tailor-made to fit the particular needs of their children and class sizes are often adjusted to meet individual learning requirements. With these advances, however, have come increased responsibilities to themselves, their schools, and their communities.

An "easy" way to attract good or better teachers, some say, is simply to raise salaries at both beginning and maximum levels. This would certainly make teaching more attractive to men who are the support of their families. However, the problem of large salary increases poses a financial problem for school boards with limited resources. There is considerable debate, too, about whether salary scales should provide for annual increments on an automatic basis or whether they should be based on merit.[3] Increases in the cost of living are such that some annual pay raise is warranted, but the idea of merit pay raises instead of or combined with the yearly increments stirs up much controversy among teachers, administrators, and school board members. Contracts negotiated between unionized teachers and school boards usually resolve these questions in a salary schedule that is, at least on the surface, mutually satisfactory.

Another suggestion is to establish "levels" of teachers in the grades somewhat resembling the professional structure in higher education. That is, have different strata for beginning teachers, experienced but not outstanding teachers, and master teachers. The last title would be conferred on experienced teachers who exhibit qualities of excellence in the classroom. The master teacher would have not only titular prestige within the profession, but would have also increased responsibilities within the teaching field, rather than moving into administration. It is assumed that the three, or more, levels would have pay differentials as well as descriptive differences. In schools where team teaching is used, the master teacher frequently heads the team.[4] Master teachers might also serve as guides to beginning teachers, a responsibility which would benefit both pupils and the novice instructor.

In terms of whom and what the teacher teaches, more opportunity for teaching one's specialty might be offered, especially in the light of revised teacher preparation programs which require each education major to have a content major as well (see Chapter 10). Such an opportunity can be provided within the framework of team teaching, or on a less formal basis. Or perhaps the teacher would simply find greater satisfaction in working with more homogeneous groups of students. Continuous progress plans such as those in Appleton, Wisconsin,[5] and Philadelphia, Pa., and elsewhere are attempts to meet this alternative.

Continuous progress or non-graded plans such as those mentioned, as well as those in other communities, reflect the increasing concern of educators for the appropriate placement of pupils in classes and for the more efficient utilization of teaching personnel. Homogeneous grouping, which is an essential ingredient of such programs, does narrow the range of abilities in a given subject matter area and thus permit the teacher to teach more efficiently. At present at the elementary level, nongraded classes are held primarily in the reading and arithmetic fields. Part of the difficulty in expanding the non-graded concept stems from this very limitation. "The second limitation on the development of a real breakthrough at the primary level is the fact that the intermediate grades consti-tute the superstructure of the elementary school. Their rigidity has stultified progress and created a major stumbling block to the full development of the ungraded primary."[6] There is also, of course, the administrative barrier to any reorganization of a school in as complete a fashion as Brown suggests—a multi-phased curriculum continuum. Translated, this means a custom-tailored curriculum for each individual student which will meet his needs and abilities rather than the system's convenience. Brown gives an example of a student at the inter-mediate level:

> . . . who is capable of doing seventh grade mathematics: he may be reading at only the third grade level while he may have a fourth grade knowledge of science and the talent of a fifth grader in art. If, rather than all ten-year-old youngsters being in the fifth grade, they spent their day being taught at the level of their achievement by various teachers, the curriculum of each individual would reflect these factors of achievement. His course of study would be so constructed that he would receive special instruction in reading in a small class, and would be scheduled for extra time in this subject.[7]

In schools that have adopted computer-assisted instruction, individually prescribed instruction, open classrooms, and simi-lar flexible plans, this type of individual progress is a daily occurrence.

It is easy to understand why teachers would sense a chal-lenge in such a school, at any grade level, and also why many of the behavior problems with which they are plagued would disappear from the classroom. Pupil frustration would be con-siderably lower. Teacher frustration, too, with the slow learner or disadvantaged would be reduced. Just as students have intra-individual differences with regard to different subject matter, so do teachers have differences within *them*selves in their ability to teach children of varying abilities. Individual progress is, however, more demanding of the teacher's time and imagination than is the more traditional form of classroom teaching.

Teachers' unions frequently demand a limit to the pupil-teacher ratio of 25:1 or 30:1 in an attempt to make teaching more attractive to their members. While this may sound highly desirable, research on class size has indicated that a standard class size is not necessarily optimal for all learning situations. Some subjects or units can be taught effectively to large lecture groups, while others are best presented to no more than a dozen students at a time. Flexibility of class size, with some deference to the teacher's capabilities and judgments, might encourage more teachers to remain in the classroom.

Working conditions in the school, as in industry, also affect teacher recruitment and retention. The masochists and the insecure enjoy working for a dictatorial employer. Most teachers, however, as most employees in other organizations, prefer to work with a helpful and cooperative supervisor.[8] Congenial colleagues, too, who work *with* one, not in competition with each other, help to create pleasant working conditions. Access to library and audio-visual resources help to make employment in a particular school more desirable. Fewer demands of a clerical nature, which can be handled by teacher aides, would also free the teacher for the job she was educated to perform. The reduction in clerical and other non-teaching tasks is also among the negotiable items in teachers' union contracts.

There are also those who propose greater flexibility of certification requirements in order to recruit more teachers. That is not to say there should be no certification requirements, but rather that it should be possible for someone with high qualifications in a particular specialty to serve as a "visiting" teacher without benefit of certification. It would be understood that such a person would have an understanding of children and an ability to communicate with them on an appropriate level. Many college professors and research scholars have not had required education courses, but are excellent teachers of astronomy, or French, or political science, and would welcome the opportunity to share their expertise with pre-college students. They cannot do so at present because they lack specific courses. Albert Einstein, in fact, could not have taught physics in a secondary school. There are also people in the community, with or without college backgrounds, who have unusual experience or ability in a field relevant to elementary or high school subjects, and who, as "visiting teachers" or "resource personnel," can add much to the curriculum. Both groups, serving in these capacities, can bring quality as well as information to public education, at least on a part-time basis. In many school districts, such resource people are used to great advantage.

Finally, there have been suggestions that outstanding public school teachers receive governmental commendations and awards, on the order of the Christian and Mary Lindback awards given at several universities to outstanding professors. These might be granted by local school boards, the state board of education, and/or the Federal government, and would include a cash grant as well as a plaque or written statement. We might take an example from the following century-old teacher evaluation:

"District No. 14. [Dame's.] Prudential Committee, Wm. Watson. Mary S. Eaton of Meredith, an accomplished lady and a superior scholar, taught this school. Everything to commend; nothing to censure. Parents do not realize how much they are indebted to a good teacher."[9]

Assuming that some or all of these suggestions might be implemented in some school districts, and that quality teachers are recruited and retained, what of the curriculum they teach?

The Curriculum

A basic question in establishing a curriculum is "Who shall determine what is to be taught?" Other questions arise from this:

1. What sources shall be used in determining what is to be taught?
2. Shall a comprehensive curriculum be provided for all children and youth?
3. How shall a balance be struck and maintained in what is taught?
4. How shall the curriculum be financed?
5. How shall the subjects taught be financed?[10]

In addition, there is a sixth question: are there alternatives to traditional curricula?

Beyond these questions, there are others. How can we measure the quality of the curriculum? Do we count the number of National Merit Scholars or other scholarship winners from a given high school? Or the percentage of students continuing on to higher education? Or the number below and above the national average on a standardized achievement test? Some comparisons among high school curricula have been based on student achievement levels on College Entrance Examination Board tests or the New York State Regents' examinations. These studies tell us the quality of preparation for the exams and a little about the ability of the students who take them, but they do not tell us much about the quality of curriculum content for these students, or for the students who do not take the tests. Again, information secured from employers does give an indication of how well the content of a curriculum has prepared an employee for a specific job, but allowance must be made for the relative native ability of the individual to master that content.

College preparatory programs until recent years were largely classical in their orientation: literature, mathematics, Latin and a second foreign language, art, music, etc. The emphasis was on learning for "its own sake" (and to pass the examinations). There was little articulation between what was taught in a high school course and a college course in the same subject-matter area, and less articulation between the elementary school and the secondary school curriculum. Professionals using the subject-matter in research or practical applications had little influence on either the textbook or the course content, particularly below the college level. Changes have been introduced in recent years, however. The growth of vocational education programs and curriculum expansion into such courses as driver education, audio-visual techniques, and sports, have caused an increase in practical applications of classroom learning. There have been strong student and professional demands to make classroom learning more relevant to everyday life. College professors have been active participants in the reshaping of curricula from the nursery level through high school. In this connection, one thinks of Suppes of Stanford working on elementary school arithmetic, Bruner of Harvard developing "Man: A Course of Study" for fifth-graders, and the numerous mathematicians who created the "new math" for students at all grade levels. As colleges have become more flexible in their attitude toward graduation requirements, their admissions directors have also permitted greater diversity in high school credits offered for college admission.

In the pre-Sputnik era, both elementary and secondary schools were strongly influenced by progressive educational theory which centered on the group and non-competition in the classroom. The result seemed to be a lack of challenge to the bright and emphasis on the average, or as some have called it, "mediocrity" in the classroom. This was roundly condemned by critics of American education such as James B. Conant, Arthur Bestor, and Martin Mayer. In his book on *Education and Liberty*, even before Sputnik, Conant urged that ". . . we must endeavor to combine the British concern for training the 'natural aristocracy of talents' with the American insistence on general education for *all* future citizens."[11] Even at that time, he urged that secondary schools be comprehensive high schools in order to uphold the principles of democracy in education. He repeated his arguments in *The Child, the Parent, and the State* (1959), and after studying high schools across the nation, synthesized much of the criticism in a constructive way.

james b. conant

The Comprehensive
High School

conclusion

I can sum up my conclusions in a few sentences. The number of small high schools must be drastically reduced through district reorganization. Aside from this important change, I believe no radical alteration in the basic pattern of American education is necessary in order to improve our public high schools. If all the high schools were functioning as well as some I have visited, the education of all American youth would be satisfactory, except for the study of foreign languages and the guidance of the more able girls. Most of the schools which I found unsatisfactory in one or more respects could become satisfactory by relatively minor changes, though I have no doubt that there are schools even of sufficient size where major improvements in organization and instruction would be in order. If the fifty-five schools I have visited, all of which have a good reputation, are at all representative of American public high schools, I think one general criticism would be in order: The academically talented student, as a rule, is not being sufficiently challenged, does not work hard enough, and his program of academic subjects is not of sufficient range. . . . As I have indicated . . . , a correction of this situation in many instances will depend upon an altered attitude of the community quite as much as upon action by a school board or the school administration.

Conant, James B. *The American High School Today* (New York: McGraw-Hill Book Company, 1959), pp. 22–32, 40. By permission of the author.

Since the publication of Conant's study of the high schools, and his subsequent books, as well as those by others, there has been a marked trend toward curriculum reform and emphasis on quality education for all whatever their ability level might be. The consolidation of school districts is in part a result of Conant's recommendations that a good comprehensive high school needed at least one hundred in the graduating class, for otherwise the school could not justify an adequate variety of courses for the academically talented, the average, and the less able. In the area of curriculum reform, a number of exciting projects are in progress, with varying degrees of success.

There has been a rash of books and studies, for example, concerned with the teaching of reading at the primary level.[12] Where the "look-say" or Gestalt method had been dominant for several years, phonics were re-instated or other techniques developed. Physics and mathematics professors became involved with the revision of courses in their disciplines at the elementary and secondary levels.

Today the college math and science departments are busy revising their lower-level offerings, because rapidly rising numbers of entrants already know what used to be introductory college work, and have gone on to what were once second- or even third-level problems. Mathematical topics like spherical geometry, matrix algebra, probability, Cartesian geometry, and calculus are to be found in large numbers of high schools, and some students will have made the acquaintance of Boolean algebra and topology. The high-school physics course is now in many schools more sophisticated than what the colleges used to offer . . . , and increasing numbers of high schools are moving into programs in biology and chemistry which give students a grasp of the real procedures as well as the descriptive vocabulary of the field.[13]

Over a dozen "new math" programs are being used throughout the country, much to the confusion of parents, and with success in some programs and lack of it in others. Under the auspices of the National Defense Education Act and the National Science Foundation, revised curricula are being taught in college workshops to teachers already in the schools. Jerome Bruner put forth his theory that even complex concepts can be taught at the primary level in simple form, expanded upon in the intermediate grades, and further elaborated upon in the secondary school—a spiral curriculum.[14] Implementation of this theory can be seen particularly in new mathematics textbooks, starting with the first grade book.

> An examination of new textbooks, experimental studies, pamphlets, and enrichment material reveals such topics as sets, numeration systems other than the decimal system, modular numbers, number line, functions, slide rule, equations, sentences, logic, operation with sets, exponents, and geometry. It is no longer correct to think of elementary school mathematics as only arithmetic. Many authors of elementary school textbooks, although the titles of the books are generally arithmetic, now include topics in algebra, geometry, sets, and numeration systems.[15]

In general, the definition of education has been re-evaluated. An attitude has developed ". . . that education was not only a memorizing of the mind to weigh facts, to arrive at rules by testing hypotheses—a training of the mind to understand."[16]

In recent years, a number of alternatives to schooling have appeared on the educational scene. At one extreme is Illich's proposal to "deschool society." He has argued that ". . . students learn that education is valuable when it is acquired in the school through a graded process of consumption; that the degree of success the individual will enjoy in society depends on the amount of learning he consumes; and that learning about the world is more valuable than learning from the world."[17] He advocates instead, "Access to reality [which] constitutes a fundamental alternative in education to a system that only purports to teach *about* it."[18] Other educational alternatives may seem only slightly less radical. The Philadelphia Parkway Program is housed in a school building only in a technical sense. It utilizes the facilities of the art museum, the

Franklin Institute, an insurance company, local hospitals, and similar public and private institutions. Alternative high schools in the area that grew out of the Parkway Program experience have relatively unstructured curricula, but a wealth of optional activities in the community from which a student can construct his schedule of learning experiences. Learning does occur, but it is a far cry from that which takes place in the traditional high school.

Work-study programs are not an innovation of the 70's, but their expansion to students of all capabilities and backgrounds is a change from similar programs in the depression era. These newer ones generally involve academic classes for half a day and work experience for the other half day, even for college-bound students. (Earlier work-study programs were designed principally for students planning to go into retailing or a trade immediately following graduation.) Such programs are frequently funded under one or another piece of Federal legislation and are administered through the Office of Education.

At the elementary level, the alternative to tradition is seen most often in adaptations of the "open classroom," imported from England. Since the best descriptions of this alternative are from Britain, the open classroom and "integrated day" concepts will be discussed in Chapter 12.

The complaints of parents about the quality of the education provided for their children and the disputes arising from desegregation efforts have led to another unorthodox alternative—educational vouchers. Under this plan, developed at the Center for the Study of Public Policy under the auspices of the Office of Economic Opportunity (OEO), parents are given vouchers equivalent to the per-pupil expenditure of the school district. They may then select the school their child will attend and pay the voucher to that school. The school must, for its part, accept those who have selected it as a first choice up to a stated proportion of the total enrollment.

"Most voucher schemes envision a diverse system of schools which are equally accessible to all students and supported totally by public funds collected according to

people's ability to pay and desire or need for education. . . .
The public monopoly over educational policy expressed
through single boards of education is replaced by a number
of boards of education which are accountable to the parents
of the school's students. . . .

"Beyond admissions and funding requirements, accountability guaranteed by state regulations of voucher schools
would be of two broad types: consumer protection and
minimum educational standards."[19]

The nation's first educational voucher experiment began
in the summer of 1972 in the Alum Rock School District of San
Jose, California. Parents of the 4,000 elementary school children in the district received vouchers worth $680 for each child
in grades K–6 and $970 per child in grades 7 and 8, which they
could "spend" on one of 21 school program options. Some of
the options were fairly traditional; six stress a single subject
area (Math-Science, Cultural Arts), others emphasize "learning by doing" or concern with the future. An Educational
Voucher Advisory Committee, composed of the involved parents, advises the Alum Rock Board of Education, which retains
control of the OEO-sponsored experiment. In this initital situation, only public schools are involved, although the original
proposal included private and parochial schools as well.[20]

Another alternative sponsored by the OEO, but one which
failed, was the much publicized and relatively short-lived "performance contracting." The goal of performance contracting
was the improvement to a stipulated amount of student performance in basic skills. Contractors were to be paid only for
each student who succeeded in reaching the goal. They were
free to use any instructional systems, instructional techniques,
and audio-visual aids that they felt would be effective. These
generally included programmed instruction and behavior modification techniques. The student populations were in schools
with the worst achievement records in reading and arithmetic,
and represented every major ethnic group. To the disappoint-
ment of the OEO and the educational psychologists who had
developed the research program: "In only two of the 20 possible cases was the mean gain of either the control or experimental students as much as one grade level."[21,22]

Related to all of these alternatives is the quest for excellence in education under the label "accountability." Demands for accountability have stemmed from negative reactions to the semiliteracy of too many high school graduates and the increase in school expenditures with decreasing effectiveness, rather than the positive goal of excellence itself. Students have long been held accountable for their learning behavior through test scores, grades, report cards, and promotion practices. What the new accountability requires is that teachers and schools be held responsible for their success or failure in having students learn at a reasonable and continuing rate of progress. First, the goals of education must be determined and clearly defined. Then the criteria by which achievement of the goals will be measured and the means of measurement must be developed. In several situations, this has led to legislative mandates for the statement of detailed behavioral objectives and the use of objective tests to assess whether or not the objectives are being met.[23] Since psychologists and educators have been trying for years to move away from the impersonal objective test, this facet of accountability is received professionally with mixed reactions. Finally, accurate reporting to the responsible authorities is a fundamental aspect of accountability.

The concept of performance goals is a familiar one in industry, but it is new to education. It is a legitimate demand in view of the escalating school taxes and deteriorating achievement of recent years. Under accountability, performance criteria will be clear for students, teachers, parents, and school administrators on a scale ranging from the goal for the school year to daily progress objectives. Some of the criteria involve the concept of mastering subjects rather than just a "passing" grade. This appears to be one appropriate response to Gardner's plea for a turn from mediocrity to excellence.

Furthermore, there have been, in the wake of C. P. Snow's little volume on "the two cultures," efforts to bring the sciences and the humanities closer together so that workers in one area may understand what workers in another field think and do. Such a rapprochement is also slowly occurring between academic (i.e., non-education) professors and educators.

Research and Development

Some of the curriculum reforms mentioned above are based on theory, others are the fruit of research. Much of the research and development activity has centered on the instruments of learning, the hypothesis being that an improvement in tools will bring an improvement in the quality of education.

Technological advances have made possible language laboratories, "teaching machines," and more sophisticated audiovisual techniques. These offer greater freedom for each student to learn at his own pace. Videotape and educational television have had a tremendous impact on education, making it possible for gifted teachers to reach thousands of students at one time or in several locations. Major corporations have coordinated their efforts with textbook publishers and producers of other educational equipment, with the result that Xerox Corporation, IBM, Time, Inc., and Minnesota Mining and Manufacturing Corporation, are now influencing American education in a direct way.

Within the framework of existing school systems, research and development are increasingly apparent. Research is supported by industry and private funds as well as the government and universities. The structure of the school system is being changed from the prevalent 6-3-3 pattern introduced some forty-odd years ago to a K-4-4-4 or 8-4 or 6-2-2-2 pattern. (This has affected teacher certification, too, as will be seen in the next chapter.) Team teaching, as noted earlier, is providing an opportunity for specialization as well as administrative responsibility combined with teaching. The use of three learning tracks, suggested by Conant, has helped individual students to learn more effectively where the track system is properly utilized, although such homogeneous grouping is still a source of controversy in education circles. Conant recommended that . . .

In the required subjects and those elected by students with a wide range of ability, the students should be grouped

Figure 9.2 Computers in Education

Patricia Hollander Gross (Stock, Boston)

Computer instructional systems (CBI) are designed to teach many pupils simultaneously. In New York City, the CBI provides individual instruction in reading and mathematics to 6000 students every day.

according to ability, subject by subject. For example, in English, American history, ninth-grade algebra, biology, and physical science, there should be at least three types of classes—one for the more able in the subject, another for the large group whose ability is about average, and another for the very slow readers who should be handled by special teachers. The middle group might be divided into two or three sections according to the students' abilities in the subject in question. This type of grouping is not to be confused with across-the-board grouping according to which a given student is placed in a particular section in *all* courses. Under the scheme here recommended, for example, a student may be in the top section in English but the middle section in history or ninth-grade algebra.[24]

This plan recognizes not only inter-individual differences in ability, but also intra-individual differences. It would enable each student to strive for excellence within the range of his own competencies.

Innovations in curriculum content and time schedules are prevalent in urban and suburban schools across the country. In an article in a popular women's magazine, in fact, the ten "top" high schools in the nation were chosen in large measure because they ". . . use new methods of teaching and new ways of learning."[25] The system which refuses to experiment or to change is the exception in these times.

Which philosophies should be retained and which modified? Which curriculum content can be discarded and which must be kept in fairness to coming generations? How much experimentation is fair to students? Who is to judge which changes are worthwhile and/or justified, and which are non-beneficial? Or, as Hanna wrote,

> How shall we as a nation move to restore a dynamic balance? How shall we face a future so difficult and yet so filled with promise for achieving the good life for all men? Shall we leave the future to luck and to chance? Or are there things we can do to assure victory for all mankind? Certainly part of the solution will be found in an improved school curriculum.
>
> The following proposal is presented with the hope that it may stimulate nationwide discussion: *Our desire to perpetuate and advance our cherished national values and institutions requires the creation of a nongovernmental, nationwide commission for curriculum research and development.*[26]

As Hanna and others have indicated, it is not feasible for small school districts, or perhaps any except the very large school districts such as New York, Philadelphia, Los Angeles, Boston, and Chicago, to maintain a research and development staff of the magnitude required today. Relatively few school districts have enough manpower to keep up with the day-to-day administrative tasks, let alone the design and development of new curricula; the evaluation of assorted experimental programs; the choice of textbooks, filmstrips, tape recordings, instructional films, television programs, etc., suitable for pupils in grades Kindergarten through 12; and the publishing of curriculum guides and evaluations of their efforts.

Why can't school districts perform all of these activities effectively? There is, first of all, a shortage of trained manpower able to work competently in the areas of curriculum research and development. Secondly, there is a veritable deluge of printed material alone each year, and the necessary time for reviewing new and revised editions of textbooks is not available. Teachers cannot do the job by themselves because of their classroom obligations, in-service training programs, and personal responsibilities. Administrators cannot always spare the needed hours at the right time for previewing visual instructional materials. A third problem is the tremendous range of knowledge which now exists. Even in one field of scholarship, mathematics, for example, there are presently ten or twelve major "new math" programs at the elementary and secondary levels. To select those most appropriate to the needs of students in a particular school district from the major and lesser well-known programs requires a high degree of scholarship, as well as ample time for visiting other school districts where the different programs are used, even before one can sit down to evaluate the relative merits of each program. Multiply this single example by the number of subjects currently offered in the schools, and the magnitude of the curriculum research and development problem is easily seen.

It is also recognized that our knowledge in various fields is expanding at such a rapid rate that what is taught in the schools is outdated almost immediately. In genetics, for example, the topic of heredity may still be taught below the college level in terms of chromosomes and genes, with little or no reference to the DNA molecule. The tendency in school districts is to use textbooks for several years, in order to derive maximum benefit from the investment in them, so that it is quite conceivable that the information known about the workings of DNA with reference to heredity may not become part of the curriculum for ten, or even fifteen, years after its original publication. Geography has suffered similarly. History books have been focused on pre-1940 events to such a degree that parents are startled to see World War II "covered" in twenty pages, and the past quarter-century telescoped into one chapter. The physical sciences have been advanced so rapidly that what a ninth-grader learns today will be out-of-date by the time he enters college.

World events and scientific developments are occurring too rapidly today for any individual to keep abreast of them all. That is why Hanna proposed a national commission for curriculum research and development. Its job would be to study the multitude of experimental programs and to encourage creative use of them at the state and local levels. Since the commission would be advisory rather than dictatorial, its influence and authority would stem from the quality of its advice. Hanna's concept is one of guidance for school districts, not prescription, and not a national curriculum such as is discussed in Chapter 10.

This proposal should be studied in conjunction with Conant's suggestion of an "Interstate Commission for Planning a Nationwide Educational Policy,"[27] and reports of meetings of the Education Commission of the States.[28]

What Do Teachers Teach?

Students of a generation ago would barely recognize some of what is taught in today's schools, and grandparents can scarcely believe that what they see is in any way related to the elementary school they attended. The pressure for quality in education has caused a revision of curriculum from the nursery school through twelfth grade and the college years.

Where the nursery school, privately-operated or church-related, was basically a "play school", today it may offer minute segments of traditional courses. Three and four-year-olds learn courtesy phrases and counting in French or Spanish; they speak of geometric shapes ("An ellipse looks like an egg.") which their parents and grandparents became acquainted with in tenth grade geometry; they learn about climate, maps, cities and states; and they still learn to function smoothly in a group.

Some nursery schools also prepare the little ones for reading by teaching the alphabet (reading and writing as well as reciting it) and numbers. Kindergarten, where the last items might have been taught ten years ago, now concentrates on reading readiness, fundamentals of arithmetic, and science, although, here, too, the atmosphere is still more relaxed than in the grades.

At the primary school level, the emphasis is on learning to read, write, and compute to a degree which will make these skills tools in the upper grades rather than having them be major subjects of the day at that time. Grades are still given in grades 4-6 for reading, mathematics, and penmanship, but the time spent on them is not as disproportionate as in the primary grades. In the first three years, social studies are introduced, usually in the form of "getting to know your neighborhood," and science experiments of an elementary nature are performed by the children as well as the teacher. In some school districts, oral French or Spanish may be taught, but this is more often begun in fourth grade or at the junior high school level. The intermediate grades (4-6) are a period of expansion, using the tools learned earlier to read about historical events and about other countries. With more people traveling around the country and abroad than ever before, and with the advent of television, the study of other peoples and countries is more meaningful to youngsters than ever before. Some literature may be introduced in the reading anthologies. Mathematics includes decimals, fractions, and a second round of concepts basic to algebra and geometry.

Probably the most common innovation in the junior high school years has been the introduction of mathematics programs which include principles and examples formerly taught only in college (see Mayer's comments, *supra*). Science, too, is of increased importance, with physics and chemistry as part of the curriculum in a general way.

At the senior high school level, students are able to take college-level courses in their twelfth year in many schools, enabling them to enter college with advanced standing. It was a most unusual high school, a generation ago, which offered courses in calculus, or philosophy, or psychology, or languages other than Latin and the modern Romance tongues. Today, Russian, Italian, Hebrew, Swahili, Chinese, and other non-Western languages are offered to high school students. English, mathematics, science, and history are still present in the curriculum, of course, but with renewed vitality.

Much of what teachers teach now reflects Bruner's "spiral curriculum" as well as the often-cited desire for quality in education. However, they often have to return to college classes to understand the more advanced materials themselves. It has been said that knowledge is doubling presently at the rate of every ten years. What the teacher learned in school is quickly outdated or updated, and part of the problem of securing quality in education is to keep the teacher well-informed in a multitude of areas. The elementary school teacher, who still often functions in a self-contained classroom, must keep ahead of her budding scholars who are exposed to much of the new information on television. The secondary school teacher frequently has to unlearn what he learned in school in order to be able to teach a new approach to his subject.

Where Do We Begin?

The renewed search for quality and excellence in education has been received well in university laboratory schools, and in many affluent suburban school districts. It is generally recognized, however, that slum schools need the greatest improvement—if only to bring them up to the minimum desirable standards. Some large cities now have or soon will have schools with enrollments composed mainly (90 percent and more) of educationally disadvantaged youngsters. These students need textbooks with meaningful content, teachers with great understanding as well as special educational qualifications, and a new relationship to schooling which provides them with both the motivation and the opportunity to learn. The emphasis on quality does need to be tempered with a liberal measure of reality, however, and with an awareness that intellectual learning is not the only road to excellence.

earl j. mcgrath

The Meaning of
Academic Excellence

In the present situation it may appear boorish to dub a few
discordant notes into the popular theme of academic excellence.
Yet that is what circumstances require to arouse a keener
awareness of the significance and direction of certain developments in higher education today. Current discussions tend to be
preoccupied with subject matter, students, buildings and
finance, and negligent of matters of basic social and educational philosophy. Too often they completely overlook two
tenets of American higher education.

The first is the revolutionary idea that all citizens in a
democracy should have the opportunity to develop their
abilities to the fullest, not only as a personal right but as a
social necessity. In applying this principle to higher education
we differ from other nations which until very recently have
largely reversed the privileges of advanced learning to the
social and intellectual elite.

The other equally uncommon doctrine holds the institutions of higher education have a responsibility to create and
disseminate knowledge related to all aspects of modern man's
multifaceted world. Hence, unlike other nations which limit
instruction to the liberal arts and the older professional
disciplines, our colleges and universities offer a great variety
of instruction and conduct research in agriculture, business
administration, pharmacy, home economics, accounting,
medical technology, food marketing and dozens of other
fields. . . .

McGrath, Earl J. By permission. "The Meaning of Academic Excellence." In Ehlers and Lee, *op. cit.*, pp. 289–292.

A basic fact on which any realistic discussion of academic excellence in American higher education must rest is, therefore, the unshakable determination of our people to open wider the doors of higher education. Accordingly, as far as our nation is concerned, academic merit cannot be defined in terms of the intellectual capacities of ten or fifteen per cent of the population. . . .

. . .

Current proposals to raise the intellectual level in colleges and universities may result in more competent engineers, physicists, historians, medical technologists, businessmen and social workers, though some thoughtful educational leaders doubt even this outcome. But efforts to strengthen and improve higher education by raising standards of performance within traditional patterns can hardly be expected to meet the larger social needs of our time.

The difficulty in enlarging the concept of academic excellence arises out of the lack of reliable measures of growth in qualities other than knowledge and a limited range of intellectual abilities. . . .

The greatest weakness in present evaluations of the outcomes of education relates to a trait not closely connected with the capacity to absorb knowledge—an abiding interest in things of the mind. Some of the so-called late bloomers, the students with mediocre or poor high school records, who were intellectually awakened by an interested and inspiring college teacher, dramatically highlight the need to appraise the outcomes of such teaching. . . .

Excellence is a highly desirable goal, indeed, but it is important also to educate highly competent carpenters as well as brilliant physicists, to permit those who hear "a different drummer" to pursue their paths, to help the handicapped help themselves toward achievement, and to provide opportunities for all to learn and to contribute to a great nation.

Summary

Excellence in education means many things. There are efforts to improve the curriculum, to be more selective in teacher selection and retention, and to implement a variety of alternative approaches to the teaching-learning process in and out of the classroom. The demand for accountability by teachers and school districts is, perhaps, one answer to the increasing problem of mediocre rather than good or excellent achievement, but ignores the multiple causes of student failure. Not even the most competent and sympathetic teacher can overcome single-handedly the effects of malnutrition, broken homes, negative self-concept, poverty, and emotional distress.

It will take more than statements of objectives and accountability reports, moreover, to remove mediocrity and promote excellence in the schools. Changes have to be made at all levels of education. Permission to enroll in a teacher education program must be based on more stringent criteria, with emphasis on the prospective teacher's attitudes and motives as well as grades. Students in all grades must be offered a variety of techniques for learning and even a variety of teachers so that no students will be adversely affected by prolonged contact with mediocre teachers, until all such teachers can be phased out of school systems.

Endnotes

1. Bonn, Myrtle. "Teachers Then and Now," *American Education*, 3, Oct., 1967, p. 15.
2. Aubrey, Roger F. "What is the Role of the Elementary-School Teacher?", *Elementary School Journal*, 68, (Mar. 1968), p. 277.
3. National Education Association. "Classroom Teachers Speak on Professional Negotiations" (Washington, D.C.: National Education Association, 1963).

4. Morse, Arthur D. *Schools of Tomorrow—Today* (Garden City, N.Y.: Doubleday and Company, 1960), p. 12.

5. *Ibid.*, pp. 27–40.

6. Brown, B. Frank. *The Appropriate Placement School: A Sophisticated Nongraded Curriculum* (West Nyack, N.Y.: Parker Publishing Company, Inc., 1965), p. 66.

7. *Ibid.*, p. 73.

8. National Education Association. "The Professional Family: a Cooperative Approach to Improving Instruction" (Washington, D.C.: National Education Association, 1965).

9. *Annual Reports of the Selectmen, Treasurer, Overseer of the Poor, and School Committee of the Town of Gilford for the Fiscal Year ending March 1, 1873.* Lake Village, N.H., 1873.

10. Herrick, Theral T. "Curriculum Problems: Some Basic Issues," *Teachers College Record*, 60, 1959, pp. 242–244.

11. Conant, James Bryant. *Education and Liberty* (New York: Vintage Books, 1953), p. 87.

12. See particularly, Chall, Jeanne: *Learning to Read: The Great Debate* (New York: McGraw-Hill Book Company, 1967).

13. Mayer, Martin. *Where, When, and Why: Social Studies in American Schools* (New York: Harper and Row, 1962), p. 164.

14. Bruner, Jerome S. *Toward a Theory of Instruction* (New York: W. W. Norton and Company, Inc., 1968) reprint.

15. Rappaport, David. *Understanding and Teaching Elementary School Mathematics* (New York: John Wiley and Sons, 1966), p. 3.

16. Keppel, *op. cit.*, p. 115.

17. Illich, Ivan. "The Alternative to Schooling." *Education Yearbook, 1972–73, op. cit.*, p. 30.

18. *Ibid.*, p. 32.

19. Arons, Stephen. "Equity, option, and vouchers." *Teachers College Record*, 1971, 72, 349–350.

20. Mecklenburger, James. "Vouchers at Alum Rock." *Phi Delta Kappan*, 1972, 54, 23–25.

21. Office of Economic Opportunity. *An Experiment in Performance Contracting: Summary of Preliminary Results*, OEO Pamphlet 3400–5, Washington, D.C.: OEO, February 1972, pp. 17–24.

22. Page, Ellis B. *Educational Psychologist*, 1972 (May), 9.

23. Woodington, Donald D. "Accountability from the viewpoint of a state commissioner of education." *Phi Delta Kappan*, 1972, 54, 95–97.

24. Conant, 1959, *op. cit.*, p. 49.

25. Faber, Nancy. "America's Ten Top High Schools," *Ladies Home Journal*, 85, (May, 1968), p. 66.

26. Hanna, Paul R. "A National Commission for Curriculum Research and Development," In *Contemporary American Education* ed., Dropkin, Full, and Schwarcz (New York: The Macmillan Company, 1965), p. 530.

27. Conant, James Bryant. *Shaping Educational Policy* (New York: McGraw-Hill Book Company, 1964) pp. 123 ff.

28. Pierce, Wendell H. "Education Commission of the States," *NEA Journal*, 56, (March, 1967), pp. 30–31.

For Further Reading

AUBREY, ROGER F. "What is the Role of the Elementary-School Teacher?" *Elementary School Journal*, 68, (March, 1968), 277–283.

BLOOM, BENJAMIN S. (ed.) *Taxonomy of Educational Objectives. Handbook I: Cognitive Domain*, New York: David McKay Co., 1956.

BONN, MYRTLE. "Teachers Then and Now." U.S. Office of Education: *American Education*, 3, (October, 1967), 13–17.

BROWN, B. FRANK. *The Appropriate Placement School: A Sophisticated Nongraded Curriculum* (West Nyack, N.Y.: Parker Publishing Company, Inc., 1965).

BRUNER, JEROME S. *Toward a Theory of Instruction* (Cambridge, Mass.: Belknap Press of Harvard University Press, 1966).

CHALL, JEANNE. *Learning to Read: The Great Debate* (New York: McGraw-Hill Book Company, 1967).

CONANT, JAMES BRYANT. *Education and Liberty* (New York: Vintage Books, 1953).

CONANT, JAMES B. *The American High School Today* (New York: McGraw-Hill Book Company, 1959).

DRUCKER, PETER. "Education in the New Technology." In *Social Foundations of Education* ed., Jonathan C. McLendon (New York: The Macmillan Company, 1966).

EISNER, ELLIOT W. "Emerging Models for Educational Evaluation." *School Review*, 80, 1972, 573–590.

FAIRLEY, RICHARD L. "Accountability's New Tool." *American Education*, 8, (June 1972), 33–35.

FEATHERSTONE, JOSEPH. *Schools Where Children Learn* (New York: Liveright, 1971).

FULL, HAROLD, ed. *Controversy in American Education* (New York: The Macmillan Company, 1967).

GARDNER, JOHN W. *Excellence* (New York: Harper and Brothers, Publishers, 1961).

GARDNER, JOHN W. "Versatility." *In Social Foundations of Education* ed., Dorothy Westby-Gibson (New York: The Free Press, 1967).

GREENBERG, J. C., and R. E. ROUSH. "Visit to the School without Walls. Two Impressions; Parkway Program in Philadelphia." *Phi Delta Kappan*, 51, 1970, 480–484.

GROSS, RONALD, and PAUL OSTERMAN (eds.). *High School.* (New York: Simon and Schuster, 1971).

HERRICK, THERAL T. "Curriculum Problems: Some Basic Issues." *Teachers College Record*, 60, 1959, 242–244.

JOHNSTON, BERNARD, ed. *Issues in Education: An Anthology of Controversy* (Boston: Houghton-Mifflin Company, 1964).

LESSINGER, L. M. "Accountability and Curriculum Reform." *Educational Technology*, 10, (May) 1970, 57.

MAYER, MARTIN PRAGER. *The Schools* (New York: Harper and Brothers, Publishers, 1961).

MAYER, MARTIN. *Where, When, and Why: Social Studies in American Schools* (New York: Harper and Row, 1962).

MORSE, ARTHUR D. *Schools of Tomorrow—Today* (New York: Doubleday and Company, 1960).

National Education Association. "Classroom Teachers Speak on Professional Negotiations" (Washington, D.C.: National Education Association, 1963).

National Education Association. "The Professional Family: a Cooperative Approach to Improving Instruction" (Washington, D.C.: National Education Association, 1965).

OLSEN, EDWARD G. "Enlivening the Community School Curriculum." *Phi Delta Kappan*, 54, 1972, 176–178.

RAPPAPORT, DAVID. *Understanding and Teaching Elementary School Mathematics* (New York: John Wiley and Sons, 1960).

RAUBINGER, FREDERICK M., and HAROLD G. ROWE. *The Individual and Education: Some Contemporary Issues* (New York: The Macmillan Company, 1968).

REYS, ROBERT N., and LOIS KNOWLES. "What is the Status of Elementary-School Mathematics?" *Elementary School Journal*, 68, (Jan., 1968), 167–171.

ROTZEL, GRACE. *The School in Rose Valley* New York: Ballantine Books, 1972. (Baltimore: Johns Hopkins Press, 1971).

SAXE, RICHARD W. (ed.). *Opening the Schools: Alternative Ways of Learning* (Berkeley, Calif.: McCutchan Publishing Corp., 1972).

SILBERMAN, CHARLES E. *Crisis in the Classroom* (New York: Random House, 1970).

TOTTEN, W. F. "Community Education: Best Hope for Society." *School and Society*, 98, 1970, 410–413.

TRUMP, J. LLOYD, and DORSEY BAYNHAM. *Focus on Change: Guide to Better Schools* (Chicago: Rand McNally and Company, 1961).

WING, CLIFF W., JR. "Student Selection, the Educational Environment, and the Cultivation of Talent." *Daedalus*, 94, (Summer, 1965), 632–641.

10

*professional
preparation of
teachers*

In chapters 2 and 9, particularly, much attention was paid to the question of what children should be taught in our schools. At least equally controversial is the question of what their prospective teachers should be taught. Are teachers born or made? Is teaching an art or a science? Should teacher preparation empasize content or techniques? These are the major questions now confronting us.

Historical Background

In ancient times, the learned man or scholar gathered about him young people with whom he discussed values, contemporary issues, ethics, and other subjects. The less learned but literate taught the illiterate, mainly young children. In this way, the tools of learning were handed down from generation to generation. Scholars produced by the great medieval universities opened schools under royal or religious auspices to teach some community children. Rarely, however, was the teacher's education designed to prepare him for his profession. Teacher education is, then, a comparatively modern phenomenon which is still in a state of modification.

The energetic and far-sighted Horace Mann was responsible, as noted in chapter 3, for the first normal schools (teacher training schools) in the United States. He was supported by Governor Edward Everett of Massachusetts and opposed by some in the state legislature of the time, as the following quotations indicate.

edward everett

The Purpose of the
New Normal Schools

In an address, delivered on the occasion of the opening of the Normal School at Lexington, 1839, Governor Edward Everett of Massachusetts contrasted the earlier monitorial instruction with that of the new normal schools, in the following words:

> The great mistake in monitorial instruction is that it supposes that the moment that the bare knowledge of a fact in its naked form is attained, it qualifies a person to teach it to others. The teacher, instead, must know things in a masterly way, . . .
>
> The first object of instruction in a Normal School, then, is as far as possible, to go over the circle of the branches required to be taught and see that the future teacher is minutely and thoroughly versed in them. . . .
>
> The second part of instruction in a Normal School is the art of teaching. To know the matter to be taught and to know it thoroughly, are of themselves, though essential, not all that is required. There is a peculiar art of teaching. The details of this branch are inexhaustible.
>
> The third branch of instruction to be imparted in an institution concerns the important art of government of the school.

The next quotation is self-explanatory.

Cubberley, *Readings, op. cit.*, pp. 338–339.

*resolution of the school committee
of salem, massachusetts, 1840*

A Defense of Mann
and the Normal Schools

During the legislative fight of 1840, the Committee on Education of the Massachusetts House of Representatives brought in
a report (and bill) recommending the abolition of the newly-
created State Board of Education and the new Normal Schools
which it had fostered. A legislative committee on retrench-
ment had made a similar recommendation. The resulting debate
in the legislature brought out numerous resolutions and
memorials in defense of both, of which the following one, from
Salem, is typical.

> The school committee of Salem begs leave to remonstrate
> respectfully and earnestly against the passage of the bill
> which has been recently reported by the Committee on
> Education. They desire to express their approbation of all
> the leading measures of the Board of Education, and, so
> far as their testimony may avail, to shield that distin-
> guished body of faithful and disinterested public servants
> from any imputations which may injure their official
> reputations or excite a doubt of the importance and useful-
> ness of their services. They desire, further, to tender an
> official tribute of commendation in behalf of the Secretary
> of the Board, who fortunately enjoys, as he merits,
> throughout the State and beyond, the measure of respect
> and confidence which is awarded only to the highest pur-
> poses and the purest motives.

Mann himself described the policies and practices of the new
state normal schools in his Tenth Annual Report in 1846.

Ibid., p. 339.

horace mann

Tenth Annual Report of the Massachusetts State Board of Education, Boston, 1846

The first three state normal schools in the United States opened at Lexington, July 3, 1839; Barre, September 4, 1839; and Bridgewater, September 9, 1840. For these schools the Board established admission requirements and a course of study, as follows:

admission and instruction

As a prerequisite to admission, candidates must declare it to be their intention to qualify themselves to become school teachers. If they belong to the State, or have an intention and a reasonable expectation of keeping school in the State, tuition is gratis. Otherwise, a tuition-fee is charged, which is intended to be about the same as is usually charged at good academies in the same neighborhood. . . .

If males, pupils must have attained the age of seventeen years complete, and of sixteen, if females; and they must be free from any disease or infirmity, which would unfit them for the office of school teachers.

They must undergo an examination, and prove themselves to be well versed in orthography, reading, writing, English grammar, geography, and arithmetic.

They must furnish satisfactory evidence of good intellectual capacity and of high moral character and principles.

Ibid., pp. 337–338.

Examinations for admission take place at the commencement of each term, of which there are three in a year.

term of study

. . . The minimum of the term of study is one year, and this must be in consecutive terms of the schools . . .

course of study

The studies first to be attended to in the State Normal Schools are those which the law requires to be taught in the district schools, namely, orthography, reading, writing, English grammar, geography, and arithmetic. When these are mastered, those of a higher order will be progressively taken.

For those who wish to remain at the school more than one year, and for all belonging to the school, so far as their previous attainments will permit, the following course is arranged:

1. Orthography, reading, grammar, composition, rhetoric, and logic.
2. Writing and drawing.
3. Arithmetic, mental and written, algebra, geometry, bookkeeping, navigation, surveying.
4. Geography, ancient and modern, with chronology, statistics and general history.
5. Human Physiology, and hygiene or the Laws of Health.
6. Mental Philosophy.
7. Music.
8. Constitution and History of Massachusetts and of the United States.
9. Natural Philosophy and Astronomy.
10. Natural History.
11. The principle of piety and morality, common to all sects of Christians.
12. The science and art of teaching, with reference to all the above-named studies.

religious exercises

A portion of the Scriptures shall be read daily, in every State Normal School.

As a result of the efforts of Mann and Henry Barnard, there were normal schools in ten or more states before the Civil War. Emphasis was on preparing teachers for the elementary schools rather than the secondary schools. First of all, secondary education was not popularly supported at that time. Secondly, few of the teachers-to-be themselves had had a secondary education. As you can see from Mann's 10th Report, part of the Normal School curriculum consisted of mastering the basic studies. A very small percentage of teachers attended even those normal schools in existence, and the quality of their education varied considerably.

For the balance of the nineteenth century, with public education becoming more and more important, both the number of normal schools (private and public) and the enrollments rose sharply. Admissions requirements to many of the schools now included a high school diploma, thus changing the curriculum in the normal schools. With this improvement, the state normal schools began to change to four-year, degree-granting state teachers' colleges in the period 1900–1950. Almost immediately, however, the teachers' colleges began another change to four-year liberal arts and education colleges, a transition now virtually complete.

Since 1900, also, however, there has been increasing acceptance by colleges and universities of their responsibility for teacher education. Often this began as a section of the department of philosophy or psychology, grew into a separate department of education, and by the 1960's became a school or

Figure 10.1 Student teacher.

T. C. Abell (Stock, Boston)

"A teacher affects eternity; he can never tell where his influence stops."   Henry Brooks Adams

college of education which is an entity within the university. Some institutions of higher learning offer only graduate work in education and have no relevant undergraduate school, such as Harvard and the University of Chicago. Master of Arts in Teaching (MAT) programs are expanding in scope and increasing in numbers as a fifth year of study is recognized to be necessary for well-qualified teachers. Some fifth-year programs (e.g., Temple University's Interne Program) are designed for persons holding non-education degrees and combine classroom experience with paid teaching internships in the public schools.

Professional Selection and Preparation

There are those who believe that teachers are born, not made, so that the professional courses they take, or the lack of them, is relatively unimportant.

> Discussions of teacher education generally focus upon instruction and programs of courses, so that the relative importance of *training versus selection* is frequently not considered, . . . If a person with the basic qualifications for being a good teacher is attracted into education, it matters less which courses he takes; he will probably wind up a good teacher if he has had practice under guidance of a wise leader. On the other hand, a person without these basic qualifications will rarely be turned into a good teacher, no matter how enlightened the curriculum to which he is subjected or how progressive the faculty to which he is exposed.[1]

That is, teachers are born, not made.

There are also those who believe that teaching the "whole child" requires breadth, but not depth, of knowledge in subject matter. Too often it is a teacher prepared in the latter way who is in charge of a self-contained classroom at the elementary level. It is true that such an all-purpose teacher would find it extremely difficult to become a master of all the subject matter areas she must teach in a four, or even five-year program. What can be done?

The first step, perhaps, is to improve selection methods at the college level. Since professors in academic disciplines too often "look down" on professors and colleges of education,

Figure 10.2

they frequently recommend to their low-achievement students that they transfer to the College of Education to earn a degree. The Colleges of Education must not accept every such poor student. Some tolerance for one weak term is understandable, but a student with a steady D+ or low C average will ultimately be no credit to the college which grants him a diploma nor will he be a help to the students he presumes to teach. Some consideration, too, should be given to the motives behind a student's application for admission to teacher preparation programs and to any marked personality disturbances he may have. With a constricted employment market in education projected for several years to come, selectivity of prospective teachers increases in importance.

To achieve the goal of producing competent teachers, what should prospective teachers learn? The following list of objectives is representative of the goals of most Colleges of Education in this country.

> The College has accepted the following objectives: 1) to enable the student to develop his role as a teacher; 2) to prepare the student to be a leader and a participating citizen in the community; 3) to assist the student in acquiring an enriched background, depth of specialization and breadth of knowledge necessary for teaching; 4) to promote in the student an understanding of the purposes and functions of public schools in our society; 5) to provide the student with a knowledge of child growth and development and an appreciation of its implications for learning; 6) to familiarize the student with different curricula, content and instructional materials common to public schools; 7) to assist students in obtaining knowledge of and improvement in techniques of guiding learners; and 8) to encourage loyalty and service to the teaching profession and a desire for continuous self-improvement.[2]

What should the "flow chart" be in teacher preparation institutions? In the days of the normal schools and state teachers' colleges, more emphasis was put on "methods" courses or pedagogy than content. Today there is general agreement on several aspects of preparation:

1. All future teachers should have basic liberal arts courses in physical sciences, biological sciences, social sciences, and humanities—that is, roughly two years of liberal arts courses.
2. There is a need for competence in the subject matter field(s).
3. There is need for competence in the pedagogical and technical aspects of teaching.
4. All future teachers should be aware of and familiar with patterns of child development and the applications of psychological principles to the learning situation.
5. Education is an academic discipline in its own right in the broad area of the social sciences.

This agreement is an outgrowth of much criticism of teacher education programs in the past decade.

Albert Lynd viewed professors of education as "illiterate" quacks, their requirements of numerous education courses as a professional conspiracy to ensnare innocent students, and the teachers they produce as inept. He was totally opposed to pragmatism and in favor of the classical curriculum as the sole means of producing literate, moral citizens. Lynd wrote that our schools were producing graduates who could not read, spell, or compute correctly, and had justification at least in the area of spelling, which was apparently a neglected subject in the schools of the post-war (1945 and after) era.[3] Bestor[4] believed that the faults of modern education stemmed from weaknesses in the teacher preparation curricula. Subject matter content, he averred, should be taught in liberal arts colleges by liberal arts professors; professors of education should present only a limited number of teaching skills courses. Mayer criticizes teacher preparation as being

> . . . insufferably generalized. It rests on observation— usually superficial observation—of what good teachers seem to do. Thus, since most good teachers are ingenious at pointing out the relevance of a study to what is in today's papers, teacher-training institutions build a philosophy around contemporaneity; since most good teachers know through peripheral vision the social relations and psychological difficulties of their students, teacher-training institutions offer techniques of sociodrama and psychodrama by which imperceptive teachers are supposed to be able to find out what gives in the buried life of the classroom. Emphasis has been placed precisely on those areas where technique cannot replace insight; and the areas where technique is valid, in the presentation of material to be learned, have been almost completely neglected.[5]

Too often, prospective teachers are taught in the very manner they are being told to avoid—dry lectures.

Conant, after a two-year study of teacher-training programs, concluded that there was great diversity in quality among them. He pointed out that not only were academic and professional professors in conflict, but the public and the students, too, argued that there were too many "pedagogy" courses which were too repetitious and ultimately meaningless. In a statement on teacher certification practices, which is largely what determines teacher education curricula, Conant compared two approaches to certification. In his book on education of teachers, a result of his study, he also recommended that certification be granted mainly in terms of competence as a student teacher.

james b. conant

Teacher Certification

the prescribed exposure approach

The first method is the one now in existence in most, if not all, of the states. If one likes this approach he might call it "the prescription of essential knowledge" method; if he does not, he will call it "the course counting method;" if he is more or less committed to it, but fears its inflexibility or considers it inadequate as a total method, he will have incorporated its requirements as "guidelines" in an approved-program system. In the latter case whether or not the guidelines are rigorously applied will vary with the commitment of the approver and the strength of the college under consideration.

I would be inclined to call this system the "prescribed exposure" approach. . . .

Conant, James Bryant, *The Education of American Teachers* (New York: McGraw-Hill Book Company, 1963), pp. 224–228. By permission of the author.

I carry coals to Newcastle in arguing before the American Association of Colleges for Teacher Education that the "prescribed exposure" approach has not worked out well. Your organization, as well as such groups as the National Commission on Teacher Education and Professional Standards, have worked diligently for years to persuade the states to abandon this traditional method. . . . groups such as yours have helped to expose the futility of the "prescribed exposure" approach. For example, you have pointed out that the mere listing of a course in a college catalog or in a state department regulation tells very little about the precise content or effectiveness of that course as taught on a particular college campus. You have also argued that teacher education is a rapidly changing and rapidly advancing field in which new patterns of organizing instruction are constantly being developed, and in which there is desperate need to innovate and experiment on individual college campuses. Some of you are even aware that those who would, for example, favor the near total elimination of courses in education have now discovered the possibility of using the state legislature to write prescriptions which would give them a captive student audience at the expense of the professors of education. For those of you who are not aware of this last point, I must warn you to expect even more powerful moves in this direction unless you can persuade the state officials that it is not their place to erect tariff barriers around the courses of any group of professors. But if you insist on using the political machinery of the state in your behalf, you must expect your opponents to do the same. Given the adoption of this tactic by the liberal arts professors as well as the professors of education, the *best* that can be hoped for is a kind of political horse trade by which, for example, a certain number of required credits in education are exchanged for a certain number of credits in chemistry. I find it hard to conceive that any professor can be happy with the thought that college curricula may ultimately be made on the basis of political deals among legislators, susceptible to the influence of varying groups of professors.

the approved program approach

I think, then, that most of us are agreed that the "prescribed exposure approach" to teacher education leaves much to be desired. The logic of the arguments against it would lead, it seems to me, to the proposition that the designation of specific courses to be required should be a function of a particular college faculty which knows in greater detail what the proposed courses are actually like, and which is in a position to design a pattern of required courses which adds up to a coherent and effective program. I assume that many of you refuse to follow this logic to its conclusion because you are convinced that certain colleges lack the ability or the integrity to exercise this responsibility seriously and well. Therefore, you have turned to the "approved programs approach," to which I, too, now turn. *Theoretically*, this approach involves "the state" examining the program prescribed within the state by each institution which trains teachers, and deciding whether the courses offered are the right courses, whether they are well given, and whether adequate standards of passing and failing are maintained.

Theoretically the "state" in examining an institution would be quite prepared to listen to arguments as to why in the institution's opinion the future chemistry teacher, for example, should be required to pass a course in calculus, or why a secondary school teacher should be required to pass a course in the history of education. Or conversely why the institution had decided both requirements had proved unnecessary and were going to be dropped. . . .

Speaking again "theoretically," a state might approve one institution in which the general education program included a great many courses in science and another in which the science offering was tightly compressed; it might approve one institution which required a great many courses in education and a second which required few. However, in practice, reality forces those who administer an approved program approach

to fall back on something which closely resembles the prescribed exposure approach.

. . .

The present type of approved program approach is not
the answer to our problem, however. These programs in large
measure continue to utilize guidelines which allocate, sometimes within broad limits to be sure, the amount of a potential
teacher's exposure to courses in general education, subject
matter specialization, and professional instruction. But though
guidelines may be stated in general terms, their application
must, in the nature of the case, be specific. Those who approve
must decide either that a college requires too much or too little
general education, that particular courses in general education
or professional education achieve the purposes for which
designed or they do not; that quality instruction is provided,
or it is not. Such decisions ultimately come down to precise,
though unstated, criteria no matter how general may be the
stated guideline under which it is subsumed. Moreover, for any
one to determine quality of instruction, or the coherence and
adequacy of a total program as it is actually taught (as opposed
to its catalog description), requires expertness in the subjects
being considered, and a great deal of time spent on the campus
and in the classrooms under evaluation. No state department
can afford a sufficient staff of experts to appraise whole
programs in teacher education, and neither their own people
nor visiting experts employed for a particular evaluation can
spend sufficient time on a campus to make adequate judgments.
They are forced therefore to fall back on formulas which
approximate exposure formulas. These already formidable
problems would be magnified many times if the approving
agency sought to examine the individuals proposed for certification to determine their degree of mastery of the material to
which they had been exposed. For this most crucial judgment
the approving agency is forced therefore to fall back on the
integrity and the effectiveness of the institution being
evaluated.

In Pennsylvania and other states, the "approved program" approach has been adopted, usually within existing certification programs. That is, the state still mandates the number of credits to be earned in a content field, but the college prescribes the particular courses to be taken to meet the state requirements, and secures state approval for that sequence of courses. Conant went on in his discussion to urge the creation of "clinical" professorships which would involve proper supervision of practice teaching by experienced master teachers of a particular subject and grade level. This proposal is now being implemented in some teacher education programs. At Northwestern University, for example, highly recommended teachers have dual appointments to the school district and university faculties (as classroom teachers and clinical professors respectively), continuing their teaching in the classroom while teaching and supervising interns and student teachers. Theoretically, each appointment is half-time, but in practice, there are conflicting demands on the clinical professor's time. Despite this and a problem of communication barriers, Northwestern has found the program to be beneficial to students and clinical professors alike.[6]

Sample Curricula

There is considerable difference among teacher-training institutions as to general (liberal arts) education requirements, professional orientation and methods course requirements, practical experience in conjunction with courses, and student teaching experience, as well as the length of the professional program. To illustrate this variability, several college catalogues were examined and the results of the investigation are included here (with the reader's indulgence asked for post-publication changes). The purpose is neither to vilify nor to glorify any institution's program, but to show similarities and differences among programs. A brief description of some experimental programs is also presented. The colleges cited are mainly publicly-supported, but they are in various sections of the country and reflect urban and non-urban needs.

1. San Francisco State College—Elementary (K-9) teaching certificate requirements:

   a. Basic requirements include a bachelor's degree plus 30 semester hours beyond the baccalaureate degree.

   b. General education requirements (for freshmen)—45 semester hours including one year of English, and five of the following: 6 s.h. in Humanities, 18 s.h. in social sciences; including state requirements in U.S. History and Constitution and California State and Local government; 8 s.h. in Natural Sciences, 3 s.h. in Mathematics; 3 s.h. in Fine Arts; and foreign language, which can be met by examination.

   c. Mathematics requirement—"Structure of the number system."

   d. Major or major and minor requirements—24-28 s.h. in upper division or graduate level work in a single major subject taught in the elementary school or a major and a minor as described in the catalogue.

   e. Professional preparation—5-10 s.h. of student teaching (minimum of 180 clock-hours), student teaching seminar (3 s.h.), Psychological foundations of education (5 s.h.), curriculum in the elementary school (9 s.h.), and three additional courses in "minor" elementary subject areas; all to be followed by a postgraduate elementary teaching interneship graduate program.

2. Northern Arizona University, College of Education

   a. Basically a 5-year program, with a Bachelor of Science degree awarded at the end of four years.

   b. Admission to the Teacher Education Program is in the third year.

   c. In elementary education, 125 s.h. for the Bachelor's degree, plus 30 s.h. in the fifth year, including 42 s.h. in Liberal Arts, 27-32 s.h. in supporting subject content, 27 s.h. in professional courses, 15 s.h. in the selected content emphasis, and 9-14 s.h. of electives.

d. At the secondary level, 125 s.h. plus 30 as above, including 42 s.h. in Liberal Arts, 19 s.h. in professional education courses, 30+ s.h. in the Teaching Major, 20+ s.h. in the Teaching Minor, and 6-12 s.h. of electives.

e. Undergraduate "field" experience—of 8 required elementary education methods courses, 6 require laboratory experience; 9 cr. of student teaching; special field experience is available for teachers on Indian reservations.

f. Certification is K–3 or 1–8 for elementary; 7–12 for secondary education teachers.

3. The Pennsylvania State University, College of Education

a. A four-year program for provisional certification, plus 24 credits in the following three years for permanent certification.

b. Enrollment in the first year with admission to teacher education majors in the second year; review of achievement and other factors at the end of the second year.

c. Elementary education—134 credits including 54 in Liberal Arts, 23 in Professional education, 26–27 in teaching methods courses, 12 in student teaching, and 18 in addition to liberal arts courses in the broad areas of humanities or science and mathematics or social studies.

d. Secondary education majors usually need 130 credits including 51 in Liberal Arts, 11–13 in Professional education, 3 in methods of teaching the major subject, 10 in student teaching, and 30–58 depending on the major subject selected (some of which are included in the Liberal Arts requirement).

e. Field experience—

1) elementary education majors have some laboratory experience with the methods courses

2) secondary education majors do "micro-teaching" in the methods course at the University

3) student teaching—one term

4) some experimental groups taking field work in their first two years of college

f. Certification: Nursery-Kindergarten-Primary; Elementary (K–6); secondary (7–12).

4. Whittier College (California)

a. A four-year program for temporary certification with mandatory completion of fifth year for full certification.

b. Admission to the teaching program in the third year.

c. Elementary and secondary education students need 124 credits for the bachelor's degree, including Liberal Arts —60 s.h.; Professional education—15 s.h. for elementary and 9 s.h. for secondary; Methods courses—up to 8 s.h.; and a major subject—20–24 s.h.

5. Syracuse University[7]

a. Secondary education experimental program requires supervised camp counseling experience in the summer before the third year.

b. In the third year, 6 credits of field experience is taken each semester, and there is a full-time interneship in the fall term of the fourth year.

6. Hunter College of the City University of New York[8]

a. Emphasis is on urban education preparation.

b. Undergraduate program includes community experience, in which the student is assigned to a settlement house or youth group concurrent with the educational psychology course, and divided student-teaching in which teams of two students are assigned to "disadvantaged" and middle class schools with the students switching assignments in mid-semester.

c. Graduate and in-service programs are oriented to needs of Puerto Rican students, and include studying the culture, language, English as a second language, acculturation problems, etc.

7. University of Florida[9]

   a. Experimental programs in teacher education.

   b. Elementary education requirements include courses in Child Psychology, Cultural Foundations of Education, Children and Learning, a 15 credit practicum, methods courses (15 cr.), and courses in elementary education (15 credits).

   c. Secondary education requirements include Child Psychology, Cultural Foundations of Education, The Secondary School Today, and three interneships including student teaching (9 cr.).

   d. There is an interdisciplinary staff which works with both elementary and secondary education students, and which uses a problem-solving approach.

   e. Laboratory-seminar experiences continue throughout the program, and there is opportunity for individual research.

8. University of Oregon[10]

   a. "An organized program of preparation for both elementary and secondary school teachers which requires five college years for its completion." There is "... emphasis on the general liberal education of the teacher at both the elementary and secondary school levels." For elementary majors, 80 per cent of the course work is in general education; for secondary majors, 85 per cent of the course work is in general education, of the liberal arts variety.

   b. Competence in a major field (subject) is required.

   c. Paid internships are part of the program.

   d. There are "... improved procedures for selection, admission, and retention of trainees in the teacher education program."

Much similarity is seen in the emphases of these eight examples of teacher education curricula, particularly the growing emphasis on competence in a major field to be taught in the schools (even at the elementary level), and the expanding programs of laboratory or field experience beyond the single student teaching experience. If the opportunity to participate in a relevant classroom or other experience setting is offered to the student in the first two years of college, two benefits are derived. For the student, there is an opportunity to "taste" the future and test his/her commitment to teaching. For the college, the early field experience serves as a screening device, picking out those who appear to have excellent potential for teaching, those who need extra help in specific aspects of teaching, and those who, by their own behavior, seem to be unsuitable for classroom leadership and are best guided in other directions as soon as possible. These and other teacher education programs also stress course work in psychology, but as William James said, "Psychology is a science, and teaching is an art; and sciences never generate arts directly out of themselves. An intermediary Inventive mind must make the application, by using its originality."[11] That is, simply taking particular courses, whether in psychology or other fields, will not in itself make a great teacher, although hopefully it will make a better one. The teacher must be able to adapt what he or she has learned to the situation at hand in an original way, not cookbook fashion. It should also be noted that the programs presented indicate a trend toward increasing requirements to include a fifth year of study to attain permanent certification. Perhaps the ultimate in increasing preparation of teachers may be found in the following article, which also presents some of the arguments for and against teacher education programs *in toto.*

lynn l. weldon

Is Teacher Education an Illusion?

Beliefs about teacher education usually fall into two categories: the liberal arts professors' position that anyone who has mastered his subject matter field can impart it, and the educationists' position that prospective teachers must have a number of educational methods courses. Although not always evident, this cleavage nevertheless exists in most colleges and universities where there are teacher education programs, and the conflict is often manifested in the form of open ridicule of each other.

The most frequent liberal arts criticisms of educationists and teacher education programs are:

1. Education courses emphasize only the how (techniques and methods), not the what (subject matter content).

2. Teacher certification requirements place emphasis on educational methods, thereby hindering subject matter mastery.

3. Education is not a valid subject matter field because it lacks a body of knowledge with form and tradition of its own.

4. Education professors and their courses are not on a scholarly intellectual level.

Weldon, Lynn L. "Is Teacher Education an Illusion?," *Journal of Teacher Education*, 19, (Summer, 1968), 193–196.

5. Education degrees are below the intellectual level of liberal arts degrees.

6. Education courses are unnecessary since the only trait needed by a successful teacher is subject matter mastery.

What causes liberal arts professors to make such devastating condemnations of teacher education programs? One answer may be that scholarship in a restricted academic field has been the center of their life since youth. To the typical liberal arts professor, the aim of education is to acquire and transmit scholarly knowledge, and in his view, the only important factors in successful teaching are advanced scholarship in a liberal arts field and a pleasingly enthusiastic teaching manner. The field of methods is a "bag of techniques" that can be quickly learned, if necessary, through apprenticeship to an advanced scholar in the field.

Educationists react equally violently to the liberal arts position:

1. Liberal arts professors hold inadequately narrow concepts of subject matter and value only academic learnings.

2. They believe that the antidemocratic indoctrination of right answers is the only teaching method.

3. They fail to realize that teaching competencies involve much more than just knowing the facts and concepts of a liberal arts subject matter field.

4. They mistakenly believe that education courses emphasize methods to the almost total exclusion of content.

5. They fight against the professionalization of the teaching profession.

6. They hold unfounded, prejudiced, inaccurate, and inadequate concepts of education degree requirements and mistakenly believe that these degrees are inferior to and easier to obtain than liberal arts degrees.

7. Instead of fostering student recognition of prejudices and provincialisms, they violate the liberalizing ideal of the liberal arts by encouraging narrow isolated subject matter specialization and irrational prejudices against education courses and educationists.

. . .

Weldon mentioned the criticism of methods courses by liberal arts professors. Teachers, students, and non-teachers have also condemned them as being too theoretical and unrealistic; or as being too superficial and an insult to the student's intelligence; or because they are not really teaching methods at all, but really quasi-curriculum courses in which the student is taught not *how* to teach, but *what* to teach at different levels and for different goals.[12] Much depends in these courses on the orientation of the school of education in which the course is offered and on the orientation of the methods course professor. No two courses in methods of teaching arithmetic at the elementary level or science at the secondary level are precisely the same, so that it is somewhat unfair to generalize after exposure to only one methods course.

In their volume on teacher education, Sarason, Davidson, and Blatt make the point that

. . . most teachers teach in a way reflecting the concept that education consists primarily of what we put into children rather than what we can get out of them. . . . teacher-training programs reinforce this conception, that is, teachers handle children in the same way that they were handled in the course of their professional training.[13]

The innovative and experimental curricula presented a few pages above represent alternatives to this situation.

Teachers in the Field

Assuming that a student gains admission to the College of Education, performs reasonably well in course work, and is ready for graduation and employment, what kind of a professional should he or she be? In the selection and admission processes, we find out our input; we should know equally well what kind of output we want. According to Highet,[14] these are the qualities of a good teacher:

1. He must know the subject he teaches, for teaching is inseparable from learning.
2. He must like the subject and have enthusiasm for it.
3. He must like his pupils.
4. He must know his pupils—their natures, their names and faces.
5. He must keep teacher-pupil relationships impersonal.
6. He must maintain wide and lively intellectual interests.
7. He must have and use a sense of humor, which helps to build "bridges" between youth and maturity.
8. He needs certain essential qualities—a good memory, determination, or will-power, and kindness.

Barzun recommends that teachers teach and be taught basic principles, flexible attitudes, thinking, and attention.[15] Kneller concludes that,

The teacher is not in his classroom primarily to impart knowledge (realism), or as a consultant in problem situations (pragmatism), or as a personality to be emulated (idealism). His function is to assist each student personally in his journey towards self-realization. A good teacher acts, himself, as a free agent; his influence is not temporary but persists into adult life.[16]

And Slick, a high school assistant principal, advises that,

. . . teaching is a profession that demands total commitment. It is more than a job; it is a way of life through which you are constantly in a fish bowl, on display to students, parents, and the community. People know you, even when you do not know them. If you are proud of what you are doing, it will show. It will show in your classroom and your students will recognize and respect that pride.
. . .
The reward in education is the satisfaction of doing your utmost to help students attain their personal goals in life through what they learn. There is no sure way of telling how much you have accomplished—even though classroom behavior and attitudes will give you a good indication of whether you are "reaching" students. Since more often than not you will not *know* whether you have helped a student, the emphasis is on faith—faith in yourself, faith in what you teach, and faith in how you teach.[17]

How much we expect of our teachers!

To aid the teacher in the classroom, perhaps certain facts of contemporary life should be faced before he graduates. Teachers in urban areas need to understand urban problems beyond the general principles offered in an introductory sociology course. They should have a course in urban sociology or social problems, and, hopefully, some experience as a teacher aide or youth worker in the "inner city" to prepare them better. Teachers-to-be should have practical experience *before* student teaching as a separate and on-going part of their education in the Sophomore and Junior years. This would be beneficial in two ways: 1) exposure to the classroom early in the college years may help a student decide whether or not this is really what he wants as a career; and 2) in student-teaching, the student will have a much better idea of how a classroom functions, thus increasing his effectiveness in the student-teaching role. Teachers in any classroom have pupils who have emotional upsets, are slow or gifted learners, and/or have physical or other handicaps. They should have some information about the problems of exceptional children and how to relate to them. It may be, finally, that all prospective teachers will need a fifth year of preparation to complete their initial education for the:

frank g. jennings

Most Dangerous Profession

Teaching is the most dangerous profession. It deals with our children, the most precious of our natural resources. It refines them into brave and wonderful adults or it grossly degrades them into dull, overaged adolescents. Its results color, mold, and determine the shape of our nation and the character of our people.

If our teachers lack luster, fewer of their charges will be as bright as they might have been. *If* our teachers are cowards, they will teach their cowardice.

If teachers are not responsible citizens, they will produce political idiots. *If* teachers become the tools of any pressure group, rather than the prime artisans of a creative society, then we will all shrink into a nation of domesticated, two-legged cattle, capable of nothing but ignorant brutality toward each other and cud-chewing obedience to the loudest shouters and the best feeders.

If teachers do not earn and keep the status and the respect which their profession requires, their role will be captured by the practical, committed members of the commercial and industrial communities, who can train people very well, but who cannot afford the expense of humane adventure.

Thus, teaching must forever live in creative danger, but teachers must hold onto the protective warnings of these terrifying *ifs*, lest these warnings become irremovable realities.

It is our great good fortune that in most of the schools in this country many pupils are met by a person for whom the magic of real respect and true love can quickly develop. This is

Jennings, Frank G. "Most Dangerous Profession," *The Saturday Review*, March 8, 1958, p. 22. By permission of the author.

so whether that teacher faces a kindergarten of five-year-olds or a seminar of graduate students. Yet sometimes this magic dies because that teacher is beset by fears and half-understood anxieties that come from the half-empty pocketbook or a half-shattered self-esteem.

The great teacher possesses a personality strong enough to free himself from these pressures. And it is this free teacher who is truly an artist in human relations. (This is something that must not be confused with some teacher's college workshop courses bearing the same name.)

Pupil and teacher begin their relationship by studying and learning *each other*. They learn by their common experience to value and use each other's words and acts and ideas. A group of human beings so learning is the closest to Eden we can ever be. For the interests of young people can encompass the whole world. All kinds of experiences press in upon them. The teacher has to know when and how to teach them to begin to be selective about these experiences.

There is great danger here! What happens if our young people are denied the ability to make and to know that they are making significant choices? George Orwell's Big Brother will come and do it for them. To prevent Big Brother from taking over, the teacher has to know and be able to show all the kinds of choices there are. To do this he must have an unquenchable thirst for delight, an insatiable appetite for wonder, and the talent to transmit these qualities to the children.

This is asking more than is ordinarily possible for anyone. But our society must ask this of its teachers. For there is this warning: the teacher who does not love poetry does a rather poor job of arranging a love affair between words and the child. A teacher for whom all painting beyond the merely pictorial is nonsense cannot follow the child into the rain forest of color and shapes that is the possible world of that child. A teacher who can think only on one level of understanding at a time cannot keep his bearings amidst the busy questions of thirty thirsty minds. A teacher who does not enjoy reading teaches this lack of enjoyment far more successfully than he can ever teach the rudimentary reading skills a young child requires.

The child learns many things quickly and permanently. Throughout childhood he is learning to be at home in this world, learning to read its signs and portents, learning its firm, unshifting names, and the volatile, shifting symbols, learning to listen and to know and to understand, learning to act less on impulse and more with purpose. And of course it is true that he begins to learn all this at home.

Whatever the quality of these home experiences may be, we ask the schools to take up these beginnings and carry them on toward those necessary goals we have set for education. The good teacher must be a person with a profound love of a subject, born of the fulness of familiarity. He must have an excellent operational understanding of basic educational principles, not the mere word-shadows of professional jargon. The teacher must have a love of people in general, and of children in particular, must have the ability to awaken and maintain the interest of students and to direct those interests toward successful experiences. Above all, the teacher must be able to foster wonder.

This is the kind of teacher our society needs. The kind of teaching that a teacher is capable of is an acquired skill. Such teachers are born in classrooms. The skill they must have can be learned by anyone with adequate intelligence who is willing to accept the hazards and the dangers of acting upon clearly accepted responsibilities.

Let the cowards and the dullards find safety in the tenure trap! The true teacher joyfully accepts the call of strange tomorrows, finds security and immortality in the healthy, happy, and intelligent citizens he has helped to shape.

Alternatives in Teacher Education

The emphases on instructional objectives and mastery learning in the schools have led to their application in teacher education as well, increasing the numbers of programs that are performance- or competency-based. The preparation of secondary school teachers at Illinois State University, City University of New York, and the University of Nebraska, for example, involves the use of self-paced instructional packages that specify the learning objectives of a particular task and the means of demonstrating proficiency by means of a variety of activities. The New School for Behavioral Studies in Education at the University of North Dakota was singled out by Silberman (1970) for its innovative teacher education programs. At the University of Massachusetts and at Indiana University there are several alternative paths to teacher certification. These involve multiple options for the prospective teacher as well as extensive field experience prior to and beyond the traditional student teaching term.

These and other new programs are a response to widespread criticisms of the performance level of recent education graduates. Even a summa cum laude graduate can be relatively mediocre in the classroom as a teacher. On the other hand, the author has personally seen students who were marginal in academic achievement perform in classroom situations with great aplomb and competence. Without the opportunity to participate in an alternative program, several good teachers would have been lost. The alternatives also offer the prospective teacher more of a chance to test his commitment to education generally and to select the specific areas in which he chooses to work.

Endnotes

1. Keppel, *op. cit.*, p. 90.
2. "Objectives," College of Education, Northern Arizona University *Bulletin*, Flagstaff, Ariz., 1967–69, p. 185.
3. Lynd, Albert. *Quackery in the Public Schools* (Boston: Little, Brown, and Co., 1953).
4. Bestor, Arthur. *Educational Wastelands* (Urbana: Univ. of Illinois, 1953).
5. Mayer, Martin. *Where, When, and Why* (New York: Harper and Row, 1962). pp. 179–180.

6. Hazard, William R., and Chandler, B. J. "The clinical professor in teacher education." *Phi Delta Kappan*, 1972, 53, 370–371.

7. Irvine, William L. "Project I: A Experimental Program for the Preparation of Secondary School Teachers," *Changes in Teacher Education: An Appraisal* (Washington, D.C.: National Education Association, 1964), pp. 77–89.

8. Schueler, "Teachers and Resources for Teacher Education," *Ibid.*, pp. 228–239.

9. Gordon, *et al.*, "The Florida Experiment in Undergraduate Education," *Ibid.*, pp. 253–256.

10. Gubser, Joy Hills. "The Oregon Program: a Design for the Improvement of Education," *Ibid.*, pp. 351–356.

11. James, William. *Talks to Teachers on Psychology* (New York: Dover Publications, Inc., 1962), p. 3.

12. Zahorik, John A. "The Trouble with Methods Courses," *Journal of Teacher Education*, 19, (Summer, 1968), p. 197.

13. Sarason, S. B., Davidson, K. S., and B. Blatt. *The Preparation of Teachers* (New York: John Wiley and Sons, 1962), p. xii.

14. Highet, Gilbert. *The Art of Teaching* (New York: Vintage Books, 1950), pp. 12–65.

15. Barzun, Jacques. *Teacher in America* (New York: Doubleday Anchor Books, 1944), p. 24.

16. Kneller, *op. cit.*, p. 66.

17. Slick, George H. "Three R's of Teaching," *Pennsylvania School Journal*, 116, (Oct. 1967), p. 80.

For Further Reading

BARZUN, JACQUES. *Teacher in America* (New York: Doubleday Anchor Books, 1944).

BIGELOW, DONALD N. (ed.) *The Liberal Arts and Teacher Education: A Confrontation* (Lincoln: University of Nebraska Press, 1971).

BROADBENT, FRANK W. "Simulating Problems of Beginning Teachers." *Elementary School Journal,* 68, (Oct. 1967), 39–43.

BRUNER, JEROME S. The *Process of Education* (New York: Vintage Books, 1960).

BURLEIGH, JUDITH C., and HAROLD W. PETERSON. "Videotapes in Teacher Education." *Elementary School Journal,* 68, (Oct. 1967), 35–38.

BURTON, WILLIAM H., ROLAND B. KIMBALL, and RICHARD L. WING. *Education for Effective Thinking* (New York: Appleton-Century-Crofts, 1960).

CLARK, BURTON R. *Educating the Expert Society* (San Francisco: Chandler Publishing Company, 1962).

CLARK, RICHARD J., and DONALD J. KINGSBURY. "Simultaneous Alternative Teacher Preparation Programs." *Phi Delta Kappan,* 54, 1973, 477–479.

CLEMENTS, H. MILLAR, WILLIAM R. FIELDER, and B. ROBERT TABACHNIK. *Social Study Inquiry in Elementary Classrooms* (New York: The Bobbs-Merrill Company, 1966).

CONANT, JAMES BRYANT. *The Education of American Teachers* (New York: McGraw-Hill Book Company, 1963).

DAVIS, E. DALE. *Focus on Secondary Education* (Glenview, Ill.: Scott, Foresman, and Company, 1966).

DECECCO, JOHN P. *Educational Technology: Readings in Programmed Instruction* (New York: Holt, Rinehart, and Winston, 1964).

DRESSEL, F. B. "Student Teaching—the Public School's Responsibility." *School and Society,* 98, 1970, 163–164.

ELLIS, JOHN F. "Who Should Teach Teachers?" *Journal of Teacher Education,* 18, (Winter 1967), 423–428.

EVJIN, MYRTLE. "The Role of the Cooperating School." *Journal of Teacher Education,* 18, (Winter 1967), 411–416.

FANTINI, MARIO D. "The Reform of Teacher Education—a Proposal for New York State." *Phi Delta Kappan,* 53, 1972, 476–479, 482.

FILBIN, ROBERT L., and STEFAN VOGEL. *So You're Going to Be a Teacher* (Great Neck, N.Y.: Barron's Educational Series, Inc., 1962).

GAGE, N. L., (ed.) *Handbook of Research on Teaching* American Educational Research Association. (Chicago: Rand, McNally, and Company, 1963; 2nd edition, 1973).

GODDU, R. J. B., and E. R. DUCHARME. "A Responsive Teacher-Education Program." *Teachers College Record,* 72, 1971, 431–441.

GOODLAD, JOHN I. "The Reconstruction of Teacher Education." *Teachers College Record,* 72, 1970, 61–72.

HIGHET, GILBERT. *The Art of Teaching* (New York: Vintage Books, 1950).

INLOW, GAIL. *The Emergent in Curriculum* (New York: John Wiley and Sons, 1966).

JAMES, WILLIAM. *Talks to Teachers on Psychology* (New York: Dover Publications, Inc., 1962 (reprint).

JENNINGS, FRANK G. "Most Dangerous Profession." In *Social Foundations of Education* ed., Dorothy Westby-Gibson. (New York: The Free Press, 1967).

KENNEDY, MILLARD FILLMORE. *Schoolmaster of Yesterday* (New York: McGraw-Hill Book Company, 1940).

KUETHE, JAMES L. *The Teaching-Learning Process* (Atlanta: Scott, Foresman, and Company, 1968).

MAYER, MARTIN. *Where, When, and Why: Social Studies in American Schools* (New York: Harper and Row, 1962).

National Commission on Teacher Education and Professional Standards. *Changes in Teacher Education: An Appraisal* (Washington, D.C.: National Education Association, 1964).

OLSEN, EDWARD G. "Operation 'Fair Chance': An Exciting Experiment in Teacher Preparation." *Journal of Teacher Education,* 19, (Spring, 1968), 79–84.

RESNIK, HENRY S. "Are There Better Ways to Teach Teachers?" *Saturday Review,* (Mar. 4) 1972, 46–50.

SARASON, SEYMOUR B., K. S. DAVIDSON, and B. BLATT. *The Preparation of Teachers* (New York: John Wiley and Sons, 1962).

SCHWARTZ LITA L., and SUNNIE R. SPIEGEL. "Field Work at Ogontz." *Penna. School Journal,* 1971, 120 (2), 21–22.

SILBERMAN, CHARLES E. *Crisis in the Classroom* (New York: Random House, 1970).

SMILEY, MARJORIE B., and JOHN S. DIEKOFF. *Prologue to Teaching: Readings and Source Material with Text* (New York: Oxford University Press, 1959).

STILES, LINDLEY J., and FRED D. CARVER. "Who Makes Policy for Teacher Education?" *Teachers College Record*, 69, 1967, 203–212.

STROM, ROBERT D., and CHARLES GALLOWAY. "Becoming a Better Teacher." *Journal of Teacher Education*, 18, (Fall, 1967), 285–292.

SLICK, GEORGE H. "Three R's of Teaching." *Pennsylvania School Journal*, 116, (Oct., 1967), p. 80.

TAYLOR, B. L., and R. C. MCKEAN. "Divergent Thinkers and Teacher Education." *Journal of Educational Research*, 1968, 61, 417–418.

TAYLOR, CALVIN W., ed. *Creativity: Progress and Potential* (New York: McGraw-Hill Book Company, 1964).

WELDON, LYNN. "Is Teacher Education an Illusion?" *Journal of Teacher Education*, 19, (Summer, 1968), 193–96.

WINTHROP, HENRY. "What can We Expect from the Unprogrammed Teacher?" *Teachers College Record*, 67, (Feb., 1966), 315–329.

WOLF, W. C., Jr. "Educators' Conceptions of Contemporary Innovation in Teacher Training." *School and Society*, 1969, 97, 378–380.

ZAHORIK, JOHN A. "The Trouble with Methods Courses." *Journal of Teacher Education*, 19, (Summer, 1968).

11

academic freedom and responsibilities

As one reads of teacher strikes, student "take-overs," "book-bannings," and controversies about loyalty oaths, it is easy to become confused about the whole concept of academic freedom. Where does "freedom" end and illegal behavior begin? This question faces students and teachers alike. At what point, if any, does the individual act as a citizen of the general community rather than as a member of the academic community? Are there different moral standards for the individual who happens to be a teacher than there are for the "ordinary" private citizen, not academically-oriented? The controversies aroused by teacher strikes and student militancy, in particular, obligate us, in the 1970's to re-examine and redefine the question of academic freedom. As is too often forgotten, moreover, academic responsibilities go with academic freedom, so these, too, must be re-considered.

Although much of the discussion on these questions is focused on freedom and responsibilities in higher education, current events throughout the country make the discussion also relevant to the secondary level of education. Certain of the points to be presented in this chapter are equally pertinent to teachers and students at all levels. Thoughtful consideration of the points of view expressed here should help to clarify the nature of the problem, and therefore help readers to take a more objective position to it.

What Is Academic Freedom?

Academic freedom is difficult to define, partly because it is a complex concept and not easily itemized, and partly because those who would define it are not in agreement. It is even difficult to decide what should not be included in such a definition. Even here, controversy develops.

There have been conflicting traditions in American education about the freedom to learn. One school has stressed conformity and education for indoctrination, stressing what is taught in the Bible and conservative textbooks. The emphasis here is on the evangelical purpose of the school as a force molding children into mature citizens. One example is that of the experience of John T. Scopes. He was an "obscure high school teacher in a small town when he volunteered to be the defendant in a test case of Tennessee's 'Anti-Evolution' law."[1] In this instance, it was prohibited to teach Darwin's theory of evolution in public schools of the State of Tennessee because it was contrary to the Fundamentalist religious orientation dominant in the state. The other point of view has emphasized freedom of inquiry and education for a free mind. This infers an "open society" in which non-conformity is tolerated.

How free is the freedom to teach? The teacher has certain rights as a teacher and as a citizen. He must exercise these rights judiciously (considering the age of the group of students whom he influences in the classroom) and responsibly. There is also a question of the freedom to learn—to read books of one's own choice, to question standard procedures and principles, and to inquire in new areas through research.

Perhaps it would be best at this point to allow three nationally-known spokesmen to present their views on this question of academic freedom, and let them try to define this elusive concept.

sterling m. mcmurrin

Academic Freedom in the Schools

the educator's freedoms

A variety of freedoms are of special importance in the life of an educator. Some of these relate directly and others only indirectly to his professional activities, but all can be major determinants of the character and quality of his teaching. Some freedoms and rights belong to the teacher as a citizen in a free society, and there is no justification for their abrogation on the ground that he is a public servant. Among these are the freedom of individuality and privacy in the community which he serves, freedom from espionage in and out of the classroom, the right to protection against defamations, slander, aspersion, and false accusation, and the right to seek redress through due process. It is unfortunately true that there are individuals and groups in our society who are willing to employ the most vicious methods of a police state in the pursuit of their ends and they sometimes enjoy strong community support when they make their underhanded attacks upon schools or upon individual teachers. No human rights or established methods of justice are sacred to the fanatic who is dominated by a conviction of his own righteousness.

Then there are the freedoms that might be called political, religious, and racial. Such freedoms are the right of free choice

McMurrin, Sterling M. "Academic Freedom in the Schools," *Problems and Issues in Contemporary Education* (Glenview, Ill.: Scott, Foresman, and Company, 1968), pp. 238–243. Originally published in the *Teachers College Record*, May 1964.

and affiliation in politics, of free political expression in private life, and the right under specified conditions to seek and hold public office. Or the right to serve in the public schools regardless of race, color, or religious belief or affiliation, and the right to profess and practice privately though openly a particular religion, or no religion at all, without reproach or public censure.

freedom of intellect

But when we defend academic freedom in the ordinary sense, of course, what is intended is intellectual freedom, the freedom of both teachers and students to engage honestly and openly in the pursuit of knowledge, to enlist fully the instrumentalities of reason and critical intelligence in that quest, and to express and communicate their opinions and ideas without liability, forfeit, or penalty. This can involve such things as policies governing invited lecturers, censorship on the performing arts or on the exhibition of painting and sculpture, restrictions on the publication of scientific research, censorship on literature employed as teaching material, or censorship on library acquisitions. Most of all, of course, it refers to what actually goes on in the classroom or laboratory. It has to do with what a teacher is free to discuss or teach or to write and publish in the fulfillment of his professional obligations. This is a complex and difficult issue—complex because of the countless variations in circumstances relating to instances of freedom or its violation, and difficult because there is no set of simple principles from which controlling rules can be derived for governing particular cases. . . . Decisions affecting intellectual freedom must often be made in situations that are ambiguous, where the issues are obscure or elusive and where the determining factors are both delicate and subtle. . . .

It is quite impossible to come to grips with the issue of academic freedom without recognizing its involvement with the fundamental aims and purposes of education, with the role of the schools as determinants of the life and character of individuals and society and of the structure of the culture. On the one hand is the compelling importance of intellectual freedom as the chief foundation of the free institution of a democratic society. On the other is the function of education as a conserver and critic of personal and social values and as protector, critic, and perpetuator of the culture. It is here that the chief problems lie in the matter of academic freedom for elementary and secondary schools, in the relation of freedom to the social functions of the schools.

. . . between elementary and graduate school there are differences . . . —differences that relate especially to the intellectual and maturational levels of the students—and those differences have an important bearing on what should or should not go on in the classroom, and on what is or is not an expression or violation of academic freedom. . . . There clearly are some things that should be dealt with at some time and somewhere in the schools, some ideas that should be aired and examined, that have, nevertheless, no place in the instruction of young children, either because no real gain would result or because the consequence might be genuine intellectual or moral harm.

. . . Just where and when an adequate maturity exists cannot be determined by rule or formula but must be decided by the best judgment and wisdom of the teacher or of the collective faculty, the parents, or the total community. In the end, however, the responsibility falls upon the teacher, who must assess the facts, interpret the public temper, and judge the value and justification of alternative actions or procedures in the classroom. He should not and cannot shed the burden of that responsibility. If he is not capable of bearing it and doing so with both wisdom and courage, he is not competent to be a teacher.

tyranny of the majority

. . . The purpose of education is not to endorse and sanctify the opinion of the many and impress it on the few, or to perpetuate whatever is common and habitual. It is rather an advancement of the individual and his society that cannot be achieved without creative change and where the full light of criticism must be thrown upon whatever claims sanction and perpetuation. This does not mean that academic freedom is to be equated with license or irresponsibility, or that the teacher is entitled to use his classroom as a forum for his private opinion, or that he has a special right as educator to impose on his students or the public what he thinks, writes, or paints. There is a proper time and place even for those things that are of unquestioned worth. . . . But what is meant by the critical presumption of education is that if the teacher is qualified to serve the public as an educator, that public should assume in him a genuine integrity of mind, sincerity of purpose, and competence of judgment, and that this confidence should not be easily dispelled by every passing fashion of opinion. That not all teachers merit such confidence is entirely obvious. . . .

Academic freedom is a two-way affair. What one has a right to teach, another has a right to learn; where there is a right to publish, there is a right to read; and if there is a right to exhibit, there is a right to observe. Censorship that is unjustified, as most censorship is, therefore, is a compound offense against a free society. Censorship in the schools that denies intellectual freedom to teachers robs the students of that same freedom. . . .

over passion and prejudice

. . .

Particular controversies over academic freedom may hinge upon individual and community taste and temperament. But the general problem is not so much a matter of personal or parochial idiosyncrasy as of traditional habits of mind that define what might be called the large dispositions of the culture. . . . The specific issues arise especially in matters having to do with religion, politics, economics, and morals, where "morals" has a somewhat limited connotation. . . .

As McMurrin points out, academic freedom also implies and creates a sense of academic responsibility. In the class-room, the teacher should have the freedom to discuss his subject. However, he is expected to present all points of view on controversial issues so that students (of sufficient maturity for the material) may think through them to their own conclusions, which may or may not agree with those of the teacher. The concept of freedom itself demands this. This freedom, though, is generally limited to topics in the teacher's own field of competence, and does not give him the right to discuss controversial matters in non-related subjects as an authority, but only as a private citizen.

richard m. nixon

The Four Academic Freedoms

Academic freedom is no "academic question"; it is one of the most powerful forces in human history.

Princes, presidents, even generals tremble in its presence.

Academic freedom is a free society's greatest single advantage in its competition with totalitarian societies.

No society can be great without the creative power it unleashes.

Yet while it can create, it can also destroy and it can consume itself.

A generation ago, "Four Freedoms" became a rallying cry for the forces of democracy: Freedom of speech and of worship, freedom from fear and from want. Today let us discuss the *Four Academic Freedoms*.

Nixon, Richard M. Commencement Address, University of Rochester, June 5, 1966. By permission of the author.

There is the academic freedom of the student to investigate any theory, to challenge any premise, to refuse to accept old shibboleths and myths.

There is a second academic freedom of the students to espouse *any* cause, to engage in the cut and thrust of partisan political or social debate, both on and off campus, without jeopardy to his academic career.

The third academic freedom is for the teacher—freedom from fear of reprisal while speaking or publishing the truth as he sees it, governed by the dictates of his own intellect and of the disciplines of scholarship.

Finally, there is a fourth academic freedom—this one within the academic community—that is, the freedom of the student from tyranny of the faculty, and conversely, freedom of the faculty from student tyranny.

These are the four academic freedoms that underlie the education you have received. Without these freedoms, teaching becomes indoctrination—a mockery of education.

Academic freedom is closely related to the freedom of expression guaranteed by the First Amendment to our Federal Constitution. Because this reference is made so often, I think it may be useful to consider at the outset one important similarity, and one important difference, between Academic Freedom and First Amendment freedom of speech.

First, I think it is clear that the same basic premise underlies both freedoms. That premise, with which we can all agree, holds that the complete free play of ideas and opinions is the best process for advancing knowledge and discovering truth.

. . .

In another sense academic freedom is different from and indeed greater than the Constitutional freedom of expression. I refer to the fact that the Constitution protects freedom of expression only from interference by government. It provides no protection from action by one private individual against another because of what he believes or says. This means that those of you who leave the academic community may find that your advancement may be retarded—or you may even be dismissed by your employer—merely because of the exercise of your right of free expression.

. . .

This special status granted the academic community does not result from some abstract principle, a privilege to be enjoyed merely at the sufferance of others. The strength of academic freedom is that it has been earned. History has taught us that teachers do their job best when they are free. *The special rights and privileges of academic freedom are conferred not so much for the benefit of the academic community but for the benefit of the society which the academic community serves.*

The American scholar stands at the height of his power. His prestige and influence reach into every sector of our national life.

In all the turbulence of crisis and change in recent years, students and teachers throughout this country have been a tremendous force—more so than any academic generation since the American Revolution.

Today's students are not merely blowing off steam in campus horseplay. They are making decisions and taking action to implement these decisions.

Woodrow Wilson's distinction between men of thought and men of action can no longer be made: The man of thought who will not act is ineffective; the man of action who will not think is dangerous.

Today's scholar has become a man of action as well as a man of thought. The challenges he faces have become infinitely more difficult.

Complex choices, without historical guidelines, potentially affecting the survival of mankind and frequently turning on narrow differences of degree, have become a condition of the daily life of our political and academic leaders.

This generation will have to maintain and extend freedom under conditions of utmost peril. It will have to learn to distinguish not only among friends, but among enemies, as the effort to secure a lasting peace without sacrificing freedom goes on.

This generation will have to live with the thought that there will never again be declared war. A limited conflict would be escalated by a declaration of war; a major conflict would be over before war could be declared.

This brings me to the paradox that confronts the academic community today and which presents all of us with real problems of choice. The power of the scholar in the United States has never been greater. Yet that enormous power of the academic community, which is the product of academic freedom, potentially threatens academic freedom.

Let us remember that we are considering here a freedom which derives its protection not from the law but from the respect and confidence the academic institution enjoys in the community in which it is located. Members of the academic community have a special status in our society for two reasons. One, a determination by society that the recipient must enjoy a maximum freedom of expression to serve society effectively; and, two, a respect by society for the judgment of the particular group, a confidence on the part of society that the privilege will not be seriously abused.

I believe that academic freedom in the United States is now so strongly supported that it will never be destroyed by its enemies—but it may be endangered by those who claim to be its friends.

Teachers must of course be free to take positions on all issues. But the position they hold in our society requires them to act with self-restraint.

. . .

Nixon's paper presents the thinking of a lawyer and moderate-conservative politician. It was addressed to and concerned principally the college-level academic community, but is relevant also to secondary school teachers who might be inclined to discuss domestic and foreign governmental policies with their older students. His concept of limited freedom deals in a sense with what is, or is not, appropriate to a situation; e.g., it is not appropriate for teachers to express hopes for victory of the dissidents or enemy—in the classroom or as an academic authority.

Commager, a respected historian and professor, also is concerned with the university level and university functions. As he points out, "The university is the chief instrument whereby society provides itself with independent criticism and advice, and with a continuous flow of ideas."

henry steele commager

The Nature of Academic Freedom

. . . Society provides freedom for scholars and for the university as an institution for the same elementary reason, because it wants to discover truth about as many things as possible.

It is out of this situation that the concept and the practice of academic freedom emerges, and on these principles that it rests. If society is to assure itself of a new generation trained to understand the world in which it will live, it must leave teachers free to transmit truth as they see it; if society is to have the benefit of disinterested advice, it must protect scholars who give that advice even when it is unpalatable; if society is to have the advantage of a flow of new ideas and discoveries,

Commager, Henry Steele. "The Nature of Academic Freedom," *Saturday Review*, Aug. 27, 1966, pp. 13–15, 37. © 1966, Saturday Review, Inc. By permission of the author.

it must leave scholars to carry on research in their own way. At its peril does any society interfere in any way, at any time, through pressure, intimidation, distraction, or seduction, with these sovereign functions of the academy.

. . .

What shall we say of university teachers and scholars who outrage public opinion by advocacy of doctrines that seem to the great majority to be erroneous? What shall we say of teachers who persistently flout the public will as expressed by resounding majorities? Once again the underlying principle is simple enough. . . . No scholar may claim that academic freedom gives him some special immunity from the law. But if what a scholar does or says does not violate any law, but merely outrages public opinion, then it is not the business of the university to do what civil authorities are unable to do.

The spectacle, common enough in the McCarthy era, of regents and trustees rushing in to punish teachers for conduct for which the civil authorities were unable or unwilling to prosecute—"taking the Fifth Amendment," for example—was a shameful one. In so far as trustees join with public opinion to intimidate or silence scholars, however much they may be misguided, they violate and betray their trust.

So it is with the punishment, by whatever means, of those who exercise their right to express ideas that are unpopular and seem dangerous—advocacy of the cause of the Vietcong, for example, or of the propriety of mixed marriages, or of the harmlessness of pornography. No doubt it is deplorable that otherwise intelligent men should entertain, let alone champion, notions of this sort, but how much more deplorable if we had the kind of society where they could not. A university is an institution where scholars are not only permitted but encouraged to think unthinkable thoughts, to explore intolerable ideas, and to proclaim their findings. There are risks here, to be sure. . . .

. . .

Those who today assure us that academic freedom is all right in ordinary times, but that in time of crisis it must give way to the importunate demands of national unity, those who argue that academic freedom is all very well in time of peace but a pernicious indulgence in time of war, are like the Southern slaveocracy and the Nazis and the white supremacists of South Africa, if not in conduct, then in principle. They are saying in effect that discussion and debate are all very well when there is nothing to discuss, but that they must be abated or suspended when there are serious matters before us. They are saying that we can tolerate freedom when there are no issues that threaten it, but that we cannot tolerate it when it is in danger.

. . .

These considerations go far beyond the confines of the academy, but they bear with special force on the academy. For the university has a special obligation to act as the critic and the conscience of society. Society has indeed created it to play this role. . . .

Commager is obviously a strong advocate of academic freedom, clear on the responsibility of the teacher to society as a whole, but in this selection, he pays relatively little attention to the responsibilities of the individual teacher. Agree or not, the public school teacher finds himself having to consider the point of view of the school authorities. Commager's article applies more to the university level where faculty obligations are somewhat different from those in the public schools and at the secondary or elementary level. Just as the individual has many inter-locking roles to play in the course of the day, so the public school teacher must remember that in his role in the classroom he is answerable to the school authorities; in his role as a citizen, he represents his profession, and again, perhaps his school system or university, deliberately or not; and even in his role as parent and neighbor, he speaks as a member of a respected profession. It is incumbent on the individual teacher, then, as has been indicated earlier, to exercise self-restraint in the use of academic freedom, and to weigh the age and/or maturity of his students in evaluating the extent to which such self-restraint is necessary. What is appropriate for the university professor to say to his students may not be appropriate for students a few years younger or of lesser intellectual maturity to hear. Outside of the school setting, the teacher must also recognize the authority which others confer upon him as a teacher, and express himself accordingly. Often, it is less a matter of *what* he says than of *how* he says it.

The teacher is, in fact, not completely free to criticize his employers negatively, for if working for a particular school board or university is that unpleasant, he should not remain with that employer any more than a workman who hates his "boss" should stay on his job. Such antipathy decreases his effectiveness in his work and reflects, in the case of the teacher, on his profession. Depending upon the nature of the criticism, it should be stated in appropriate places at appropriate times. As a teacher, special obligations are incumbent upon the individual. One of these is that his statements should be accurate and show respect for (and awareness of) the opinions of others.

In the foregoing excerpts, one area of academic freedom was explored lightly. This is the freedom to do research, as long as it does not interfere with teaching or other academic responsibilities. This means that the teacher can select his topic, obtain subjects (within ethical limits), and publish the results. There have been conflicts over research areas, mainly in higher education, but they have in general been resolved in line with the concept of academic freedom.

Faculty and Student Responsibility

Teaching is a profession that carries certain responsibilities that go hand-in-hand with academic freedom. These include ethical behavior, commitment to doing one's job well, accountability to society, and helping students to grow, in turn, into adults with a similar awareness of and commitment to freedom with responsibility, not license. The teachers' code of ethics states these obligations succinctly.

Code of Ethics of the Education Profession

preamble

The educator believes in the worth and dignity of man. He recognizes the supreme importance of the pursuit of truth, devotion to excellence, and the nurture of democratic citizenship. He regards as essential to these goals the protection of freedom to learn and to teach and the guarantee of equal educational opportunity for all. The educator accepts his responsibility to practice his profession according to the highest ethical standards.

The educator recognizes the magnitude of the responsibility he has accepted in choosing a career in education, and engages himself, individually and collectively with other educators, to judge his colleagues, and to be judged by them, in accordance with the provisions of this code.

principle i
commitment to the student

The educator measures his success by the progress of each student toward realization of his potential as a worthy and effective citizen. The educator therefore works to stimulate the spirit of inquiry, the acquisition of knowledge and understanding, and the thoughtful formulation of worthy goals.

In fulfilling his obligation to the student, the educator—

"Code of Ethics of the Education Profession," *NEA Journal*, 57 (April, 1968) pp. 42–43.

1. Shall not without just cause restrain the student from independent action in his pursuit of learning, and shall not without just cause deny the student access to varying points of view.

2. Shall not deliberately suppress or distort subject matter for which he bears responsibility.

3. Shall make reasonable effort to protect the student from conditions harmful to learning or to health and safety.

4. Shall conduct professional business in such a way that he not expose the student to unnecessary embarrassment or disparagement.

5. Shall not on the ground of race, color, creed, or national origin exclude any student from participation in or deny him benefits under any program, nor grant any discriminatory consideration or advantage.

6. Shall not use professional relationships with students for private advantage.

. . .

principle ii
commitment to the public

The educator believes that patriotism in its highest form requires dedication to the principles of our democratic heritage. He shares with all other citizens the responsibility for the development of sound public policy and assumes full political and citizenship responsibilities. The educator bears particular responsibility for the development of policy relating to the extension of educational opportunities for all and for interpreting educational programs and policies to the public.

In fulfilling his obligation to the public, the educator—

1. Shall not misrepresent an institution or organization with which he is affiliated, and shall take adequate precautions to distinguish between his personal and institutional or organizational views.

2. Shall not knowingly distort or misrepresent the facts concerning educational matters in direct and indirect public expressions.

3. Shall not interfere with a colleague's exercise of political and citizenship rights and responsibilities.

4. Shall not use institutional privileges for private gain or to promote political candidates or partisan political activities.

5. Shall accept no gratuities, gifts, or favors that might impair or appear to impair professional judgment, nor offer any favor, service, or thing of value to obtain special advantage.

. . .

Nowhere in the Code of Ethics are teacher organizations, of the labor union type, really discussed, other than to abide by the requests of the National Education Association as a professional association. Such requests might include abiding by sanctions imposed by the national or state association on a state or local school system. Specific instances of unsatisfactory educational conditions reported by state education associations are published frequently in the *NEA Reporter*, generally referring to a school district, although both a junior college and a Head Start program were listed in late 1972.[2] When sanctions are imposed, teachers are forewarned that some aspect of employment in that school district or state educational system is undesirable, and in some cases, are advised not to seek employment in systems under sanctions. There have also been those who have stated that teachers should become more militant and more tolerant of student militancy, as long as it is non-violent.[3] This inevitably leads to the question of faculty and student responsibilities in instances where protest is appropriate or contemplated.

It goes without saying that educators must oppose violence and unrelated or unnecessary demonstrations. But there are those who insist that teachers should not fear the wide variety of peaceful demonstrations, including civil disobedience, when such marches, boycotts, and sit-ins are designed to correct or to cause to be remedied long-standing and deep-seated grievances which are contrary to moral and/or ethical principles. It is even conceded that teachers might have to strike or boycott for themselves if that is the only way to secure needed changes in salary scales, curriculum innovations, school equipment, and the like.

There are presently two major teacher organizations which differ in the degree to which they urge militancy. The National Education Association regards itself as a professional organization, including classroom teachers, school administrators, and even some higher education faculty. It had, in 1972, over one million members in many subdivisions which included the Council for Exceptional Children, the Association of Classroom Teachers (ACT), the Association for Higher Education, the National Association of Secondary-School Principals, and others, and state and local associations. The NEA has become increasingly militant, and no longer prefers to call collective bargaining "professional negotiations," or strikes "professional holidays." The American Federation of Teachers, part of the AFL-CIO, has a smaller membership than the NEA, and limits its membership to classroom teachers. The AFT is strongest in the large cities of the nation, and functions largely through its local affiliates. The organization does not use euphemisms: it engages in traditional collective bargaining with school boards, and it calls a "strike" a "strike."[4] The AFT has stimulated the NEA in recent years to more political action on behalf of the profession, and it is not beyond the realm of possibility that, one day, the two organizations might merge or a third one arise, having a politically and economically impressive membership of more than two million educators. In late 1973, discussions began between these two organizations about a possible merger. A third organization, limited to higher education faculty, is the American Association of University Profes-

Figure 11.1 Teachers strike

Copyright © *The New York Times, June 4, 1967, p. E-11.*

Teacher walkouts, such as the one above in New York City in 1967, became commonplace in the late 1960's. Issues have centered in administrative matters, wages, and, notably in the 1968 New York City strikes, community-school relations.

sors. The AAUP has joined the other two organizations in collective bargaining activity in addition to its work of protecting academic freedom, tenure, and other professional rights for its members.

Tenure is granted to a teacher after a probationary period of service in a school district or college. It means, basically, that the teacher, having proved to be competent, cannot be fired except for due cause (e.g., criminal conviction). The tenure concept was originally designed in part to protect teachers from the personal and political influences on school board members as well as to protect their right to speak freely in the classroom. In two 1972 cases, however, the Supreme Court ruled that *non*-tenured faculty are not automatically entitled to administrative hearings prior to non-renewal of their contract, except under certain circumstances. According to faculty organizations, then, the non-tenured teacher can only be assured of due process hearings (that is, hearings on the reasons for non-renewal) if such a procedure is stipulated in a legal binding contract such as a collective bargaining agreement.[5] The frequency of problems arising from non-renewal of contract, inadequate salaries, course overloads, and other working conditions have led college faculties to unionization, much as public school teachers and lay parochial teachers had done earlier.

It is still difficult for many citizens to accept the idea of a teachers' strike, although there have been several major ones in Florida, Ohio, New York City, Philadelphia, and Pittsburgh. Even college faculties, particularly those at community colleges, have been on strike. Community shock is registered because teaching is regarded as a profession, dedicated to the service of the public, and professionals simply don't go on strike. Many teachers also see themselves in this way. On the other hand, it is a known fact that many teachers who are underpaid are also geographically immobile for personal reasons, and need some weapon with which to secure salary increases. Working conditions, the desire for improved curricula, and the need for adequate and appropriate educational resources are also considered to be legitimate reasons for teachers to oppose their administrators or the school board. Before they march out on strike, however, they should remember that they do have a primary responsibility to their students. Closing down the schools does a great disservice to the students, for it reduces the quantity and often the quality (if strike-breakers are hired to teach) of the education the students receive, as well as altering the "image" of the teacher which the students have. The courts have usually ruled, nevertheless, that teacher strikes are not a menace to community well-being, notably except in Philadelphia's lengthy strike in early 1973.

Don't students also have responsibilities? Indeed, they do. If they would imitate their elders by sit-ins, boycotts, and similar protest activities, then it is their responsibility also to avoid damage to personal and private property, to people, and to the global image of the student population. Wanton destruction of private property, as in the case of papers in administrative offices at Columbia University being destroyed in the spring of 1968, the burning of a Stanford professor's lifelong accumulation of research notes, laboratory explosions at the University of Wisconsin, and similar acts have no place in legitimate protest demonstrations.

Similarly, student militancy at the University of California at Berkeley has caused negative public reactions not only toward Berkeley students, but also toward college students in general. In the 1968 election campaign, student uprisings on public and private college campuses, particularly those activities sponsored by the Students for a Democratic Society, were condemned by some as unAmerican and Communist-inspired. The Kent State (Ohio) and Jackson State (Mississippi) demonstrations of 1970, both tragically fatal, further alienated the public. Sitdown strikes and student marches further intimidated many college administrators, and were mimicked at the secondary school level with similar results.

Students need to remember, too, that public education is supported by the public, and the general public is afraid of, and unwilling to support, violent demonstrators. This has been reflected in reduced alumni support at many institutions and in the voting down of school bond issues in the area of public education. The restrictive attitudes of state legislators have also been aroused in part by these events.

donald s. seckinger

Freedom and Responsibility in Education

. . .

In the light of protestations and slogans about freedom and responsibility, there is a curious relationship between propaganda and philosophy in education. Frequently, educators look on propaganda as a useful tool for blunting criticism, enlisting support, and getting on with the job of keeping school. Philosophy, in contrast, is viewed as an impractical, visionary enterprise, far removed from everyday learning situations with real students in real schools.

Yet, it is the propaganda of education which treats the individual as an object by abstracting him into a typical learner. Genuine philosophizing in education, on the contrary, insists on dealing with concrete, and often paradoxical, ethical and moral situations faced by real human beings, and with obligations of schools to face these situations.

. . .

Not surprisingly, programs of instruction based on the propaganda of education are geared to the same safe averages and norms, the same social expectations, as is the propaganda itself. These programs must stress the comfortable and the conformable. They must purvey knowledge which is prepackaged and procedures where the getting of this knowledge, as a commodity to be stored and fed back to the school on demand, are spelled out. Rewards and punishments also are spelled out, and skillful teachers are encouraged to exploit social pressures in the name of individual freedom.

. . .

Seckinger, Donald S. "Freedom and Responsibility in Education," *School and Society*, 96, (Summer, 1968), pp. 278–279.

Freedom in education demands occasions for learning. These occasions require teachers who are open to the intellectual risks involved in sharing discoveries in knowledge with their students. Freedom involves students in the uncoerced appropriation of knowledge that may lead on to self-discovery and the awareness that one is responsible for his own decisions.

We live in a time of social unrest and social progress, of technological achievement which sees us poised between unprecedented material well-being and a new age of incredible barbarism and suffering. In such a time, the desire for escape is understandable, but there is no escape.

For the educators, there is no tuning out of society, whatever its imperfections, nor is there any really comfortable retreat from freedom in the conformities of educational propaganda. There is only the facing of freedom, the responsibility to answer for oneself, and the obligation we have as educators to provide the occasions wherein others may seek their own commitments to themselves and to the world.

It is the responsibility of the student, too, to face freedom, to be able to face himself in adulthood, and to take advantage of the occasions provided for learning in order to make of himself a better person.

Loyalty Oaths

What is a loyalty oath? Generally, a loyalty oath is a statement of support for the government and nonentanglement in foreign governments or "subversive" groups. Such a statement has been presented to prospective teachers for their signature at many points in our history—usually during crises of a political sort. In some cases, the oath may require the teacher to teach or not to teach specific aspects of patriotism, for example,[6] principles of democracy but not principles of Communism. Or, as was mentioned at the beginning of the chapter, particular subject-matter may be prohibited in the curriculum, such as Darwin's theory of evolution. The most recent era in which teachers were required to sign loyalty oaths—or not be hired— began in the early 1950's, particularly while Senator Joseph McCarthy of Wisconsin was conducting his investigations of Communists in the government. His investigations occurred in a period when it was found that atomic secrets had been stolen and given or sold to Russia during and after the Second World War. Fears of Communism rose. McCarthy investigated principally alleged subversives in the Federal government, but the panic of "guilt by association" and anxiety about possible "Reds" in the classroom also affected education. The loyalty oaths were the result. These oaths have been prescribed individually by the states, but have not been required in every state.

A question that immediately arises is whether the required signature as prerequisite to employment infringes on the individual's rights as a citizen. Involved in this question is also the concept, as mentioned above, of freedom or guilt by association. In the case of Adler v. Board of Education (342 U.S. 485, 1952), Adler brought suit against the New York Board of Education, charging that the state's Feinberg Law abridged his rights of freedom of association which are guaranteed under the First Amendment. The Feinberg Law empowered the Board of Regents of the state to make a list of "subversive" organizations, membership in which disqualified an individual from teaching in the school system. The Supreme Court majority opinion stated that this was a reasonable procedure for self-protection on the part of the state, and that those who joined such organizations innocently could so plead at their dismissal hearings. (Note the year well—it was during the "McCarthy era.") In his dissent to the decision, Justice William O. Douglas pointed out, however, that ". . . innocence in this case turns on knowledge; and when the witch hunt is on, one who must rely on ignorance leans on a feeble reed."[7] He decried the implied guilt by association. It was indeed contrary to the long-held principle that the innocent are innocent until proven guilty.

Fifteen years later, the Adler decision was reversed.

In a decision estimated to affect at least 26 states, the U.S. Supreme Court declared unconstitutional New York State's "complicated and intricate scheme" of teacher antisubversive laws and regulations.

The High Court struck down the entire New York teacher "loyalty" program and rejected the theory that teachers' rights are secondary to considerations of internal security . . .

In a 5–4 decision, the Supreme Court assailed New York's antisubversive laws as being unconstitutionally vague and posing a grave threat to academic freedom.

In the majority opinion, Justice Brennan said: "Our nation is deeply committed to safeguarding academic freedom, which is of transcendent value to all of us and not merely the teachers concerned. That freedom is therefore a special concern of the First Amendment, which does not tolerate laws that cast a pall of orthodoxy over the classroom."[8]

It is important to note that the case in point, Keyishian v. Board of Regents (1967), drew particular attention to the area of academic freedom, as well as restating the constitutional right of the individual to freedom of association. Contrary to the Adler and other decisions, "Teachers may work in a 'sensitive area,' but they do not have to relinquish their rights to freedom of speech and association because of public employment."[9] To those who were too young during the McCarthy years of power to know, or who do not recall the atmosphere he created, let it be said that people in "sensitive" position became suddenly afraid of their neighbors, their employers, their group affiliations. The atmosphere was not unlike that found in totalitarian states where friend is encouraged to report on friend for the slightest infraction of state law. The Keyishian decision, therefore, has great meaning to all who do remember the days of the "witch-hunt," to those who even now have to contend with extremist and prejudiced views, and to teachers, especially.

Another aspect of the loyalty oaths concerns the freedom to teach and to explore. The most notorious example of this may be the afore-mentioned teaching by John Scopes about Darwin's theories of evolution in defiance of Tennessee's fundamentalist law banning such discussions in the state's schools.

> The never-ending battle for academic freedom is waged at all academic levels, in schools as well as in colleges, in small towns as well as in the great cities. And the public school teacher who engages in the battle faces a far greater risk, and hence needs greater courage, than does the professor in a famous university. The professor who defends the right of his students to learn the truth knows that he can count on the support of his colleagues and of the academic community throughout the Western world. But the public school teacher who demands the same right for his students rarely can count on such support. For him it is often a lonely battle, judged by an audience unable to grasp the significance of the issues at stake.
>
> The experience of John T. Scopes was an exception. . . . in the gaudy carnival that H. L. Mencken dubbed the "Monkey Trial" he had the support of some of the best legal talent in the nation. When he was convicted the American Civil Liberties Union paid his $100 fine . . .
>
> . . .
>
> Even today, after forty-two years, it is not entirely clear which side won at Dayton. No one denied that Scopes had broken the law; it was the law that was on trial. Because the defense was unsuccessful in its attempt to test the law's unconstitutionality in higher courts, that issue remains unsettled. However, a similar law in Arkansas was declared unconstitutional by a Chancery Court only last May [1966] as a result of a suit filed by a high school biology teacher . . .[10]

In his trial, Scopes was defended by Clarence Darrow, and William Jennings Bryan prosecuted for the state. Although the law continued to be in the statute books in Mississippi and Arkansas in 1968, its existence was terminated for all practical purposes by a United States Supreme Court ruling of Nov. 12, 1968. The decision declared such laws to be in violation of the First and Fourteenth Amendments.

The freedom to teach is not circumscribed by loyalty oaths and legislative prohibitions alone, however. Community prejudices may place the teacher in the uncomfortable position of being constantly under surveillance, with every sentence scrutinized for "disloyal" or "subversive" or "immoral" content. Since principals and supervisors rarely enter the classroom, such scrutiny is conducted by students, who may misinterpret, quote incorrectly, or simply decide to gain revenge against a disliked teacher by causing him difficulty. If a teacher has to watch literally every word he says for fear of such scrutiny or attack, then his freedom to teach is abridged. If his freedom to teach is abridged, so is the student's freedom to learn. If one of the functions of education is to maximize freedom of inquiry and to stimulate critical thinking, then the teacher must be free to teach all sides of a question so that the students may learn how to think through conflicting opinions to arrive at a decision for themselves. Related to this aspect of the freedom to teach and to learn is the opportunity to hear about and to read about matters which may be unpopular with various groups—Communism, the United Nations, racial integration, and so on. If such groups are influential enough with school authorities, they can have books about such topics banned from school library shelves, and teachers discussing these matters "called on the carpet" for dismissal. Closing one's ears and eyes to controversial issues does not make them disappear. What does disappear is academic freedom.

The freedom to teach is not unique to teachers under the Constitution as teachers, but as citizens. In the nineteenth century, academic and personal freedom for the public school teacher was not a concern.

While nineteenth-century society hammered out the rationale for academic freedom at the university level, it remains for twentieth-century society to do the same for the elementary and secondary school teacher. As America moved in the twentieth century to a more cosmopolitan perspective and local regulation of teachers' personal lives decreased, the possibility of defining an area of responsible freedom was enhanced. But the threat of international Communism slowed this progress. A society under external threat is reluctant to extend its boundaries of freedom. In the Supreme Court cases, one can sense a real struggle to maintain a free education in the face of a threatened society. If successful here, teachers may yet have the opportunity to prove they are capable of exercising that responsible freedom which alone is at the heart of any profession. The role of the teacher, then, has been changing. Through these decisions, one can also see a pragmatic court repeatedly making judgments not only on the basis of the traditions of the past, but, more important, on the expected consequences of these decisions for the present and the future. The Constitution, then, has become a living, changing document, relevant to the major issues of the times. In maintaining the life of the Constitution, the court has, in effect, concurred with the opinion of Oliver Wendell Holmes: "The Constitution is an experiment, as all life is an experiment."[11]

Endnotes

1. Woodring, Paul. "The Editor's Bookshelf," *Saturday Review*, March 18, 1967, p. 64.

2. *NEA Reporter*, Oct. 1972, 11, p. 11.

3. Kraft, Ivor. "The Politicalization of America's Educators." In *Social Foundations of Education*, ed., Dorothy Westby-Gibson (New York: The Free Press, 1967), pp. 281–288.

4. Moskow, Michael H. "Teacher Organizations: an Analysis of the Issues," *Teachers College Record*, 66, (Feb. 1965), pp. 453–463.

5. *The Pennsylvania Professor*, October 1972, 5 (1), p. 1 (referring to Sindermann v. Texas and Roth v. Univ. of Wisconsin-Oshkosh cases).

6. Stone and Hempstead, *op. cit.*, pp. 113–117.

7. Quoted in Karier, *op. cit.*, p. 322.
8. *School Boards*, X, March 1967, p. 6.
9. Karier, *op. cit.*, p. 325.
10. Woodring, 1967, *op. cit.*, p. 64.
11. Karier, *op. cit.*, pp. 326–327.

For Further Reading

ALTBACH, PHILIP G., ROBERT S. LAUFER, and SHEILA McVOY (eds.) *Academic Super Markets* (San Francisco: Jossey-Bass, 1971).

American Association of University Professors. "Academic Freedom and Tenure." *AAUP Bulletin*, March 1958.

American Association of University Professors. "Statement on Collective Bargaining." *AAUP Bulletin*, Winter 1973, 423–424.

BLANCHARD, PAUL. *The Right to Read: The Battle against Censorship.* (Boston: Beacon Press, 1955).

BURRUP, PERCY E. *The Teacher and the Public School System*, 3rd ed. (New York: Harper and Row, 1972).

DOHERTY, ROBERT E. "The Law and Collective Bargaining for Teachers." *Teachers College Record*, 68, 1966, 1–12.

FORSTER, ARNOLD, and BENJAMIN R. EPSTEIN. *Danger on the Right* (New York: Random House, 1964).

HOOK, SIDNEY. *Heresy, Yes. Conspiracy, No.* (New York: John Day Company, 1953).

KARIER, CLARENCE A. *Society, and Education* (Glenview, Ill.: Scott, Foresman, and Company, 1967).

KING, JOSEPH A. "Books and Banners: a Case History." *Saturday Review*, (Nov. 9) 1963, 28–29, 66.

KRAFT, IVOR. "The Politicization of America's Educators." *Social Foundations of Education* (Dorothy Westby-Gibson, ed.) (New York: The Free Press, 1967), 281–288.

KRUG, MARK M. "'Safe' Textbooks and Citizenship Education." *School Review*, (Winter) 1960, 463–480.

LIPSET, SEYMOUR MARTIN. "Students and Politics in Comparative Perspective." *Daedalus*, 97, (Winter 1968), 1–20.

MACIVER, ROBERT M. *Academic Freedom in our Times* (New York: Columbia University Press, 1955).

MCMURRIN, STERLING M. "Academic Freedom in the Schools." *Problems and Issues in Contemporary Education* editors of *Harvard Educational Review* and *Teachers College Record*, eds. (Glenview, Ill.: Scott, Foresman, and Company, 1968), 238–243.

MOSKOW, MICHAEL H. "Teacher Organizations: an Analysis of the Issues." *Teachers College Record*, 66, (Feb. 1965), 453–463.

MYERS, DONALD A. *Teacher Power: Professionalization and Collective Bargaining* (Lexington, Mass.: D.C. Heath-Lexington Books, 1973).

NAGI, MOSTAFA H. "Social Psychological Correlates of Membership in Teachers' Organizations." *Teachers College Record*, 74, 1973, 369–378.

NEA Committee on Professional Ethics. "Code of Ethics of the Education Profession." *NEA Journal*, 57, (Apr., 1968), 42–43.

NELSON, JACK, and GENE ROBERTS, JR. *The Censors and the Schools* (Boston: Little, Brown, and Company, 1963).

NIXON, RICHARD M. "The Four Academic Freedoms." *College and University Journal*, 5, (Summer, 1966), 4–9.

PETERSON, RICHARD E. "The Student Left in American Higher Education." *Daedalus*, 97, (Winter, 1968), 293–317.

POUNDS, RALPH L., and JAMES R. BRYNER. *The School in American Society*, second edition (New York: The Macmillan Company, 1967).

Problems and Issues in Contemporary Education ed., Editors of *Harvard Educational Review* and *Teachers College Record* (Glenview, Ill.: Scott, Foresman, and Company, 1968).

ROBINSON, DONALD W. "The Teachers Take a Birching." *Phi Delta Kappan*, (Feb. 1962), 182–188.

SMITH, G. KERRY (ed.). *Stress and Campus Response* (San Francisco: Jossey-Bass, 1968).

TAYLOR, HAROLD. *On Education and Freedom* (New York: Abelard-Schuman, 1954).

THAYER, V. T., and MARTIN LEVIT. *The Role of the School in American Society*, second edition (New York: Dodd Mead and Company, 1966).

WESTBY-GIBSON, DOROTHY, ed., *Social Foundations of Education* (New York: The Free Press, 1967).

WOODRING, PAUL. "The Editor's Bookshelf." *Saturday Review*, March 18, 1967, p. 64.

12

a national educational policy

Is there a need for a national educational policy? Are there feasible methods with which to implement such a policy? Could such a policy be consistent with our traditional view of states' rights in education? What is done in other nations?

In an attempt to answer these questions, the basic problems relevant to the questions will be discussed in this chapter, and the alternative possible solutions will be presented. Since other countries do have a national educational policy, a very general introduction to the world of comparative education is also included.

The Problems

We have previously noted that there is a high and increasing rate of population mobility in the United States. This creates sizable problems for school-age children. If their families move from one community to another even within the same state, they generally have to face not only new teachers and classmates, but also new texts and approaches to education. Even in adjacent school districts, for example, one system may offer "Illinois math" another "SMSG math." Depending upon the student's grade-level, he may or may not be adequately prepared to make the shift from one to the other successfully. It is equally possible that in one district, French is introduced in fourth grade, carried through succeeding years, and articulated with the secondary-level French program, while a second near-by district does not offer French until 9th grade. The result is that students moving between the two are either "behind" in sixth grade, or lose some of their competence through lack of reinforcement while waiting for the ninth-grade language course.

A second complication arising from this mobility involves grade placement. An average student from an "average" school in one district may be dropped back a grade when moving to a district with brighter pupils and a more difficult or accelerated curriculum. This practice both reflects poorly on the original district and may be a psychological blow to the individual student.

Thirdly, there is the question of whether an academic or business diploma from one high school "means" the same in terms of accomplishment as either diploma from some other high school. Of course, one must admit that the same is true of college degrees.

If these are the problems which occur in adjacent school districts of a single state, consider their magnification on an inter-state basis! Children of military families, in particular, face frequent changes of assignment. If they move four to six times in their basic twelve years of education, it is likely that they will need an additional year to complete the requirements of the state in which they reside as seniors. Most states require a course in state history at some point in the grades, and students have reported that they encountered graduation difficulties because, in one of the earlier schools, they had learned state history for that state and it was not transferable. Similarly, one state may accept a non-laboratory general science course for a diploma, and a second state may mandate a laboratory course.

In different sections of the country, because of the local historical development and/or ethnic background of the state's population, certain cultures and languages are emphasized to the omission or de-emphasis of others. If a student moves from the Scandinavian-German culture of Minnesota or Wisconsin, does he "lose out" when he moves to the Spanish-oriented culture of Southern California or New Mexico?

Finally, there is the fundamental variation in quality of education from school to school, district to district, which can be found within and between any state(s).

There are many possible solutions to these problems, some of which are acceptable to many and few of which are acceptable to all. Before presenting them, however, let us examine how these situations are handled at home and abroad.

Patterns at Home and Abroad

There is one state, New York, which has uniform achievement tests at the secondary level. The New York State Regents examinations strike "terror" into the hearts of many students when they are merely mentioned. They are comprehensive in subject matter, are intended to be fair in design, and ensure that when passed, the student has learned at least a minimum desirable amount in that subject (or is an unusually talented guesser). The tests may be taken, for example, after one year of work in mathematics, the sciences, and American History; two years in a foreign language (or three or four); and four years in English. Those who pass the examinations in a sufficient number of subject areas are awarded a Regents diploma in addition to their regular high school diploma. (Note: Many, if not all, New York state colleges require the results of Regents examinations among the credentials submitted for admission to them by New York residents.) Although the system is a century old, it is still a source of controversy among educators as well as students. One critic, chairman of a suburban New York high school social studies department, has commented that in his field,

> A state exam cannot adequately test the historical method; nor can it test the student's knowledge of how historiographical opinions have changed over the years. Such things are arbitrary, independently taught and independently understood. The test, therefore, must rely upon fact recall. It fosters the type of educational emphases generally conceived to be most deadly to classroom interest and student improvement.[1]

And, further,

> The State University Board of Regents has the legal au-
> thority to test. Like other State Boards, it is obliged to
> emphasize patriotism and citizenship. But do centralized
> examinations in American history achieve these goals?
> Theoretically, a centrally produced, expertly created test
> might be of some value. But consider the differences be-
> tween students from a socio-economically deprived neigh-
> borhood of New York City and those from a central high
> school in a rural area, or those from a wealthy suburban
> community. Can one detailed and intricate test, given to
> all students in American history, be an instrument for citi-
> zenship education, when American history and citizenship
> have had quite different meanings for the children from
> each of these areas? A sense of irony alone should dictate
> against using a standard test to evaluate the achievement
> of non-standard children.[2]

Again, if one extrapolates this situation to a national scale, the
problems engendered in a national testing program where the
differences are magnified, becomes apparent.

College Entrance Examination Board and similar examinations are voluntary in the sense that they are not school or
state-imposed, but otherwise present difficulties similar to
those of the Regents. They are mass-testing programs; they are
oriented to the collegebound; they are designed for machine-
scoring, so that usually only one answer may be considered
correct, which curbs academic nonconformity. There is considerable complaint by teachers, students, and parents, that
all of these tests reduce the flexibility of the curriculum, because teachers tend to "teach for the tests."

Abroad, national educational policies and testing programs
are the rule. Traditionally, a testing program has been used
with ten and eleven-year-olds to select those who will be sent
to university preparatory schools, to vocational schools, to
"general" secondary schools, or in some instances, to no
school at all beyond the mandatory eight or nine grades.[3] High
rates of selectivity continue to be common in Great Britain,
France, and Germany, as well as other countries, for the aca-

demic programs. However, there is a recent trend toward increased education, since the school-leaving age in England and on the Continent has been raised from 14 years of age to 15 or 16 years.

England now has secondary modern, technical, and comprehensive high schools in addition to the traditional grammar (university preparatory) schools, to which all students move from the primary schools. The secondary modern schools are state schools which are non-selective, and which offer a combination of academic and vocational courses.[4] Placement in the post-primary schools is determined by the famous (or infamous) "11+" examination scores, particularly those in English and arithmetic. In recent years, there has been a decrease in the use of these tests, varying with each local school authority. The curriculum of the first two years in these schools is sufficiently similar today to permit some reassignment to other schools at the end of the second year, if the pupil's achievements warrant it. The external or national examination for university admission may be taken at the conclusion of the grammar or the secondary modern school course. This is an improvement over the situation which existed until the Second World War, for at that time in England, as in other European countries, ". . . there were elementary schools for the working class and for the peasants on the one hand, and a system of academic schools based on a classical curriculum for the middle class. The degree of social exclusiveness varied from country to country . . ."[5] The system of external examinations was so rigid, that in 1916, Alfred North Whitehead stated that,

> The machinery of our secondary education is rigid where it should be yielding, and lax where it should be rigid. Every school is bound on pain of extinction to train its boys for a small set of definite examinations. No headmaster has a free hand to develop his general education or his specialist studies in accordance with the opportunities of his school, which are created by its staff, its environment, its class of boys, and its endowments. I suggest that no system of external tests which aims primarily at examining individual scholars can result in anything but educational waste.[6]

Heresy, indeed, at that time!

At the primary and junior levels, equivalent to our pre-kindergarten through grade 5, the "open classroom" and "vertical grouping" by age offer a marked contrast to the traditional British school. Learning appears to be incidental, but is really neatly structured by the teacher's selection of materials available in the classroom. The children learn by doing, with those who "can" helping those who "can't," and the teacher knowing exactly what each child's performance level is at a given time. There is greater awareness of individual differences that ultimately must lead to changes in the upper schools. There is increased emphasis on adapting the school to the child rather than the other way round.

France has had a highly centralized national system of education since the days of Napoleon. This begins at the primary level, and since entrance to primary schools depends upon pre-school preparation, many children go to pre-primary schools for that preparation. The "weeding-out" process gathers strength from that level, and becomes increasingly selective. In recent years though, France, too, has re-evaluated its educational system, and becomes aware of the need to change the pattern of distribution of children at the secondary level. French educators have developed a unique plan to do this.

Presently all French children attend the common primary school for five years. At eleven they are sorted either into a type of secondary school or remain, as in Germany, in extended years of primary until the school-leaving age of fourteen. The January 1959 Education Law indicates, however, that the school-leaving age will be raised to sixteen, . . .

. . . the extended elementary years will be abolished, every adolescent to age sixteen will be attending a secondary school, and the special sorting process to assure that each child gets the proper secondary education will be in operation.

Mainly there are four types of secondary school, the classical *lycée*, comparable to the *Gymnasium* or grammar school, the modern secondary, the professional secondary, and the terminal secondary. Henceforth children will be sorted into one of these school types, but whatever the school name, all children will commence their two years in a common program known as the *cycle d'observation*, or determination block. At the end of the initial term of three months an orientation committee will decide the gross shunting of each child into either a classical or a modern stream.

The orientation committee here should be introduced, for it will presently be met again. It comprises the teachers who have taught the child in his first term, plus a psychologist, plus an M.D. This committee makes a recommendation to the child's parents, and if at any step the parents object to the professional decision, the child is entitled to a reappraisal through testing.

Just halfway through the *cycle* (at the end of the first year) the orientation committee reviews the student's progress and fitness for the stream he is in. A change to the alternate channel is possible here, again subject to the challenge of parents.

Finally, after the end of the two-year *cycle* and when the child is thirteen years old, the orientation committee reviews each child's case on the basis of achievement records. It recommends assignment to the most appropriate type of secondary school. This may mean a shift in school building for the child, or it may mean he continues his secondary education in the building where he has undergone the *cycle d'observation*. Even after this final assignment the parents are entitled to challenge the committee's judgment, but again the student must pass a test to permit him to shift streams.

The Plan conforms to the familiar pattern of Continental respect for the judgment of the school, and it perpetuates the parental privilege of asking for retrial, yet the main lesson for American consideration would seem to be in the several levels of re-appraisal which are built into the two-year progression of the *cycle*.[7]

Such a strong evaluation and guidance program at the equivalent of our sixth and seventh grades is rare in American education. It is more common at the end of eighth grade in an 8-4 pattern or ninth grade where there is a junior high school. Even then, the multiple re-evaluations rarely exist, at least not in such definite form, and not on a national basis.

Further to the east, Czechoslovakia now has a unified school system under its 1960 Education Act, presenting a unified curriculum which combines the principles of Comenius with the principles of socialism. There is compulsory attendance from ages six to fifteen, with a basic nine-year school whose purpose is ". . . to give the pupils basic general and polytechnical education, provide correct vocational guidance with full regard to the needs of society and the talents, interests and inclinations of the individual."[8] The aims and mandated program for each of the ten major and six minor subjects offered during the nine year course are spelled out in syllabi. The curriculum, syllabus, and texts for each subject are identical throughout the country, although in a report to UNESCO for the school year 1965–66, some differentiation in curriculum was reported for the ninth year of study, with homogeneous grouping of students and modifications in the curricula of the secondary cycle.[9] Special education, for which Comenius himself stressed a need, is provided for the retarded, the physically handicapped, the maladjusted, and the highly talented (art, mathematics, languages, and physical training).

> . . . The schools of the second cycle basically provide three basic directions, three ways whereby young persons can pursue their aims in life. All these three schools follow specific aims; yet they each have certain features in common. None of them places obstacles in the way of higher education. Under capitalism apprentices were quite unable to reach the university. Now in the course of two years they are able to pass the School-Leaving Certificate at schools for employed persons. The School Certificate opens the way to enrolment at the university.[10]

In 1965, about forty percent of school-leavers continued at secondary schools, and Vodinský states that this number is expected to increase to about sixty-seven percent in 1970. Admission to the universities is based on possession of the School-Leaving Certificate (obtained by examination), recommendation from the secondary school, and an entrance examination to the student's particular faculty, or school of study, at the university.[11] The State determines the job placement of each school-leaver and university graduate according to where his services are needed most. As in other Soviet satellites, the Ministry of Education and Culture operates what we might call this "complete" national education policy.

Moving further east, to the theocratic State of Israel, we find religious, military, and economic problems affecting educational policies. Due to the survival problem, in both military and economic realms, highly-valued but relatively low-priority education had been compulsory for only eight grades, but a required ninth grade has been added and there is movement toward a tenth required year of schooling. This has resulted in a shift from an 8-4 pattern of schooling to the more familiar (to us) 6-3-3 pattern.

The religious factionalism prevalent in Israel has led to two state-supported school systems plus a private parochial system operated by ultra-Orthodox Jews. The State determines the curriculum in both of its school systems (one for the religiously observant) as well as in schools operated for Bedouin and Arab children. Conant's advocacy of a flexible, multiple track system of homogeneous grouping is practiced in Israel from the sixth grade on. Homogeneous but parallel classes exist in Hebrew, foreign languages, and mathematics. This permits easy reassignment of pupils as their academic performance changes. At the secondary level, those students who are able to attend specialize in humanistic studies, sciences and mathematics, Oriental studies, or vocational programs with or without "matriculation." The British influence from the Mandate period (pre-1948) is still felt in terms of matriculation (degree-seeking) and examinations. Although secondary education is neither required nor free, abundant scholarships are available for able students so that secondary education is not strictly divided by socio-economic status.

There is a State Ministry of Education as well as local Departments which deal with problems peculiar to their own areas.[12] The Education Department in Jerusalem, for example, operates six schools for retarded children, one for the physically handicapped, and one for the blind and deaf, divided according to the secular and religious systems described above. This Department also operates the schools for Arab children in the East part of Jerusalem and nearby communities, integrating the "culturally different" children into the overall educational system. Incidentally, these are not the only "culturally different" children in the state. There are, in addition, those children from Jewish families which have fled from Egypt, Yemen, Tunisia, Morocco, and Iraq. Their way of life was centuries behind the twentieth, and behind and incomprehensible to the European or Ashkenazic Jews of modern Israel.

> Israeli officials, teachers, and other professionals are aware of the problems created by the absorption of these Oriental immigrants. Some of the steps they are considering are analogous to those suggested for solving our own racial problems in the United States. Often mentioned is preferential treatment—special schooling and job opportunities—for those children of Oriental Jews who show promise. Overall, the emphasis for equalizing society is on education; in this respect, Israel and the United States put faith in the same method.

> There is, however, a wide educational gap between Oriental and *Ashkenazic* Jews. All children go through nine years of schooling. Then competitive examinations are used to select those who will go on to higher education. Oriental Jews coming from impoverished backgrounds, from cultures where there has been no great value placed on education, are unable to compete with the children of the European group. Parenthetically, it is somewhat of a shock to find that, in a country so dedicated to equal education and equal opportunity for its citizens, children receive only nine years of public schooling.[13]

In discussing this problem with Jerusalem's Minister of Education, it was found that the situation resembles not only our difficulties with racial differences, but with all of the educationally disadvantaged.

India, also formerly under British rule, found, when it became independent in 1947, that it had a tiny minority of well-educated intellectuals and a huge mass of illiterates in the population. Under a centralized national education policy, Gandhi proposed a system of free elementary Basic Education, which opposed the traditional emphasis on intellect at the expense of imagination and emotions. The goals India set itself in its early years of independence were: free elementary education for all children, education for illiterate adults, reorganization of secondary and higher education, rapid expansion of scientific and technical education, and enrichment of the national cultural life—for a population numbering in the hundreds of millions, and to be achieved almost simultaneously. In half a decade, substantial progress was made simultaneously in all the indicated directions.[14] In more than a decade since Kabir's book, even more progress has been made, although much has yet to be done. There has been a de-emphasis on the national examination system, recognition of the several sub-cultural languages and societies, and an expansion of schooling to rural areas.

In Communist China, the entire school structure has been reorganized in the years since 1949. The average level of formal education has been more than tripled (from 2.0 years to 6.5 years), and the extremely conservative emphasis on rote memorization and classical texts has been almost completely altered.

"Mao's special concern with educational reform stems from his long-held conviction that traditional education has been the prime device by which ruling classes perpetuated themselves in China. . . . Mao believed that only by demolishing this system could the time-honored distinction between scholar and peasant, intellectual and manual worker, be made to disappear; then his new homogenized man (at once worker, peasant, soldier, and intellectual) could emerge."[15]

The goal in the rural areas is a 9-year school. Instruction and practical labor are integrated in keeping with current governmental philosophy.

From this glimpse of American and foreign educational patterns, it is easy to see that each centralized policy has its problems. Let us examine some possible solutions for the United States, considering both positive and negative viewpoints.

Implementing a National Education Policy

As early as 1796, the American Philosophical Society (Philadelphia) offered a prize for the best proposal for a national educational system. Rep. George F. Hoar of Massachusetts introduced a bill to establish a system of national education in 1870. Apart from the sections of the bill dealing with state and local administration of schools, he included a provision that schoolbooks ". . . to be used in all the national schools shall be such as are prescribed by the said superintendent, under the direction of the Commissioner of Education."[16] None of the books to be used in the national schools, nor any of the instruction, was to favor the beliefs of any religious group. Taxes for the support of education in each State were to be assessed on real estate owners and the monies raised to be spent within each state.

In 1881, Sen. Henry W. Blair proposed the establishment and support of schools by the national government, with financial aid given in decreasing amounts over a ten-year period. There were to be common (elementary) schools providing free instruction to all, without regard to race, national origin, or socio-economic level.[17]

"The fact is, of course, that without a drastic Constitutional amendment nobody is in a position to establish an educational policy in the United States . . . We cannot have a national educational policy, but we might be able to evolve a *nationwide policy.*"[18]

What kinds of a nationwide policy might we develop? Some suggest establishing minimum teacher education standards throughout the country, so that every child would be guaranteed a teacher with at least a certain minimum amount of education and competence. This is one way of beginning, although it is doubtful whether it would have as much effect on unifying the curriculum across the country as it would on lifting the quality of education.

Another suggestion is that a national body establish minimum standards to be met in a sequence of grades (e.g., grades 1–3, 4–6, 7–9, 10–12). Any state or local board of education would be permitted to set higher standards, but none could function below the national minimums. The purpose here would be to ensure a citizen population with at least a certain degree of literacy and information on which to base their opinions and with which they would be more easily employable. Enforcement would probably have to be through withdrawal of Federal and/or state support funds. Since some localities might have higher standards, as is the situation at present, the problem for mobile students would not be very much reduced. To aid in their correct grade placement, however, it might be possible for them to take a single battery of tests (Stanford, SRA, or other achievement tests), which is used by the receiving school district. With minimum standards operating at each group of grade levels, most children should not have to be placed a grade lower than in their original school. If non-graded schools were in operation, the problems would be further diminished.[19]

With regard to the respective value of different high school diplomas, it might be possible to establish a voluntary certification program. Nationwide high school certification tests would be offered in several fields (e.g., English, history, mathematics, foreign languages), with a certificate awarded to those who pass at a standardized proficiency level. Such certificates would be similar to the Regents diploma awarded in addition to New York high school diplomas, but the tests might be subject to the same criticisms voiced by Littlefield (*supra*). In 1962,

Admiral Rickover proposed a National Standards Committee, one of whose functions would be to formulate a national scholastic standard with accompanying tests. "This . . . would be accomplished by providing examinations set at different ability levels. Those who agreed to take the tests and passed would receive national accreditation. 'By offering the reward of a certified diploma to our children, many who now drift through school would be encouraged to aspire to higher academic goals,' he said."[20]

What Rickover said applies in a way at lower school levels, too. Do all children get promoted automatically (social promotion)? Or must each student meet certain standards of achievement, assuming normal intelligence, in order to be promoted? This is a very practical problem, relating to one's philosophy of education and one's values.

The Commonwealth of Pennsylvania, for one, has undertaken a statewide assessment plan. It sets forth goals to be measured and the techniques to be used. Other states, as noted earlier, have established demands for accountability that might lead to state-mandated achievement objectives and standards.

State accountability programs and the national assessment programs now in progress are designed to evaluate the quality and progress of education provided across the nation. The assessment plans have been criticized on the grounds that they are an invasion of privacy, are an attempt to centralize education, and are anti-democratic.

One needs to weigh what critics say about national assessment and what its advocates claim it will accomplish. Leading critics, preferring to call national assessment by what they believe to be its truer name—national testing—claim that it will test individuals; will compare unfairly different regions whose problems, resources, curricula, and goals are different; will force teachers to teach toward the tests; will result in a national curriculum made out by the test-makers, rather than by local and lay people; in effect, will rank the 50 states unfairly; and, by withholding

Federal funds, will force districts and states to participate in national testing whether they want to or not. Once the results of national testing are known, critics say, the public will rank the states and districts; business and industry and their professional staffs then will leave poor school-image areas for good ones. These are some of the coercive features seen in national testing.

Advocates defend national assessment for many reasons. First, it will provide the nation, as a whole, with reliable information about the strengths and weaknesses of American education. Since it will measure a wide range of curriculum programs and goals, it can not lead to a national curriculum or force teachers to teach toward the tests. Groups by age, school level, and regions will be assessed, and not individuals. . . .

. . . When Congress, in 1867, established the U.S. Office of Education as a fact-finding and statistics-gathering agency, it laid the basis for national assessment. The same national concern, the same international danger, and the same economic, social, and technological problems that prompted large scale Federal aid to education also require some form of national assessment. Congress and the people have a right to know where their money goes and what good it does. . . . We are headed toward a national direction of higher quality in American education, and national assessment would seem to be part of that process.[21]

Much of the controversy and confusion lies in the equating of national assessment and national testing programs. The purposes, as will be seen, are different. The national testing program is more closely related to Rickover's certification idea than to evaluating the quality of education provided in various parts of the country.

The following three excerpts present divergent points of view about a national testing program. You will have to determine for yourself which has the most validity in terms of what is best for our national educational goals *and* the students. Some of the criticisms levied at the national assessment program will be repeated; others are directed more at the concept of more mass testing with less room for divergent thought.

frederick m. raubinger

A National
Testing Program—No

Thoughtful educators and parents are beginning to look with growing misgivings on national examinations and on the abuses of standardized testing in general.

The threat of federally controlled examinations is perhaps less now than a year ago, but it would be naive to think it does not exist. Should such examinations ever be imposed upon the schools, a large degree of federal control would follow inevitably. There would be no way to avoid a national lock step in education.

And even short of federally controlled testing, there is reason to take a hard look at other programs which, for all practical purposes, are becoming national examinations.

The College Board examinations are a case in point. These were formerly required by only a limited number of colleges. Now an increasing number require candidates for admission to take these tests.

In spite of warnings by College Board officials about the limitations of the tests, use of the tests often produces undesirable effects on the schools.

A creative English teacher spent a full semester cramming her students for College Board examinations by dull drill on word derivation and vocabulary. Private coaching schools are springing up in many communities. Several boards of education in one area met to compare College Board examination

Raubinger, Frederick M. "A National Testing Program: Viewed with Misgivings," *NEA Journal*, 48, (Nov., 1959), p. 29.

results in the misguided belief that they could thus identify strengths and weaknesses in their systems.

The questionable impact of the tests on the curriculum is being felt in mathematics. Schools are advised to adopt the new mathematics program recommended by a commission of the College Entrance Examination Board because future tests will be geared to the approach used by that program.

In an effort to improve on their records in examinations, schools are urged to push high-school subject matter down into junior high and elementary schools, where they do not belong. . . .

. . .

The dangers of defects of national or state-wide testing programs are becoming more obvious as testing increases at a phenomenal rate. Some are inherent in the testing itself, and some come from misuse of test results.

Present testing theory encourages attempts to make too early predictions about pupils, to classify and label them too inflexibly, and to draw conclusions about capabilities based upon insufficient evidence. Great injustice to young people frequently results.

Tests cannot possibly reach some of the most important outcomes of education. Intellectual curiosity, persistence, moral values, the attitude of competing with one's self instead of one's fellows—all proper objectives of good teaching—cannot be measured by tests.

Undue emphasis on testing, particularly on a national or state comparative basis, encourages poor teaching—the kind that concentrates on coaching children for tests and helping them learn the tricks of guessing the right answer even though they don't really understand it.

. . .

The amount of testing which is being done in many of our schools at present is so great that it interferes with teaching, simply because it takes up too much time, makes proctors out of teachers, and gives the false impression that education is largely a matter of taking and passing examinations.

Tests have their uses, but each school should determine the tests and have complete freedom to choose those that suit its purpose. Testing agencies should exist to serve the schools, not to set educational policy. In no event, should they exercise undue influence or attempt to determine what should be taught.

A partial rebuttal to Raubinger's statements may be found in this excerpt from:

joshua a. fishman and paul i. clifford

Mass Testing in American Education

. . . One way to obviate the potentially deleterious effects of testing programs upon the school would be to institute constant review committees composed of school representatives . . . and test-makers. These committees would seek to revise testing programs constantly so that they would more adequately sample the degree to which a student has acquired the kinds of behavior which are implied in the statement of the school's objectives. If the behavior sampled in the testing programs were congruent with the behavior implied in the statement of

Fishman, Joshua A., and Paul I. Clifford. "What Can Mass-Testing Programs Do for—and to—the Pursuit of Excellence in American Education," *Problems and Issues in American Education* (Glenview, Ill.: Scott, Foresman Co., 1968), p. 158.

the school objectives, then the testing program and the school instructional program would be mutually reinforcing. At this point, it would still be necessary to educate teachers, administrators, and the public at large not to employ test results for comparisons or evaluations for which the tests were not intended.

Mass-testing—like all standardized testing—is also misused in that its norms become goals. . . . Test norms should be regarded merely as descriptions of the status quo rather than as prescriptions for better education. . . . Even *Project Talent*, the most grandiose mass-testing venture in world history, should not be thought of as discovering talent or as indicating positive standards. Like all mass-testing, it merely hopes to identify talent that is already recognized and then to describe its distribution.

Finally, there is the view of those who believe that nationwide testing is a good idea. Many believe that a nationwide program would reduce provincialism in education. "Extended sharing in a nationwide or worldwide pool of knowledge and competence—a sharing that occurs at higher levels of training—reduces provincialism. Developments of this kind move American educational experience in the direction of a national curriculum regardless of the vocabulary used in discussing it."[22] There are already movements in this direction: for teachers, there are summer workshops or graduate study, national journals, regional and national conferences, telephone lectures and conferences. Also, textbook publication has been centralized, as have been the manufacture, distribution, and purchasing of audio-visual equipment and other school requirements, Punke and others point out that a centralization program should be selective. "A nationwide emphasis seems appropriate in many fields of vocational training—with due regard to variants in agriculture and in recreation at some resorts.

Qualifications for secretaries, mechanics, physicians, and teachers, and to a large extent for lawyers and engineers, are much the same in Alabama and Iowa. So are qualifications for food-handling service, the banking and finance vocations, electrical services, or work in international relations—one of the most rapidly growing areas of concern for Americans. The mobility of the population, because of vocational or other interests, further emphasizes the value of nationwide similarity in educational programs—partly to reduce the handicaps of children who transfer from one school to another.[23]

While voicing advocacy of a national testing program (below), Robert L. Ebel has stated that "Tests, including external tests, can be powerful, useful educational tools. Like all educational tools, they are always more or less imperfect, and sometimes they may be used improperly."[24] Nevertheless, he believes that a national testing program is a good idea.

robert l. ebel

A Nationwide Testing Program—Yes

There are some basic educational goals that all pupils must pursue. All need to know how to read with understanding, to write effectively, to calculate accurately. All need to understand the nature of our physical world, our cultural heritage, our contemporary problems.

I believe that we can, if we will, develop generally acceptable yardsticks for measuring the achievement of these

Ebel, Robert L. "A Nationwide Testing program: Viewed with Favor," *NEA Journal*, 48, (Nov., 1959), p. 28.

common goals. I believe that such yardsticks could contribute substantially to the pursuit of excellence in education. I believe that this can be achieved—without impairment of individualized education or infringement of local control—by a *voluntary* nation-wide achievement-testing program, shaped and guided by educational leaders.

. . .

A good nationwide achievement-testing program has values difficult to obtain in local programs:

It can marshal our best minds to the task of defining our common goals of achievement; of devising valid, efficient tests of these achievements.

It can utilize modern test-scoring and data-processing equipment to achieve efficiency and economy and to relieve teachers of the tedious and educationally unrewarding clerical burdens often associated with testing.

It can provide the large number of broadly representative, highly comparable test scores that are required as a basis for truly valid norms and accurately meaningful score interpretations.

Above all, it can provide dependable evidence of the degree to which pupils are achieving common educational goals.

Some educators are so fearful over what a nationwide testing program might do *to* them that they fail to see clearly what it could do *for* them. Measurement of achievement is essential to the evaluation of a program, and evaluation is a necessary prelude to guidance toward future improvements. The greatest value of a good nationwide achievement-testing program lies in its stimulation and guidance of educational improvement.

One specific fear is that nationwide testing would standardize and freeze the curriculum in a national pattern of deadly uniformity. But if the tests measure only what all need to know, how can the pursuits of these goals be "deadly?" Only as much uniformity in curriculum and methods will appear as can contribute to the attainment of common goals. If new tests are developed annually, as they should be, there need be no freezing of these goals.

Another fear is that teachers will emphasize the tested achievements unduly and neglect others of equal importance. If a community or its school administrator or its teachers are easily induced by a program for testing to overlook other equally important achievements, then it is their lack of wisdom, not the testing program, that should be indicted.

A third fear is that nationwide testing will force teachers to abandon creative teaching for drilling, coaching, and cramming. But good tests do not reward superficial, rote-learned responses.

A fourth fear is that nationwide testing will result in unfair evaluation of teachers and invidious comparisons of schools. It is indeed foolish to evaluate a teacher or a school solely on the basis of achievement-test scores, even when all pupils have been tested and dependable norms are available. But it is only a little less foolish to assume that the achievements of pupils have nothing whatsoever to do with the quality of a school or the teaching it provides.

Would increased participation in nationwide achievement-testing programs indicate that the schools are being overrun with testing and in danger of being taken over by the testers? Not if the program is voluntary. Not if it is under the control of educational leaders. Not if less useful testing is restricted.

All of us who ask for better schools and better teachers owe it to those who pay the bills to do the best we can to show that the money is being well spent. Effective use of a good voluntary nationwide testing program would be a long step in this direction.

Much of the controversy about evaluation, minimum teacher and curriculum standards, and promotion stems from the simple fact that we have fifty state offices of education, some 10,000-plus school districts and local school boards, and no single centralized Ministry or Department of Education. We are probably the only country in the world where lack of a high school diploma, in the current generation, marks an individual as an exception to the general rule. We are also the only country right now which has such a large proportion of late adolescents and young adults in college, and we continue to seek to move all those with the ability to do college work into college. The question is often raised whether, in attempting to educate so many, we dilute the quality of education offered. Is one of the proposed solutions the right answer to this question?

Summary

The issue of a national system of education is examined from several points of view in this chapter. There is, first, the decision whether or not to adopt such a policy. Secondly, a brief lesson in comparative education presents the patterns employed in several countries that have a national educational policy. Third, the possibility of assessing educational output through mass testing, rather than standardizing educational input, is discussed. Clearly the need to maintain diversity in educational programs while developing transferability among programs offers a real opportunity for creative thinkers in the field to provide a solution.

Endnotes

1. Littlefield, Henry M. "Who's Afraid of Regents Exams?" *Teachers College Record*, 68, 1967, p. 481. By permission of the author.

2. *Ibid.*, p. 483.

3. An excellent review of what is "new" in European education on this point may be found in: Conant, James B. "The Changing Educational Scene on Both Sides of the Atlantic." In H. Full, ed., *Controversy in American Education* (New York: Macmillan, 1967), pp. 377–387.

4. "Common English Educational Terms," *Saturday Review*, Jan. 21, 1967, p. 63.

5. Vaizey, John. *Education in the Modern World* (New York: World University Library McGraw-Hill Book Company), 1967, p. 157.

6. Whitehead, *op. cit.*, p. 25.

7. Belding, Robert E. "The Junior High Years Take Over in Europe." In *Controversy in American Education*, ed., Harold Full (New York: The Macmillan Company, 1967), pp. 392–393. By permission of the author.

8. Vodinský, Stanislav. *Schools in Czechoslovakia* trans., Gottheimer and Kohoutova (Prague: State Pedagogical Publishing House, 1965), p. 22.

9. *Report on the Czechoslovak Education System in the School year 1965–66* (Prague: State Pedagogical Publishing House, 1966).

10. Vodinský, *op. cit.*, p. 50.

11. *Ibid.*, p. 79.

12. Much of this information was acquired in conversation with M. Kubersky, Director of the Department of Education in Jerusalem, August, 1967.

13. Kolack, Shirley M., and Sol Kolack. "Can Israel Surmount its Internal Problems?" *Transactions*, 5, 4 (1968), pp. 40–41.

14. Kabir, Humayan, *Education in New India* (New York: Humanities Press, 1955).

15. Fraser, Stewart E., and John N. Hawkins. "Chinese education: Revolution and Development." *Phi Delta Kappan*, 1972, 53, p. 489.

16. H.R. 1326, Feb. 25, 1870. Microfilm of the bill is in the Southern Historical Collection, University of North Carolina. In Knight, *op. cit.*, pp. 458–463.

17. In Knight, *op. cit.*, p. 464.

18. Conant, James Bryant. *Shaping Educational Policy* (New York: McGraw-Hill Book Company, 1964), p. 110.

19. See, for example: Brown, B. Frank. *The Appropriate Placement School: A Sophisticated Nongraded Curriculum* (West Nyak, N.Y.: Parker Publishing Company, 1965).

20. "Admiral Rickover Assails U.S. Education," Phila. Inquirer, Sept. 16, 1966.

21. Parker, Franklin. "Federal Influences on the Future of American Education," *School and Society*, 96, 1968, p. 278.

22. Punke, Harold H. "National Curriculum," *Elementary School Journal*, 68, (April, 1968), p. 345.

23. *Ibid.*, pp. 347–348.

24. Ebel, Robert L. "External Testing: Response to Challenge," In *Principles and Practices of Teaching in Secondary Schools* ed., Florence Henry Lee (New York: David McKay Company, 1965), p. 389.

For Further Reading

BELDING, ROBERT E. "The Junior High Years Take Over in Europe." In *Controversy in American Education* ed., Harold Full (New York: The Macmillan Company, 1967), pp. 387–394.

BLANCHARD, B. EVERARD. "A National System of Education for All American Youth." In *Contemporary American Education* ed., Dropkin, Full, and Schwarcz (New York: The Macmillan Company, 1965), 523–528.

Children and Their Primary Schools. A Report of the Central Advisory Council for Education (England), Lady Plowden (Chairman), 2 vol. London: H. M. Stationery Office, 1967.

CONANT, JAMES B. "The Changing Educational Scene on Both Sides of the Atlantic." In *Controversy in American Education* ed., Harold Full (New York: The Macmillan Company, 1967), 377–387.

CONANT, JAMES B. *Shaping Educational Policy* (New York: McGraw-Hill Book Company, 1964).

CONAWAY, LARRY E. "Some Implications of the National Assessment Model and Data for Local Education." Presented at American Educational Research Association annual meeting, New Orleans, 1973.

FISHMAN, JOSHUA A., and PAUL I. CLIFFORD. "What Can Mass-Testing Programs Do for—and to—the Pursuit of Excellence in American Education." *Problems and Issues in Contemporary Education* ed., Editors of *Harvard Educational Review* and *Teachers College Record* (Glenview, Ill.: Scott, Foresman, and Company, 1968), 151–164.

FRASER, STEWART E., and JOHN N. HAWKINS. "Chinese Education: Revolution and Development." *Phi Delta Kappan,* 1972, 53, 487–500.

FULLER, EDGAR, and STERLING M. MCMURRIN. "Pro and Con: Should There be a National Board of Education?" In *Student, School, and Society* ed., John A. Dahl, Marvin Laser, Robert S. Cathcart, and Fred H. Marcus (San Francisco: Chandler Publishing Company, 1964), 349–354.

GUSTAFSON, MATTI. *Education in Finland* (Helsinki: Ministry for Foreign Affairs, 1967).

HAND, HAROLD C. "Recipe for Control by the Few." *The Individual and Education: Some Contemporary Issues* ed., Frederick M. Raubinger and Harold G. Rowe (New York: The Macmillan Company, 1968), 275–283.

HANSEN, JOHN W., and COLE S. BREMBECK eds. *Education and the Development of Nations* (New York: Holt, Rinehart, and Winston, 1966).

KABIR, HUMAYAN. *Education in New India* (New York: Humanities Press, 1955).

KOLACK, SHIRLEY M., and SOL KOLACK. "Can Israel Surmount Its Internal Problems?" *Transaction,* 5, (March, 1968), 40–43.

LITTLEFIELD, HENRY M. "Who's Afraid of Regents Exams?" *Teachers College Record,* 68, 1967, 480–486.

MARKLUND, SIXTEN, and PAR SODERBERG (Albert Read, trans.). *The Swedish Comprehensive School* (London: Longmans, Green, 1967).

National Education Association. "National Educational Assessment: Pro and Con." (Washington, D.C.: The Association, 1966).

NELLEMANN, AKSEL. *Schools and Education in Denmark* (Copenhagen: Det Danske Selskab, 1964).

PARRY, J. P. *The Provision of Education in England and Wales: An Introduction* (London: George Allen & Unwin, Ltd., 1971).

PARTRIDGE, JOHN. *Life in a Secondary Modern School* (Harmondsworth, England: Penguin Books, 1968).

PUNKE, HAROLD H. "National Curriculum." *Elementary School Journal*, 68 (April, 1968), 343–348.

RANDAZZO, JOSEPH D., and JOANNE M. ARNOLD. "Does Open Education Really work in an Urban Setting?" *Phi Delta Kappan*, 1972, 54, 107–110.

ROGERS, VINCENT R. *Teaching in the British Primary School* (New York: Macmillan, 1970).

Report on the Czechoslovak education system in the school year 1965–66 (Prague: State Pedagogical Publishing House, 1966).

VAIZEY, JOHN. *Education in the Modern World* (New York: World University Library McGraw-Hill, 1967).

VODINSKÝ, STANISLAV. *Schools in Czechosclovakia* trans., Gottheimer and Kohoutová (Prague: State Pedagogical Publishing House, 1965).

WALTON, JACK. *The Integrated Day in Theory and Practice* (London: Ward Lock Educational Ltd., 1971).

WEBER, LILLIAN. *The English Infant School and Informal Education* Englewood Cliffs, N.J.: Prentice-Hall, 1971).

WHITEHEAD, ALFRED NORTH. *The Aims of Education* (New York: Mentor Books, New American Library, 1958).

WOODRING, PAUL. "National Assessment." *Saturday Review*, Sept. 17, 1966, 71–72.

13

anticipations and conclusions

As noted in the preface to this edition, the rate of change, particularly in the field of education, has accelerated markedly in recent years. After studying our current problems and issues in the field, there is a need to try to foresee those that lie ahead and the alternatives that are projected as potential solutions.

A major problem with which we are constantly wrestling has to do with the objectives of education—our philosophy of education. What *are* these objectives? What *should* they be? To these questions, there are at least a dozen different responses, each with several modifications. From one point of view, education is, or should be, the key to changing our whole society. This is an enormous assignment and would require financial, moral, and political support that is unlikely to be forthcoming unless there is a radical change to the level of socialization found in Scandinavian countries.

If we succeed in reducing educational and other inequalities, will we raise or lower the level of opportunity? Will it help us to have a society in which brotherhood and equality flourish among the ignorant?

A second point of view urges that the goal of education is the maximum self-actualization of every individual. Since we have no way of knowing the maximum potential or even the optimal performance level of anyone, this task becomes almost as impossible as the first. We also do not know what lies ahead for any individual, and can therefore hardly plan for him as efficiently as for the Betas and Gammas of Huxley's *Brave New World.* As long as we have personal freedom, the future is unpredictable. To prepare for the unknown, we need people who have information, the intellectual and motor skills to use it, and a healthy respect for the rights of other people. Finding the balance between individual freedom and group dependence is a job that can be done by paying increased attention to moral education even as we provide the opportunities for cognitive learning and the acquisition of various skills.

Do we want to stress cognitive learning foremost among all educational objectives, as the essentialists would have us do? There are predictions that the future will require even better-informed citizens, but does this mean that we should return to the concept of an intellectual elite, with the less capable left by the wayside as was true until compulsory and universal secondary education were introduced?

Can we define educational objectives so well as to have accountability be a realistic and viable concept? Are children

Figure 13.1 Open classroom.

Anna Kaufman Moon (Stock, Boston)

or their parents always wise enough, or informed enough, to put vouchers to their best use? Are these appropriate means of implementing educational objectives?

A second problem area is the duration of schooling. Will post-secondary education be as important in the next ten or twenty years as it has been for the past twenty years? Are we going to be better off expanding infant and early childhood education to prevent some of the learning problems we have today? At present, we seem to be moving toward the latter course, one which will not reduce years in school but might result in more learning occurring in the same period of time, and with a reduced need for remedial services. The population to be served and the economy of the nation will determine to some extent whether or not it is feasible to extend compulsory education (really compulsory school attendance) with respect to the needs of the labor market. In the early 1970's, many governmental leaders severely criticized the emphasis on higher education and urged recognition of the fact that we were creating a population over-qualified for many of the occupations that exist.

Related to the two major questions above is the item of curriculum. What should be taught? To whom? For how long? The liberal arts tradition is a strong one in this country. History, for example, should not necessarily be taught for its own sake as was once the case, although there is much of intrinsic interest in this field, but for the community of culture and events to which we are all heir and for the perspectives on new problems that the lessons of the past can provide. Not everyone can or should be a scientist, but the increasing technology and influence of science on our lives make it imperative that we have some comprehension of the major principles, techniques, and discoveries of both the life sciences and the physical sciences. A shrinking political world and more international business as well as social contacts demand a greater appreciation of foreign cultures, at least, and hopefully a marked increase in foreign language competence among more of our people. Mutual respect for the different disciplines and an increase in interdisciplinary efforts are encouraging moves in the direction of increasing our awareness in these areas. One never knows when something learned at some point in life can be applied in a new situation. A case in point: in the study of child development, Breughel's painting of children at play (art history, art appreciation, museum tours, as possible sources of learning about this) can provide an excellent point of departure for class discussion, a lecture, or a paper.

The early 1970's saw several additions to curricula across the country, many of them interdisciplinary and all of them controversial. Several were formerly perceived as parental functions. Drug education begins in the primary grades in an attempt to counteract this mounting social problem. Sex education has moved from the home to the classroom, albeit with many voices raised in opposition, as yet another function of education. Environmental studies, related to contemporary and future ecological problems, make even the youngest pupils aware of pollution hazards and shortages of needed fuels. Career education, also beginning in the primary grades, initially exposes students to the vast array of potential occupations in the labor market and gradually leads youngsters to narrow their foci to those areas in which they have the most appropriate abilities and greatest interest. Even the fundamentalist view of man's origins is once again part of the curriculum in California and a few other states, accompanied by a watered-down emphasis on theories of evolutionary development.

Intertwined with subject matter must be the development of skills for further learning in formal or informal settings. The Community Schools Programs Act of 1971 will result in thousands of adults returning to classes for the high school courses they have never had or for instruction in new fields of interest. They will neither expect nor accept rote memorization, the distribution of disembodied facts, or lack of application as a mature approach to learning. Also, as external degree programs are introduced and become more widespread, adults will find that they need to read for main and supporting ideas, to be able to abstract concepts from concrete details, and to be able to think divergently as well as convergently to solve academic and practical problems. These skills can and should be taught throughout the school years. They are still basic to further learning in any setting. The curriculum as well as the level of skills demanded of the learner must keep pace with the strong motivation that adults bring to their voluntary learning experiences, for they anticipate that these activities will bring them not only personal satisfaction, but also an increase in competencies.

The "open university" concept, another import from England, is another attempt to contribute to adult education. As practiced in New York, New Jersey, and elsewhere, it offers adults the opportunity to earn external degrees from college, through study in their spare time at home and by receiving credit for non-academic experiences. Learning is self-paced and occurs through correspondence or television instruction plus periodic conferences with a faculty advisor. A few colleges have practiced a modification of this program, with the student required to spend one or two weeks per term or a summer term "on campus." The open university, however, offers fewer conflicts with the adult's full-time responsibilities. It also offers heretofore unavailable opportunities to the family-committed woman and to the homebound handicapped.

School financing will continue to be a problem until an equitable alternative to property taxation is found. This will probably also affect control of education. The Federal government already exercises some control of curriculum, pupil placement, and personnel selection when it offers funds for limited special programs with built-in specifications. Will there be an expanded role for Federal control if a nationwide "value-added" tax or revenue-sharing plan replaces the property tax as the main source of funds for public education? Is year-round schooling an effective means of reducing the tax burden? What if, after a century of effort, a cabinet level Department of Education is established? Will national uniform standards follow?

Related to school funding is the expansion of collective bargaining among teachers. Not only are salary increases negotiated, resulting in increased costs for personnel, but union demands also include smaller classes (more personnel needed), more supportive personnel, shorter working hours, and more ancillary materials—all of which raise the annual school district budgets, and thus the costs to the taxpayer. Also, as the population shifts, new school buildings are needed or it becomes unprofitable to continue to operate old and under-populated ones. Here, too, funds are being increasingly restricted, with much criticism leveled at the "Taj Mahal" constructions of the affluent 1960's. Educational costs continue to spiral, but most American taxpayers are not ready to accept confiscatory taxes even for such a noble purpose as educating their children.

In return for meeting union demands, school boards and legislatures are examining teacher qualifications more carefully. Tenure may become a thing of the past, since teachers will be protected by union contracts against unfair dismissals. However, it will be more difficult to become and remain a teacher as more stringent teacher selection practices and periodic re-evaluations become realities. Prospective teachers will be screened more carefully before they reach the student teaching experience, so that we can look forward to having more teachers with more competencies at a higher level of mastery than has been true in the recent period of rapid expansion in education.

Alongside the many innovations and alternatives already described is the growing involvement of industry in education. The application of technological systems approaches to education is becoming more widespread, although the validity of this application to people rather than products is in doubt. Accountability legislation, for example, reflects industry's cost analysis procedures, although these, too, may not be appropriately applied to education. Several major companies, such as IBM, Xerox, and General Electric, own subsidiaries that produce learning tools—both hardware (e.g., computers) and software (books, films, tapes). The impact of technology on education is perhaps most clearly seen in the rise of new personnel classifications: media specialist, educational programmer, systems analyst, etc.

An important and continuing consideration for the future is whether we provide education for everyone or only for those who want to learn—again, a question of our educational and social philosophy. If the latter, we will be reversing the principles and practices of a century's duration, but at the same time reducing educational costs (fewer students = fewer teachers and classrooms needed), dropout problems, classroom behavior problems, and similar educational challenges prevalent today. On the other hand, if we say that learning in formal school settings is open only to those positively motivated for learning, it may become a highly prized privilege. Experience with adult students, (married women, veterans, dropouts who drop back in) suggests that those who attend college voluntarily are so strongly motivated that they are excellent students. It is doubtful, however, that American society will accept such a reversal easily. To the contrary, we will probably try to expand equal educational opportunity on an ever larger scale while simultaneously trying to restrict financial outlays. This will be a worthwhile effort only if education has top priority, philosophically and financially, for the public in general as well as leaders in government.

For Further Reading

"Career Education in Syracuse." *Today's Education*, 62 (2), 1973, 24–29.

CARLSON, KENNETH. "Equalizing Educational Opportunity." *Review of Educational Research*, 42, 1972, 453–475.

GORDON, GEORGE N. "The End of an Era in American Education." *Educational Technology*, 12 (12), 1972, 15–19.

HOLT, HOWARD B. "Year-Round Schools and System Shock." *Phi Delta Kappan*, 54, 1973, 310–311.

KAY, PATRICIA M. "Defining Teaching Competency: Emerging Issues in the Developmental Period of an Assessment Approach to Competency-Based Teacher Education." Symposium, American Educational Research Association annual meeting, New Orleans, February 1973.

MUIRHEAD, PETER P. "Career Education: The First Steps Show Promise." *Phi Delta Kappan*, 54, 1973, 370–372.

WARD, BEATRICE A. "Teaching Competency: Can It Be Assessed?" Symposium, American Educational Research Association annual meeting, New Orleans, February 1973.

14

a concluding statement

If, in these pages, the prose has sometimes been less than objectively pedagogical or the comments impatient with those who quibble while millions of pupils wait for decisions, it is because the author's involvement with education is parental as well as professional. In addresses to undergraduate education students, and to their parents, the statement of faculty dedication to the better professional preparation of teachers has always been that we are doing our best to teach them well because four years hence, they may be teaching *our* children.

After high school, undergraduate, and graduate education in institutions strongly influenced by the liberal arts tradition, a bias may also be found in favor of a solid liberal arts foundation in all curricula. These courses are of value to every student, because ultimately he lives in a world of people, not things, and he must be able to relate to those people. The liberal arts courses also open new vistas for personal enrichment and pleasure.

At the same time, teaching students from a large metropolitan area at a campus of a large state university, the author has become increasingly aware of the students' problems in their own lives and school experiences. The problems of education majors, specifically, as they go out to teach in this same area will reflect whatever strengths and weaknesses they brought to college with them and carried through their college years. Those students from middle-class homes, in particular, usually have an inadequate knowledge of what goes on in "inner-city" schools or what happens "on the other side of the fence." Part of their teaching preparation must include a growth in knowledge of and empathy with people different from themselves. Indeed, they must have as much exposure to and interaction with children of all backgrounds as possible. This is one of two principal ways, it seems, in which we can hope to improve the teacher's ability to work with all students. The other way is to increase the level of mastery of basic skills needed by the prospective teacher. Mastery should be a prerequisite to enrollment in the teacher preparation curriculum. Elementary school teachers who fear and find difficulty with arithmetic, who can't spell with reasonable proficiency, and who learn, themselves, primarily through visual aids because they dislike reading, are poor excuses for teachers in any classroom. Similarly, secondary school and college teachers should be expected to be well-informed in their content fields and to be willing to continue to learn.

The problems with which we have been concerned here are not the only ones in American education. They do represent, however, the major critical areas in contemporary thinking about the nation's schools and school children. Before we can resolve these issues to the majority's satisfaction, we must determine a philosophy of education and establish meaningful educational goals for the present and the future. Hopefully, we will not continue to live in a world where total war seems always imminent, but rather in one where the considerable efforts of which this nation is capable can be concentrated on people as our greatest asset.

Periodicals of Interest

AAUP Bulletin. American Association of University Professors. Quarterly.
Articles on higher education and academic freedom.

American Education. Dept. of HEW. 10 issues annually.
Brief articles on a variety of educational programs across the country; statistics on Federal support of education and on student and teacher populations.

American Educational Research Journal. American Educational Research Association. Quarterly.
Empirical and theoretical articles in all fields of education; includes book reviews on research methods and measurement and evaluation.

American School Board Journal. Bruce Publishing Co., Milwaukee, Wisc. Monthly.
Articles on current topics and problems of school administration, school business administration, educational plant planning, and illustrations and descriptions of newly completed school buildings.

American Teacher Magazine. American Federation of Teachers, AFL-CIO. Four issues during school year.
Articles on all fields of education.

Bulletin. National Association of Secondary-School Principals. Monthly (Sept.-May).
Articles relevant to secondary education.

California Education. California State Department of Education. Monthly (Sept.-June).
Education articles relating primarily to the California public school system.

Canadian Journal of Behavioural Science. Canadian Psychological Association. Quarterly.
Includes articles on many aspects of education, including social class, language development and differences, educational psychology, testing.

The Catholic Educational Review. Catholic University of America. Monthly (Sept.-May).
Scholarly articles in the entire field of education.

Catholic School Journal. Bruce Publishing Co., Milwaukee, Wisc. Monthly (Sept.-June).

Articles on all aspects of elementary and secondary education, including school building planning.

Chicago Schools Journal. Board of Education, City of Chicago, Ill. Monthly (Oct.-May).
Articles on all fields of education at all levels.

Childhood Education. Association for Childhood Education International. Monthly (Sept.-May).
Articles on education of children ages 2-12.

The Clearing House. Fairleigh Dickinson University. Monthly (Sept.-May).
Articles on the broad field of education relevant to junior and senior high schools, and to professional growth.

Comparative Education Review. Comparative Education Society. Three issues per year.
Scholarly articles, descriptive or advanced analytical, relating to comparative or international education.

Community Educational Journal. Penndell Co. (Midland, Mich.) Bimonthly.
Brief articles relevant to this expanding field of education.

Daedalus. American Academy of Arts and Sciences. Quarterly.
Each issue is focused on a major problem in the arts, social sciences, education, or the nation.

The Educational Forum. Kappa Delta Pi. Bimonthly (Nov.-May).
Articles on the entire field of education.

Educational Horizons. Pi Lambda Theta. Quarterly.
Articles on the entire field of education, but each issue usually follows a theme determined by the editors.

Educational Record. American Council on Education. Quarterly.
Articles principally on higher education and on the relationship of education to society.

Educational Theory. Published at University of Illinois. Quarterly.
Scholarly articles and studies in the history and philosophy of education primarily.

The Elementary School Journal. Department of Education, University of Chicago. Monthly (Oct.-May).
Articles of general interest to elementary school teachers, principals, and other personnel. Focus is on problems and practices at the elementary school level, and national events as they are related to the elementary school.

Exceptional Children. The Council for Exceptional Children. Monthly (Sept.-May).
Articles in the entire field of special education.

Grade Teacher Magazine. Teachers Publishing Corp., Darien, Conn. Monthly (Sept.-June).

Harvard Educational Review. Harvard Graduate School of Education. Quarterly.
Scholarly articles on the entire field of education, especially those relating to research, theory, and policy positions.

Illinois Education. Illinois Education Association. Monthly (Sept.-May).
Articles on general education, professional organization problems and practices.

Journal of Educational Research. Dembar Educational Research Services, Inc. 10 issues per year.
Reports and critiques on research in the whole field of education.

Journal of Experimental Education. Dembar Educational Research Services, Inc. Quarterly.
Reports of sophisticated research in the entire field of education, usually specialized and technical.

Journal of General Education. The Pennsylvania State University Press. Quarterly.
Articles in education for the non-specialist, educated reader; interdisciplinary articles; articles about curricular design, great teachers and their teaching methods.

Journal of Higher Education. Ohio State University Press. Monthly (Oct.-June).
Articles are usually non-technical, and focus on important problems in higher education.

Journal of Negro Education. Bureau of Educational Research, Howard University. Quarterly.
Articles center on problems pertaining to the education of Negroes; and broader problems in the areas of social, cultural, and historical phases of Negro life and other minority groups.

Journal of Secondary Education. California Association of Secondary School Administrators. Monthly (Oct.-May).
Articles related to research, experimentation, and unusual aspects of secondary education.

Journal of Teacher Education. National Commission on Teacher Education and Professional Standards, NEA. Quarterly.
Concerned primarily with methods of educating prospective teachers and the problems involved.

Junior College Journal. American Association of Junior Colleges. Eight issues per year.
Articles deal with information and ideas of interest pertinent to junior colleges.

Michigan Education Journal. Michigan Education Association. Nine issues per year.
Articles on the entire field of education.

Minnesota Journal of Education. Minnesota Education Association. Monthly (Oct.-May) ; semimonthly in Sept.
Articles on all aspects of education.

National Catholic Educational Association Journal. National Catholic Educational Association. Quarterly.
Articles in the entire field of Catholic education.

NEA Journal (Today's Education). National Education Association. Monthly (Sept.-May).
Articles of interest in the general field of education.

New York State Education. New York State Teacher's Association. Monthly (Oct.-June).
Articles in all fields of education.

Ohio Schools. Ohio Education Association. Monthly (Sept.-May).
Articles on the entire field of education.

Peabody Journal of Education. George Peabody College for Teachers. Bimonthly.
Articles on all aspects of education.

Pennsylvania School Journal. Pennsylvania State Education Association. Monthly (Sept.-June).
Includes articles of general interest to educators and prospective teachers, at all levels.

Phi Delta Kappan. Phi Delta Kappa. Monthly (Sept.-June).
Articles on the general field of education, with some research papers.

Quarterly Review of Higher Education Among Negroes. Johnson C. Smith University, Inc. Quarterly.
Articles on the entire field of education.

School and Community. Missouri State Teachers Association. Monthly (Sept.-May).
Articles on the broad field of education.

School and Society. Society for the Advancement of Education, Inc. Biweekly (Oct.-May).
Articles emphasize comparative education, controversial issues, higher education, educational theory, educational history, and research.

School Life. Department of Health, Education, and Welfare, U.S. Office of Education. 9 issues per year.
Articles are on the entire field of education.

School Review. University of Chicago Press. Quarterly.
Research reports, theoretical presentations, and critiques of theory and policy in education.

Sociology of Education. American Sociological Association. Quarterly.
Articles and research notes on the sociological aspects of education.

Teachers College Record. Teachers College, Columbia University. Monthly (Oct.-May).
Articles dealing with crucial issues in education.

Virginia Journal of Education. Virginia Education Association. Monthly (Sept.-May).
Articles on the entire field of education.

Information gathered in part from: Lins, L. Joseph, and Robert A. Rees. "Scholar's Guide to Journals of Education and Educational Psychology." Dembar Educational Research Services, Inc. (Madison, Wisc.), 1965.

Index

Academic freedom, 21, 319,
320-49
"Code of Ethics," (NEA),
333-35
definition, 320-32
reflection of local tolerance, 111
responsibilities, 320-49
Academy, forerunner of high
school, 29
Accountability, 160-61, 264-
65, 384, 388
Acculturation, function of
education, 39, 132-53
Adult education, 47, 88,
138, 141, 386-87
Agricultural areas, changing,
17, 131-32
Aid to education (see Federal aid to education)
Alkendhi, 15, 69
American Association of
University Professors,
102, 336-37
American education (see
specific topic of in-
terest)
American Federation of
Teachers, 102, 336
American Indian
disadvantaged, 147, 148-
52, 240
federal responsibility, 186
and parochial schools,
207-8
American Philosophical Society, 29-30, 364
Ancient cultures, 3-8
Antioch College, 35
Appalachia
disadvantaged, 147, 148
teacher volunteers, 148
Apprenticeship
in American South, 31

in Rome, 6-7
and vocational education,
47
Aristotle
"Ethics and Politics," 77-
78
philosophy of realism, 4,
12, 13, 15, 76-80
Assessment, national policy,
364-67
Automation, and the un-
skilled, 134, 153-54
Avicenna, 15

Bacon, Francis, 17, 80
Bagley, William C., 49, 91,
92
Bailey, Thomas D., 103-105
Behavioral sciences and re-
constructionism, 91
Binet, Alfred, 172
Boston, and school segrega-
tion, 236
Brameld, Theodore, 48-49,
89, 91
British education (see
English education)
Bruner, Jerome S.
goals of education, 52-53
spiral curriculum, 262, 272
Business, concern with edu-
cation (see Industrial-
ist concern)
Busing, 230, 231-33, 236,
240
Butts, R. Freeman, 203-6

California
continuation education,
146
junior college founding, 39
migrant workers and
school system, 139-41
standards of education,

107-8, 146
Catholic school system (see
Parochial schools)
China, early education in, 7-
8
China, education under Mao
in, 363-64
Christianity, early, 8
Church (see also Religion
and education)
education and Aristotelian
influence, 12, 79-80
history, 8
schools, 12-13, 224
Civil rights, application in
education, 20, 120,
223-43
Civil Rights Acts of 1954
and 1964, 50, 132-33,
183, 228, 234, 235
Class size, 256
Clifford, Paul L., 370-71
"Code of Ethics" (NEA),
333-35
College Entrance Examina-
tion Board examina-
tions, 258, 356, 368-
70
College preparatory course,
95, 258-59
College of William and Mary,
29, 30, 32
Colonial period in American
education, 13-31, 193
Comenius, John Amos, 4,
16-17, 82, 360
Commager, Henry Steele,
329-31
Communist contemporary
teaching, 50-51, 67
Community participation in
school, 239
Community Schools Pro-
grams Act, 386-87

Compact for Education, 123-25
Compensatory education, and poverty cycle, 138-39, 237, 240
Compulsory education, 27, 30, 36, 39, 46, 50, 214-15
Computer instructional system, 255, 266
Conant, James Bryant
  competition, 95
  consolidation of schools, 120-22, 261
  dropouts, 138
  Education and Liberty, 259
  high schools, 259-61
  National Advisory Council on Education, 186
  progressive education, 259
  "Slums and Suburbs," 134-37
  talented, education for, 260, 266-67
  teacher certification, 294-97, 298
  tracking, 266-67, 361
Congress, and education, 102-3, 170, 177, 367 (*see also* Federal aid to education)
Consolidation of districts, 120-21, 132, 261
Core curriculum, 48, 90
Cost of education, 20, 154-61
  local board concern, 109-18
  per pupil expenditures, 155-57
  relation to G.N.P., 155, 161
Council for Basic Education, 91
Counts, George S., 48-49, 89, 91
Curriculum
  core, 48, 90
  differentiation beginnings, 47-48
  essentialist *vs* existentialist demands on, 93-94
  establishment of excellence, 251, 255, 257-65, 268-69
  issue in 19th-century schools, 35, 36

minimum standard, 365
modern, 270-72
redesign and reconstruction, 53, 87-88, 91-93, 115, 131, 138-39, 186, 261, 267-70, 385-86
teacher educational institutions, 288-290
sample curricula, 299-302
Cuban refugees, 152
Czechoslovakia, education in, 17, 360-61

Dame school, 28-29
Dartmouth College, case, 136
Decentralization, 238-39
De facto segregation, 228, 230, 234
Degler, Carl N., 198-202
De jure segregation, 228, 230
Democracy
  education in, 101
  and pragmatism, 82
  and reconstructionists, 91
Department of Education (federal), establishment, 171-72
Dewey, John
  and Comenius, 4, 17
  on Plato, 68
  pragmatists, 12, 40-46, 84, 85, 91
Dialectic method, 3-4, 67
Disadvantaged, 147-54, 272
Discrimination
  pupil attitudes after integration, 236-37
  and reconstructionism, 91
Districting, and reconstructionism, 91
Dropouts
  characteristics, 137-38, 142-43
  and local school boards, 113
  a problem, 132, 142-47
  recommendations for, 138-39, 145, 146, 235
  relation to country's economy, 132, 144
  teachers, 138
  vocational guidance for, 138, 145
Drury, Robert L., 112-14

Dutch education in early New York, 29

Earnings compared for educational levels, 144
Ebel, Robert L., 372, 375
Economic Opportunities Act of 1965, 132, 169, 177, 183, 235
Economics, effect on education, 20, 131-66
Education (*see also* specific topic of interest)
  alternatives, 262-65
  department of, establishment, 171-72
  early history, 3-24
  economic concerns, 20, 131-66
  excellence in, 21, 247-79
  goals in America, 20, 27-62
  government responsibility in, 20, 100-28
  innovation concept, 48-50
  national policy, 27, 353-79
  nature of, 21
  quality, 132, 247-79, 261
  religious emphasis, in early history, 27, 193
  responsibility, 323-25, 332-35, 340-41
  standards, effect of minimum, 180
  state (governmental) responsibility, 13-15, 20-21, 101-28
  statistics, 156-57
  of teachers (*see* Teacher education)
  vocational, 47, 102, 259
Educational Opportunities Center
Educational parks, 91, 120, 232-34
Educational Policies Commission, 48-53
Educational television, 266
Education colleges, 288-94
  objectives, 292
Elementary and Secondary Education Act of 1965
  economic purpose, 132
  establishment, 183
  federal aid to education, 115, 169, 183
  migrant workers, 140

religious school teaching,
Empiricism, 82
Endowed free schools, 28
English education, 50, 90-91, 263, 356-58, 387
Environment, 41-46
Essentialists, 91-93, 95
Examination system, basis in dialectic, 67
Excellence in education, 21, 27, 247-79 (see also National education policy)
  foundation for, 251
  Gardner on, 248-50
  meaning, 247, 273-75
Existentialism, 65, 93-94, 95
Experimentalism, 82

Faculty psychology, 92
Federal aid to education, 20, 21, 169-89 (see also Economics; Parochial schools; War on Poverty)
  arguments advocating, 178-80
  arguments against, 180-82
  bills proposed in 1960's and 1970's, 182-86
  development, 170-77
  historical precedents, 169-74
  Nixon years, 184-86
  parochial schools, 183, 197-207
  present questions, 187
  school lunch program, 173
  state allotments, 1972, 185
Federal control of policy at local level, 179, 387
Feedral legislation (see Legislation)
Federal period in American education, 31-38
Financial aid to schools, 20, 21, 169-89
Fishman, Joshua A., 370-71
Flag saluting, school issue, 211-12
France, education in, 15, 358-59
Franklin, Benjamin, 29-30
Free compulsory education, 27, 29-30, 35, 36, 39, 46-47, 50

Freedom, academic (see Academic freedom)
Freedom of association, 342-43
Freedom to teach, 345
Froebel, Friedrich, 19
Fulbright Act, 186
Functionalism, 82
Funds, granting as weapon, 365, 366-67

Gardner, John W., 172, 247-50
German education, 13-15, 18-19, 356
G.I. Bill, 173-74, 201
G.N.P., relation to educational expenditures, 155, 161
Goals (see also Excellence in education; National education policy)
  of American education, 20, 27-62
  contemporary, 50-57, 94-95, 102, 383-84
  of education colleges, 292
  local decision, 104-105
  post-Sputnik, 50-52
  post-World War I, 48-49
  twenties and thirties, 48-49
Government responsibility for education, 13, 15, 20-21, 169-89 (see also Federal aid to education)
Grammar school in early Rome, 7
Greek culture, 3-5

Hanna, Paul R., 268, 270
Harvard, 29, 290
Hatch Act, 172
Headstart (Operation), 56, 177, 238
  for American Indians, 151
  instituted in New York, 235
Health, Education, and Welfare, Department of, 102, 172, 179, 184, 186
Hebrews, ancient, 3, 5-6
Herbart, Johann Friedrich, 18-19
Higher Education Act of 1965, 183
Higher Education Facilities Act of 1963, 183

Higher Horizons, 235
Homogeneous groupings, 254-55
Howe, Harold, 228, 230
Humanism, 13
Hutchins, Robert Maynard, 70-76, 92

Ibn Khaldoun, 15-16, 80
Idealism, 49-50, 65-82
India, education in, 88, 363
Indians, American (see American Indians)
Individual
  ability differences, 267-68, 358
  early educational emphasis on, 17-19, 47-48
  idealism and, 67-68
  pragmatism and, 82
  purpose of education for, 18
  realism and, 79
  worth concept, 31
Industrialist concern with education
  and dropout, 145
  early, 34
  research and development, 266, 388
Industrial Revolution, 33, 36
Innovation philosophy, 48-50
Instrumentalism, 82
Integration of schools (see Segregation and education)
Intelligence testing, 47, 172
Islam, 15
Israel, education in, 361-63

James, William, 82, 83, 303
Jennings, Frank G., 309-11
Jewish schools (see Religion and education)
Job Corps, 173, 183
Johnson, President Lyndon B.
  educational bills presented, 177, 178, 182-84
  and goals of education, 55
  Indian programs, 151
Junior colleges, first public in California, 39

Karier, Clarence J., 88-90, 95

403

Kennedy, President John F.
  educational bills presented, 177, 178, 182-83
  and goals of education, 38, 55
Keppel, Francis, 50, 132, 134, 247
Kilpatrick, William H., 90, 95
Kindergarten, 19, 28, 271
Kneller, George F., 91, 307
Knowledge proliferation, 269-70

Labor unions, teacher, 102, 335-38
Land grants to colleges, 171
Latin grammar schools, 29
Learning by doing, 82
Legislation (*see also* specific acts)
  early period, 170-71, 176
  federal aid to education, 169-89
  Kennedy-Johnson administration, 177, 182-86
  parochial school aid, 193-202, 208-11
  poverty, 132-34
  religion and education, 211-15
  segregation, 224-28, 232, 233, 235
Letter to Laeta, 8-12
Liberal education (Robert M. Hutchins), 70-76
Local school board
  responsibility, 109-12, 117-19
  rules and regulations, 112-16
  setting standards under national policy, 365-66
Local school districts
  best judge of needs, 105, 178
  citizens' influence, 104-105
  consolidation, 110, 120-22, 132
  control of education, 103-19, 125
  enrollment, 110
  number, 110
  restructuring, 91
Locke, John, 80
Loyalty oath, 341-42
Luther, Martin, 13-15

McCarthy investigations, 50, 342-43
McGrath, Earl J., 273-74
McMurrin, Sterling M., 321-25
Magnet schools, 120, 121, 233, 228
Mann, Horace
  education efforts, 19, 33-36, 46, 283, 285-88
  influence on Dewey, 41
  introduced European education ideas to America, 18, 19
  school and social reform, 46
Massachusetts in early education, 3, 27-28, 35, 193, 283-88
Massachusetts Act of 1852, 36, 39
Mathematics programs, 259, 261, 262, 269
Mather, William G., 153-54
Mentally retarded, programs for, 56
Migrant workers, 132, 139-41
Militancy
  of students, 339
  of teachers, 336, 338
Minimum standards of education, effect, 180-81, 233
Miscegenation, 231
Mohammedans, 1
Montessori method, 12, 80
Moravians, 29
Morrill Land Grant Act of 1862, 170, 171
Morrill Act of 1890, 172

National Advisory Commission on Civil Disorders, report, 121, 233, 234-35
National Advisory Council on Education, recommendation for, 186
National defense, concern in education, 102
National Defense Education Act of 1958
  amendments of 1963-1964, 183
  establishment, 169, 177
  excellence concept, 250
  federal aid provided, 169

religious school benefits, 202
revised curricula, 262
National Education Association
  "Code of Ethics," 333-35
  Commission on Reorganization of Secondary Education (1918), 48
  federal aid advocate, 178
  lobbyists, 102
  organization, 335-36
  and parochial school dispute, 190
National education policy
  assessment evaluated, 20-21, 366-67
  history, 364
  implementing, 364-84
  need, 272, 353-79
  patterns extant, 355-64
  problems, 353-55
  responsibility, 102-103
  testing, 365-84
National Foundation for the Arts and Humanities, 183-84
National Institute of Education, 56, 184
National Institute of Health grants, 169
National Science Foundation and curriculum, 262
Negro (*see also* Segregation and education)
  colleges, 224-25
  despair in slum, 134-37
  disadvantaged, 147
  post-Civil War education in South, 37, 224-25
Neighborhood Youth Corps, and migrant workers, 120
New York State
  Board of Regents examination, 89, 258, 355-56
  and school segregation, 233
  variance in school district costs, 156, 159
Nixon, President Richard M., 173, 184-86, 232, 325-29
Nongraded concept, 254-55
Normal schools, 34, 35, 283-88

404

Office of Economic Opportunity, 140, 177, 185, 214
Office of Education, 102, 125, 171-72, 186, 228
Open Classroom, 91, 263, 358
Open University, 387
Operation Get Set, 56, 177
Operation Headstart, 177, 238
Ould Deluder Act of 1647, 27-28, 112

Parks, educational, 91, 120, 233, 234
Parkway Program, Philadelphia, 146, 262-63
Parochial schools
  development, 194
  legal basis for existence, 208
  present-day problems, 160, 195-97, 206-207
  public aid to
    arguments advocating, 197-202
    arguments against, 203-206, 209
    qualifications for, 20, 183
    shared programs, 121, 196, 202
    U.S. Supreme Court decisions, 207-15
Peace Corps, 168, 170
Pennsylvania
  costs, suburban school district, 157-58
  counties, 108
  educational standards, 106-107
  federal period of education in, 31-32
  goals for education, Pennsylvania plan, 366
  statewide assessment, 366
  teacher education, 106-107, 298, 300
Perennialism, 69-70, 95
Performance contracting, 185, 264
Performance, excellence in, 248-50
Personnel of schools
  appointed by boards, 115
  statistics, 156-57

Pestalozzi, Johann
  introduced object lessons, 18, 19
  teaching influenced American education, 33-34, 82
Philadelphia Academy, 29
Philosophies of education, 65-98, 383, 389 (see also Excellence in education)
Pittinger, John C., 116-19
Plato, 3, 5, 65-68, 77, 152
Play in curriculum, 19
Poverty
  cycle, 137, 139
  economic problem of education, 131-66
Practice teaching, 298, 303, 308
Pragmatism, 65, 82-90
Prayers in school, 212
Preschool programs, and poverty cycle, 139
Private schools (see also Parochial schools)
  federal aid to, 183, 197-207
  legal basis for existence, 208
  problems, 160
Problem-solving techniques, 52-53, 56, 87, 95
Progressive Education Association, 89-90
Progressive education movement, 46-48, 88-91, 259
Project Re-Entry, 127
Protestant schools, 194-95 (see also Religion and education)
Psychology
  culture-free tests, 138-39
  in curriculum, Pestalozzi influence, 18
  testing introduced, 47
Public tax support of secondary education, 36-37
Puerto Ricans, 149, 153, 233, 240
Puritans, 5, 69

Quadrivium, 7
Quakers, 29
Quality in education, 132 (see also Excellence in education)

Raubinger, Frederick M., 368-70
Ray, Kenneth C., 112-14
Realism, 65, 76-82
  and individual, 79
  and pragmatism, 81-82
Reconstructionism, 48-49, 91, 95
Released time for religious study, 213-14
Religion and education, 31, 193-219, 288
Research and development, 266-70
  industrialist aid, 266
  national commission proposed, 268, 270
Resource personnel for schools, 256-57
Rhetorical schools in Rome, 7, 50-52, 174-75, 366, 367
Rome, education in ancient, 6-7
Rousseau, Jean Jacques, 17-18, 40, 80
Rugg, Harold S., 48-49, 91
Rural areas
  changing, 131-32
  and poverty, 132-34, 152
Russell, Bertrand, 49, 80
Russian education, 51-52, 174-75

St. Jerome, 8-12
San Francisco, and school segregation regulations, 235-36
Santayana, George, 80
Saslow, Dr. Harry, 150
School district consolidation, 120-21, 132, 261
School lunch program, 110, 173
School superintendent, 115, 117-18
Schooling, alternatives, 262-63
Schools
  early church, 12-13, 29
  early free, 33
  nonpublic, 20, 193-219
  urban vs suburban, 121-22, 131-32
  "without walls," 94
Science in curriculum, 92, 102, 261-62, 265, 270

405

Scientific studies, government impetus, 102
Scopes, trial, 320, 344
Seckinger, Donald S., 340-41
Secondary education, public tax support ruled constitutional, 36-37
Segregation and education, 223-43
early history in North and South, 223-27
economic problem, in New York City, 131, 235
legislation, 224-28, 232, 233, 235
problems continuing, 238-40
types, 228
Separate-but-equal doctrine, 225, 226
Seven Cardinal Prinicples (1918), 48, 54
Slums
Conant report, 134-37
schools poorest, 132, 134-37, 234
today's vs 1900's, 136-37
Smith, Mortimer, 54-55, 91
Smith-Hughes act of 1917, 47, 170, 172
Socrates, 66
Soviet education, 51-52, 174-75
Spanish-Americans of southwestern U.S., 152
Spartan education, 4-5
State-level control of education, 101, 106-109
allotment of Federal funds, 177
board of education, first in Massachusetts, 34
inequalities, 178
philosophy supporting, 171
State (government) responsibility for education, 13, 15, 20-21, 35-36
Strikes, by teachers, 21, 234, 319, 336-39
Student involvement, 119

Student militancy, 115, 339
Superintendent of schools, hiring, 117-18

Talented, education for, 56, 67, 92, 261-63, 267
Teacher (see also Academic freedom)
awards, 257
certification, 256, 294-97, 303
collective bargaining, 387-88
Conant on, 293-97
excellence, 252-54
grades of, 254
idealistic concept of, 68
master, 254
organizations, 335-37
parochial school, 195
pay, 157-58, 253-54
personal freedom, 251-52
professional selection, 21, 290-94, 388
qualities of good, 307
ratio to pupils, 256
recruitment and retention, 251-57
role, 252, 331, 332
salaries relative, 157-58, 178, 180, 254-55
strikes, 21, 319, 336-39
tenure, 337-38, 388
Teacher education
alternative programs, 311-12
controversy on content, 293-94, 304-306
education courses, 292-307
history, 283-90
minimum standards, 104, 365
objectives, 292
occupational program proposal, 296-98
professional preparation, 283-316, 388
recruitment and retention, 251-57
sample curricula, 298-303

Teaching
a "dangerous profession," 238
rewards, 308, 309-11
Teaching machines, 266
Team teaching, 254, 266
Terman, 172
Testing, national program, 365-75
Textbook decision, parochial schools, 208-10
Totalitarian society education, 91
Tracking, 266-267
Trivium, 7

Unemployment of youth, 137
University of Pennsylvania, 29
Upward Bound, 151
U.S. Constitution
academic freedom under, 345-46
interpretation for federal aid to education, 20, 100, 170-71, 180
Preamble, 123, 171
and religion, 193
U.S. Office of Education, 102, 169, 170-72, 186, 367

VISTA
in Appalachia, 148
establishment, 183
Vocational education, 47, 93, 121, 138, 183, 259, 371-72
Vocational Education Act of 1963, 183
Vocational guidance for dropouts, 138, 145
Voucher plan, 263-64

War on Poverty, 141, 177
Weldon, Lynn L., 304-06
Whitehead, Alfred North, 49, 80-82, 357

Yale University, 29
Youth, unemployment statistics, 137